POLICING THE WORKSHY

This book is dedicated to my mum
who died on 13th October 1990

Alex

Policing the Workshy

Benefit controls, the labour market and the unemployed

ALEX BRYSON
JOHN JACOBS

Avebury

Aldershot · Brookfield USA · Hong Kong · Singapore · Sydney

Published by
Avebury
Ashgate Publishing Limited
Gower House
Croft Road
Aldershot
Hants GU11 3HR
England

Ashgate Publishing Company
Old Post Road
Brookfield
Vermont 05036
USA

A CIP catalogue record for this book is available from the British Library and the US Library of Congress.

ISBN 1 85628 357 7

Printed and Bound in Great Britain by
Athenaeum Press Ltd , Newcastle upon Tyne

Contents

Acknowledgements

With such a range of data needed to conduct this research, its completion was reliant on a number of organisations.

For the benefits casework we thank the National Association of Citizens Advice Bureaux, the Federation of Independent Advice Centres, and the advice agencies in our four labour markets. In addition Judge Derek Holden, President of the then Social Security and Medical Appeals Tribunals and its Regional Directors not only agreed to be interviewed but gave us access to invaluable tribunal records.

We are grateful to the Employment Service, the DSS (much of which is now the Benefits Agency), NUCPS, and CPSA for enabling us to interview staff at regional and local office level in jobcentres, UBOs and DSS offices.

Jane Ritchie and Andrew Thomas at Social and Community and Planning Research ensured that the claimant group interviews were conducted to the highest standards. Their advice in analysing the qualitative data was very welcome.

We thank all the employers, advice workers and benefit claimants in the local labour markets who agreed to give their time for interviews.

Special thanks to Professor William Brown and Professor David Piachaud who acted as academic supervisors and, in conjunction with Low Pay Unit colleagues Louie Burghes and Chris Pond, were crucial in providing their expert comments on various drafts.

Many thanks must go to Barbara Jacobs, not only for putting up with the mess of papers lying around the dining room for months but more importantly for her patient listening to the ramblings of one temporarily obsessed with the niceties of social security regulations. The frequent discussions of abstruse points of the law and practice of unemployment benefit and income support in which she was ever willing to take part were way above and beyond the call of the marriage vows and were always helpful and much appreciated.

Finally, without the support of the Nuffield Foundation and Ms Pat Thomas in particular we would not have been able to do anything. Thanks!

Glossary of abbreviations

AO	Adjudication Officer
AOG	Adjudication Officers' Guide
ASW	Actively seeking work
BTWP	Back to work plan
CAB	Citizens Advice Bureau
CAO	Chief Adjudication Officer
DE	Department of Employment
DSS	Department of Social Security
EAS	Enterprise allowance scheme
ES	Employment Service
ET	Employment training
FTA	Failure to attend
HC	House of Commons
IS	Income Support
IVB	Invalidity Benefit
LV	Leaving (work) voluntarily
NACAB	National Association of CABx
NI	National Insurance
PQ	Parliamentary question
RA	Restricted availability
RE	Refusal of employment
RMO	Regional Medical Officer (of the DSS)
R(S)	Reported commissioners decision on supplementary benefit
R(U)	Reported commissioners decision on unemployment benefit
SSA	Social Security Act
SSAT	Social Security Appeals Tribunal
(T)	A tribunal of commissioners' decision
TTWA	Travel to work area
UB	Unemployment Benefit
UBO	Unemployment Benefit Office
VUD	Voluntary unemployment deduction

Introduction

This book considers two connected issues. Firstly, whether legislation intended to make claimants more flexible in their job expectations and improve their job seeking actually increases claimants' prospects of obtaining employment.

Secondly, even if one were to accept that failure to comply with such legislation should lead to benefit withdrawal, one must still consider whether formulators and administrators of public policy have succeeded in balancing employment advice against benefit checking, or whether the fear of 'benefit scrounging' (which goes all the way back to the Poor Laws of 1834) has made the system more 'penal' than 'good' labour market policies alone would dictate.

Concentrating on the impact of the legislative changes contained in the Social Security Act 1989, and recent organisational changes within the public job placement service, we assess the benefit claiming process and the opportunities for claimants to take work.

We have evaluated:

- the recruitment requirements of employers in four different parts of England and Wales, their attitudes to the legislation, the claimant unemployed and various recruitment channels, including the Employment Service;

- the attitudes of the unemployed to the legislation and arrangements made for them in claiming benefits, searching for work and taking work and training; and their experiences in applying for jobs and benefits;

- the role of the public job placement service and how it is viewed 'from the inside' by staff at local and regional level, and claimants;

- and how the Employment Service and the Department of Social Security (and, since April 1991, the Benefits Agency) perform against their own criteria for adjudicating on benefit eligibility, a story told through official statistics, internal circulars, benefit advice agencies, reports on tribunal decisions and the words of tribunal staff and those working in the Employment Service and DSS.

The research came to some striking conclusions (Chapters 13 and 14). It identified a set of unintended consequences which threaten rather than improve claimants' prospects of work; highlight employers' disquiet over the direction of the ES and its value as a source of potential recruits; and reveal a number of shortcomings – both legislative and operational – which are undermining many claimants' legitimate rights to unemployment benefits.

The unfortunate thing is that none of this needs to be so. The precept on which the legislation is constructed (whereby an 'inflexible' pool of claimants are failing to take available work) is largely unfounded. We go some way to disposing with the 'scrounger' myth, pointing instead to the ways in which a public job placement service can play a constructive 'brokerage' role for employers and the unemployed alike.

The title of this book is taken from Sir Derek Rayner's report,
Payment of Benefits to Unemployed People, 1981.

Part 1
THE GOVERNMENT'S PLANS FOR THE UNEMPLOYED

1 The research: Objectives, design and conduct

This study, funded by the Nuffield Foundation, assesses the impact that the Social Security Act 1989 has had on those claiming unemployment benefit and income support.

In particular the study focuses on the introduction of a new provision requiring claimants to actively seek employment, and on alterations made to existing legislation governing benefit penalties for refusing employment, neglecting to avail oneself of employment, and restricting one's availablity for employment.

Chapter 3 explains how the legislation was designed to ensure that claimants engage in effective job search each week and, with Employment Service counsellor advice if necessary, maintain realistic expectations about the wages and occupations they can command. The intention was to facilitate claimants' movement off the unemployment register into employment. It was also intended that the 1989 Act should improve the flexibility of the labour market and thereby facilitate economic competitiveness.

In designing the study it was felt necessary to consider the Act's implications not only for claimants but for employers and the Employment Service if a clear understanding of both the claiming process and the labour market implications was to emerge.

The pilot study

A pilot study was conducted in April 1990 in Hammersmith and Fulham.

It consisted largely of unstructured interviews with employers, advice agencies, local Employment Service and DSS staff, and the council's Economic Development Unit.

It revealed that the Act's impact depended crucially on:

- claimants' awareness of the social security changes and the extent to which significant changes in claimants' behaviour would increase the take up of jobs and government schemes;

- employers' propensity to employ the unemployed;

- and the way in which the ES and DSS administered the system.

The Employment Service said:

> We would agree with the findings of your pilot study that claimants' labour market behaviour; employers' willingness to take on the unemployed; and the way in which we administer the regulations will all have an important role... (letter from William Smith, Claimant Services Branch, 30th July 1990).

The pilot study also revealed that it was necessary to treat the legislative changes in the context of wider organisational and functional changes within the Employment Service, including the Back To Work Plan, the New Framework, Active Signing and Agency Status (Chapter 2).

Research design

The research comprised of:

- statistical data on benefit suspension, adjudication decisions, benefit penalties and tribunal decisions;

- case work and tribunal reports highlighting the problems of claimants;

- local labour market analyses involving semi-structured in-depth interviews with the unemployed, those who had recently left the unemployment register, employers, advice agencies, benefit administrators, Social Security Appeals Tribunal (SSAT) staff, and union representatives;

- interviews at regional and national level with policy and administrative officials in the DSS, ES and SSATs.

Lists of those interviewed in the local labour markets are contained in Appendix 1. In addition there were group interviews with the unemployed and those who had recently left the register (see below).

The case work material was collected from a variety of sources throughout the UK but chief among them were the National Citizens Advice Bureaux's Information Retrieval System which records problems raised by clients and noted by advisers; and members of the Federation of Independent Advice Centres.

Access to tribunal decisions was agreed with the President of the SSATs and his Regional Directors.

Interviews were conducted with DSS and ES staff with the help of the ES's Claimant Services Branch, local contacts and the NUCPS and CPSA trade unions.

The local labour markets

In order to say something worthwhile about local labour demand and supply decisions it was necessary to pick discrete, well-defined geographical localities. The four studied were St Helens (Merseyside), Hammersmith and Fulham (London), Brighton and Hove (Sussex) and Newport (Gwent). They were chosen for their differing labour market characteristics in relatively distant parts of England and Wales.

A London Borough was chosen because the London labour market was cited in the White Paper *Training For Employment* which led to the legislative changes.

Appendix 2 provides a background to each area.

How the interviews were conducted

Interviews with the unemployed and those recently leaving the unemployment register

Social and Community Planning Research were commissioned to conduct group interviews with claimants and those who had recently left the unemployment register in the four labour markets.

The purpose of these interviews was to:

- assess the total impact of the benefit claiming process on individuals' work intentions and job search in the light of the Employment Service's benefit checking and advice priorities through counselling interviews and signing on; and

- focus more particularly on their awareness and understanding of the 1989 changes, and their impact on job search and the type of employment and/or schemes sought/taken.

The sample of respondents was recruited using a household screen. In order to check that individuals met the quota requirements a screening questionnaire was used prior to inviting them to take part in the group discussion (Appendix 3).

Where the person agreed to take part an introductory letter was left with them, containing information about the study and a contact name and telephone number in case they were unable to attend. Respondents were also advised that they would be given £12 to cover any inconvenience or expense.

Twelve people were sought for each group on the assumption that nine would turn up. In fact 35 people attended in the four groups. About half of those recruited had to be unemployed and claiming benefit. The remainder had to have been out of work and claiming benefit at some point since October 1989 and currently either in work, attending a government scheme or in full-time education.

In total there were five quota variables: employment status, length of unemployment, sex, age, and marital status.

There was no weighting towards those who may have had direct experience of benefit sanctions.

The aim of the recruitment process was to obtain a broad spread of recruited respondents, in terms of the above quota characteristics. The profile of the sample of those who attended the group discussions differed slightly from the recruited samples because some people chose not to attend once they had been recruited.

The group interviews were conducted on four separate days in January and February 1991. Attendees were asked to fill in a short questionnaire giving household, income and employment history details (Appendix 4). The interviews were conducted in a semi-structured fashion according to a topic guide produced by the Low Pay Unit and SCPR (Appendix 5).

Other labour market interviews

As with the group interviews, the employer samples were chosen to obtain a broad spread of interviews in each labour market, in terms of size, sector and location.

Employers and others such as advice agencies were initially contacted by telephone.

The pilot study showed that structured interviewing was not appropriate. The interviews were conducted in a relatively informal manner. To meet the objectives of the study certain topics had to be covered but the unstructured nature of the interviews allowed interviewees to raise issues that they considered important.

How the interview material was analysed

The qualitative data was analysed according to a process used by Social and Community Planning Research.

Interview transcripts were transferred onto A3 'graphs' and information organised according to type of respondent (ie unemployed, employer or other) and region. Each A3 graph represented a topic area which was itself broken down into between 4 and 7 sub-headings.

The 'grids' produced allowed for each respondent's interview to be recorded, either in paraphrases or direct quotes, according to region, topic and sub-topic.

Reading the 'grids' in conjunction with the transcripts and, in the case of the claimant interviews, with taped recordings of the interviews, assisted in locating the key issues raised by different sets of respondents.

2 Brokerage in the labour market: The role of the Employment Service

Since the introduction of the Social Security Act 1989 the Employment Service has undergone much change.

This chapter briefly explains some of those changes and how they have altered Employment Service practices and the process that claimants have to go through in claiming benefit and seeking work.

Employment Service aims and objectives

The prime functions of the Employment Service – the administration of unemployment benefits and assisting claimants to find employment – have been in place since its creation in 1987. However it was not until it became an executive agency under the Government's Next Steps Initiative that its performance targets were made public and explicit.

Agency status

The relationship between the Employment Service and its 'parent' government department, the Department of Employment, is governed by a Framework Document which lays out the conditions under which the Agency acts in a quasi-independent fashion to implement Department of Employment policy objectives with respect to the unemployed.

This is supplemented by an Annual Performance Agreement 'between the Secretary of State for Employment and the Chief Executive of the Employment Service' which 'sets out the specific aims, operational objectives and targets to be met by the Employment Service as an Agency' (Annual Performance Agreement 1991/2).

In addition the Employment Service produces an Operational Plan each year which, once agreed with the Secretary of State, 'sets out how the Agency plans to meet the performance requirements contained in (the) Agreement' (Annual Performance Agreement 1991/2). It also describes in detail the annual priorities for the Agency.

Objectives

The ES's policy objectives cited in the Operational Plan for 1990/1 were to:

- provide unemployed people, particularly those who have been unemployed for longer than six months and those in the inner cities, with job opportunities and help in job search skills, or opportunities to become self-employed or to find appropriate training;

- provide particular assistance to people with disabilities to take advantage of work and training opportunities and to help and encourage employers to make such opportunities available;

- pay benefit and allowances promptly, accurately and courteously;

- encourage unemployed claimants to seek work actively and check that they are entitled to unemployment benefit, income support or national insurance credits in accordance with social security legislation;

- discourage benefit fraud by identifying, investigating and where appropriate prosecuting those suspected of, or colluding in obtaining benefit by deception.

This translated into a set of specific targets including:

- 1.65 million placings of unemployed people into jobs or 80 per cent of placings of unemployed people among the total number of placings of people into jobs;

- 65,000 Enterprise Allowance Scheme entrants;

- 335,000 Employment Training starts;

- 275,000 placings for the long-term unemployed;

- a 'reference level' of 400,000 for new claims not pursued following inital contact.

Achievements

Three quarters of the way into the first Operational Plan – that is, between April and December 1990, the ES had:

- placed 1,088,286 unemployed people into jobs (66 per cent of its target);

- placed 165,400 people claiming benefits for six months or more (60 per cent of the target); and

8

- achieved 320,034 'non-pursuals' of benefit claims following inital contact (80 per cent of target) (Source: *Hansard*, 14th February 1991, col. 590).

Resources

'ES resource allocation and likely business volumes will be linked to outputs through the annual performance agreement' (Operational Plan 1991/2) so that the ES is accountable through the achievement of targets according to agreed financial criteria.

It employs 35,000 staff. In 1990/1 its annual budget was £860 million. This rose to £939.7 million in 1991/2 – not including the £3 billion it pays out in benefits on behalf of the Department of Social Security.

Office integration

In 1987 the ES inherited around 1,000 jobcentres and 1,000 unemployment benefit offices. According to the Chief Executive:

> The granting of Agency Status was coupled with the decision to bring together these two local office networks to provide the full range of benefit payment and job placement functions under one roof (*Employment Gazette*, April 1991).

The process should be completed with the creation of 1,100-1,200 integrated offices in the mid-1990s. Currently there are around 400 integrated offices. This study shows that the extent of integration has a major impact on claimants' attitudes towards using the local Employment Service office for counselling and as a channel for job search. The research suggests that integration, and the creation of 'multifunctioning' counsellors – that is, advisers with responsibility for both benefit checking and job placement functions – has been detrimental to claimants' experiences in using ES facilities to help them get back into work.

Making the 1989 Act effective

In its Operational Plan for 1990/1 the Employment Service had been content that, in 'ensuring that claimants are available for and actively seeking work and that offers of employment are not refused without good reason' the '1989/90 levels of achievement will be at least maintained'.

It was soon apparent that the Secretary of State for Employment was not satisfied with this 'stand still' position. In April 1990 he announced a new Back To Work Plan which would '(make) sure that the recent legislative changes which require those in receipt of benefit to be actively seeking work are properly enforced'. It offered:

- individual guidance for each unemployed person on how best to find work;

- a new booklet 'emphasising that the need to look for work is a fundamental responsibility of everyone who expects to receive unemployment benefits';

- a new advisory interview after 13 weeks of unemployment with a check on activity in looking for a job and subsequent help for those who have been unable to get work even though their skills are in demand in the local labour market;

- a unified advisory service which will abolish the distinction between restart counsellors and claimant advisers;

- ensuring 'that each unemployed person after the fresh claim stage is seen by the same adviser during any period of unemployment';

- a more systematic follow-up of those who do not take up places on ET, in jobclubs or on restart courses even though they have agreed to do so (*Hansard*, 4th April 1990).

The Secretary of State summed up these changes by saying that:

together.. (they) will improve the effectiveness of the help that the ES is able to give to unemployed people in getting them away form dependency on benefit and into work or other opportunities that will improve their chances of getting a job (*ibid.*).

In the year to April 1991 greater and greater emphasis was laid by the Secretary of State and the ES itself on assisting with job search and continually reviewing claimants' progress.

In November 1990 the Secretary of State made an announcement that was tantamount to a change in the emphasis of public policy, away from 'training the workers without jobs for the jobs without workers' towards more assistance with jobsearch techniques. He said:

Jobsearch techniques, help in getting an interview and particularly in securing the offer of a job have proved to be highly effective ways of getting back to work... training is not always the best solution for all unemployed people (Department of Employment press release, 12th November 1990).

To that end the Secretary of State allocated extra resources to the jobclub programme and the Job Interview Guarantee Scheme, with a view to increasing available places by 100,000 (Press Release, 13th December 1990). On 30th April 1991 Job Interview Guarantees were opened up to all those unemployed for six months or more. At the same time the funds available for ET were reduced in real terms, although the ES in conjunction with Training and Enterprise Councils maintained their commitment to guarantee ET offers (as well as jobclub, JIGs, and EAS) to those claimants aged 18-24 and unemployed between 6 and 12 months, and aimed to do the same for claimants under 50 and unemployed for more than two years, or claimants with disabilites.

Finally, in March 1991 the Secretary of State announced:

For the first time all unemployed people who reach 13 weeks of unemployment and have no job to start will have the guaranteed offer of an interview – a chance to review their plans and to assess further options for getting back to work (Department of Employment press release, 20th March 1991).

The greater emphasis on getting claimants back to work, and making the 1989 Act more effective through guaranteeing continual review is reflected in the Annual Performance Agreement for 1991/2, which states that the ES will ensure the provision of 'advice to new claimants on their permitted period'.

In monitoring their success in making claimants aware of their duties to seek and be available for work, as well as not to refuse work without good reason, they would track the number of ASW warning letters issued, the number of claimants moving on to other benefits, the number of adjudication decisions on availability, restricted availability, actively seeking employment and refusal of employment; as well as the proportion of Adjudication Officers' decisions leading to disallowance of benefit.

At the operational level, the ES sought to introduce a New Framework[1] by Christmas 1990 (memorandum from Regional Director, ES, London and South East Region to Area Managers, 27th September 1990.) The research shows that this had not occurred in Brighton and Hove or Hammersmith and Fulham by Christmas, and that St Helens had yet to make it fully operational by February 1991.

It was intended to provide the conditions under which continual claimant review would occur. All new claimants (an estimated 4 million in 1991/2) would undergo a New Claims Interview where their Back To Work Plan (BTWP) would be agreed. At 13 weeks counselling interviews would occur to review the BTWPs of around 10-15 per cent of claimants.

In addition signing clerks would become more involved with the counselling process. The Active Signing initiative envisaged clerks checking claimants' eligibility for benefit at signing on, and referrals to Claimant Advisers for counselling interviews if necessary.

If still unemployed at six months claimants would have to attend a restart interview – as well as at 52 and 78 weeks. Here job seeking and availability would be checked and restart menu options offered.

At any point Claimant Advisers may decide to 'caseload' a claimant. This involves intensive counselling for up to eight weeks with a view to securing a positive outcome (leaving the unemployment register, usually through job placement or participation in a government scheme).

Regulations came into effect on 17th December 1990 (Income Support (General and Transitional) Amendment Regulations 1990) requiring those registered unemployed for two years to attend a restart course. Claimants were forewarned of this 'mandatory' course at their 18 month restart. 'Intensive help' could follow if they had not achieved a positive outcome after that.

Together, these changes signify a more intensive effort on the part of the ES to enforce the 1989 regulations by continually reviewing claimants' job search, employment expectations and benefit eligibility. Because it was not fully in place during the course of the research, it is by no means clear what practical implications the New Framework and Active Signing could have on claimants.

The labour market as a whole

The claimant unemployed represented about four fifths (83 per cent) of all those seeking and available for work in Spring 1990, according to the ILO/OECD definition (those without work in the reference week, looking for work in the four weeks prior to interview and available to start work within two weeks). Under-counting is particularly acute among women, with only 52 per cent of those seeking and available for work being claimants (*Unemployment Unit, Working Brief*, April 1991).

Although the ES, as the interviews with local staff revealed, are seeking to concentrate resources on claimants, non-claimants continue to be big users of jobcentre services. They are not, however, subject to the counselling process and benefit eligibility rules that apply to claimants.

Job readiness

Of the claimant unemployed moving through the Employment Service counselling system most are subject to the availability and actively seeking work rules. There are exceptions (e.g. lone parents). However, their status may change (for instance when a lone parent's youngest child reaches 16 years of age) and so their claims are kept under review for that reason.

There are numerous options counsellors can offer claimants. In practice they tend to distinguish between those who are job ready and those who are not. Those who are not may be directed towards basic skills courses, confidence building methods, specialist outside advice, government training programmes, with some jobsearch advice. Throughout their job readiness will be kept under review.

For the job ready, there is the possibility of work experience (e.g. Action Credit in some areas), structured job search assistance, government funded on-the-job training, and – often after six months' registered unemployment – Job Interview Guarantee Schemes, the Enterprise Allowance Scheme and intensive job application assistance in a jobclub. Further encouragement will be offered through advice on in-work benefits.

For the purposes of benefit eligibility the distinction is not so clear since, after the first week of claiming those subject to the availability rules are expected to take steps to seek work, whether they are job ready or not. That said, the type of steps they can take must be 'reasonable' in his or her case in offering the best prospects of obtaining offers of employment. Consequently what is reasonable for the job ready may not be reasonable for the 'unready'.

The role of benefit sanctions

The flowchart describes the theory behind the use of benefit sanctions – and the threat of benefit sanctions – in materially altering claimants' jobsearch behaviour and work expectations.

The Use Of Benefit Sanctions

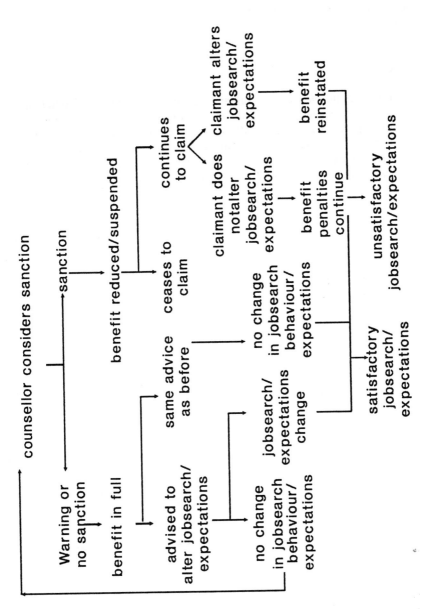

It assumes that benefit sanctions are able to affect claimants' behaviour and expectations without benefit penalities actually being implemented. The prospect that claimants will alter their behaviour and expectations clearly relies heavily on claimants' belief that threats to benefit might be used.

Note

1. Details of the New Framework and Active Signing are taken from: *Employment Service Framework For Customer Management Guidance*, Claimant Services Branch August 1990, NF/90/11; *New Framework For Advising Claimants, Active Signing Guidance*, Claimant Services Branch September 1990; *New Framework – 13 Week Reviews*, Management in Confidence, NF/90/29, *Target Caseload*, NF/90/30, and *Target Caseload – Guidance for Managers*, NF/90/31.

3 Eligibility for income support and unemployment benefit after the Social Security Act 1989

In 1988 (*Training for Employment*, Department of Employment, 1988) the Government gave notice of its concern that failure to seek work, ineffective job search methods, and the wage and occupational inflexibility of the claimant unemployed were major causes of unemployment.

This chapter explains the legislative changes to benefit eligibility made by the Social Security Act 1989 which were intended to alter claimants' behaviour in these respects.

Background to the legislative changes

Throughout the 1980s changes were made in the administration of the availability rules which are a condition for receiving unemployment benefit and income support (some claimants such as lone parents, those incapable of work, and people aged 60 or older, are exempt from 'signing on' and are not subject to availability testing). The changes began with the Rayner Scrutiny (Report of the Joint DE/DSS Rayner scrutiny, *Payments of Benefits to Unemployed People*, 1980) whose recommendation that unemployment benefit offices (UBOs) administer a stricter availability for work test was implemented in October 1982. However with the National Audit Commission subsequently pronouncing the changes to have been ineffectual, far more rigorous availability testing was introduced for all new claimants with the UB671 questionnaire in October 1986.

In the same year restart interviews were introduced for those who had been unemployed for a year. Later they were extended to all those who had been unemployed 6 months. The fusion of jobcentres and UBOs brought together job search advice and checks on benefit eligibility and, in may 1988, formal availability for work testing was introduced into restart interviews held in jobcentres. The launch of the Employment Service as an Executive Agency in April 1990 and the announcement of its "Back To Work Plan" completed this fusion: the Secretary of State has announced that the "unified advisory service... will abolish the increasingly artificial distinction between restart counsellors and claimant advisers" *(Hansard,* 4th April 1990, col. 647).

Pressures on the unemployed have been stepped up with the Secretary of State stressing that the "new booklet (which replaces the old UB40) emphasis(es) that the need to look for work is a fundamental responsibility of everyone who expects to receive unemployment benefits". He has also announced "a new advisory interview after 13 weeks of unemployment with a check on activity in looking for a job" (ibid). By March 1990 the Secretary of State was announcing that "for the first time all unemployed people who reach 13 weeks of unemployment and have no job to start will have the guaranteed offer of an interview – a chance to review their plans and to assess further options for getting back to work" (Department of Employment press notice, 20th March 1990).

But where does the legislation fit in with all this? The basic statutory framework for eligibility for unemployment benefit has been in place since 1975 (Social Security Act 1975), adopted and adapted by the Social Security Act 1986 for income support. Important changes have been made through statutory instruments, perhaps the most significant being the extension of the maximum period of disqualification for unemployment benefit from 6 to 13 weeks in 1986, and from 13 to 26 weeks in April 1988 for those refusing/failing to take up suitable job opportunities and for those who have made themselves 'voluntarily unemployed' by leaving a job without 'just cause' or who have been sacked for misconduct. Although the change has had considerable impact on those actually disqualified *(Disqualified From Benefit,* Low Pay Unit, 1988), recent evidence suggests that the general lack of awareness of the changes and a failure to understand them means that they have had little impact on claimants' behaviour generally *(Voluntary Unemployment – Benefit Sanctions,* Social and Community Planning Research, 1989).

Nevertheless, the Government puts great store by the changes it can effect to claimants' behaviour through legislation. It anticipates that the new requirement for claimants to actively seek employment each week, and changes to rules governing restrictions placed on availability for, and refusal of, employment, contained in the Social Security Act 1989 will reduce net expenditure by £100 M in a full year and take 50,000 claimants off the unemployment register *(Independent,* 19th October 1989, p.2). Their actual impact, however, will depend upon the way in which the DSS and ES administer the system; the extent to which claimants are aware of the changes and, if they are aware of them, the extent to which job take-up will increase through significant changes in claimants' behaviour, and employers' propensity to take on the unemployed.

Restricted availability

The Social Security Acts (SSA) 1975 and 1986 and established case law require claimants to be willing and able – generally at once – to take up suitable employment,

16

unless deemed or not required to be available (SSA 1975 s17 (1)(a) for unemployment benefit and SSA 1986 s20 (3)(d) for income support; and R (U) 1/53 and R (U) 5/80). If claimants can show that they have reasonable prospects of obtaining, on their stated conditions, the kind of employment they are holding themselves available for, then the question of restricted availability should not arise.

Under the old regulations (Social Security (Unemployment, Sickness and Invalidity Benefit) Regulations 1983 SI No 1598 reg.7 (1)(a) and Income Support (General) Regulations 1987 SI No 1967 reg.10(1)(d)), if claimants could not show "reasonable prospects", they could still be eligible for benefit if the restrictions

- would not have prevented the claimant from having reasonable prospects but for temporary adverse industrial conditions;

- were nevertheless reasonable in view of the claimant's physical condition;

- were reasonable "having regard to both the nature of his usual occupation and also to the time which has elapsed since he became unemployed".

While the regulations under the Social Security Act 1989 are similar there are some notable changes with practical implications (all the amendments relating to UB are contained in the SS (U, S and IB) Regs.1989 SI No 1324, and those for IS in IS (General) Regs.1989 SI No 1323).

In the first place, prior to October 1989, claimants only had to be available for "suitable" employment. Now the legislation regarding "suitability" no longer applies (IS Regs.1987 reg.10 (1)(a) and SSA 1975 s20 (1) as amended; and Adjudication Officers' Guidance (AOG) 86040). Unlike the UB test, for the IS test there is a commonsense qualification. That is, that the job must be one which the claimant can "reasonably be expected to do", allowing for age, experience, health, education and other factors (IS Regs.1987 reg.7 (1)(a), AOG 25209 and R (S) 11/51 (T)). The SSA 1975 may provide such a rider for UB. It states that " 'work' in this paragraph (means) work which the person can reasonably be expected to do" (SSA 1975 s17 (1)(a)). However the availability (and actively seeking work) tests refer to "employment" rather than "work" (which is used in "capable or incapable of work") . Nevertheless, since the two words are commonly used interchangeably, the point is arguable.

Secondly, they allow for restrictions which are reasonable in view of a person's mental condition.

Thirdly, under previous regulations, claimants could only be restricting their availability where "as a consequence" of the restrictions they imposed they had no reasonable prospect of securing the employment for which they held themselves to be available. While this is still the case for IS claimants (IS Regs.1987 reg.10 (1)(d) as amended), if UB claimants place any restrictions on their availability an Adjudication Officer is able to take into account personal factors which mean the claimant has no reasonable prospects of getting work, even if it is not her/his restrictions which affect those prospects (UB Regs.1983 reg.7B (1)). It is thus possible to fail the UB test whilst passing the IS test.

Perhaps the most significant change is the determination of the time in which it is permissible for a claimant to cite occupational restrictions to her/his availability: this no longer depends upon what the Adjudication Officer considers reasonable in the light of the time the claimant has been unemployed, but on any period up to a maximum of 13 weeks, the actual period being determined by the Officer with regard to the claimant's usual occupation, skills, qualifications; the length of time the claimant has spent in that occupation or training for it; and the availability and location of employment in his/her usual occupation (UB Regs.1983 reg.7(B)(5) and (6); IS Regs.1987 reg.10(1)(d)(iii) and 10(4) to (6)).

After a maximum of 13 weeks, no claimant can stipulate occupational restrictions. All must be available for employment, regardless of whether or not it is "suitable" (AOG 86040).

Actively seeking employment

Arguing that a stock of job vacancies remained unfilled whilst unemployment was high, the Government believed that "unemployment... could be considerably reduced and many vacant jobs filled if unemployed people looked more intensively and more effectively for work" (*London Labour Market*, HMSO, 1988). It was not content to rely on case law suggesting that availability was itself an active state whereby the claimant had to draw attention to his/her availability (R (U) 1/53; R (U) 5/80). The Minister of State, Nicholas Scott, argued that the case law was equivocal and that "the state of the law does not enable the Department to warn people that unless they take those steps, they will no longer qualify for benefit" (Standing Committee F, 21st January 1989, col.173). In the report stage of the Social Security Act 1990, Under Secretary of State Gillian Shephard, said that the previous test meant that "one simple step, such as attending a jobcentre, would be enough" (*Hansard*, 3rd April 1990 col. 1093).

Consequently, the 1989 Act's amendment to Section 17 of the 1975 Social Security Act requires that claimants actively seek work each week, as well as being available and capable for it (SSA 1975 s17 (1)(a)(i) and SSA 1986 s20 (3)(d)(i)). The claimant must "take steps which are reasonable in his case as offer him his best prospects of receiving offers of employment". In determining the reasonableness of the steps the Adviser or Adjudication Officer must have regard to all circumstances, including the claimant's skills, qualifications, physical and mental limitations; the time that has elapsed since his last employment; steps taken in previous weeks; activities which contribute to actively seeking such as training, and conditions in the local labour market. The actual steps to be taken by claimants are set out in the regulations and include oral and written applications for jobs, and seeking information on the availability of employment (UB Regs.1983 reg.12B and IS Regs. reg.10A).

The claimant must actively seek jobs for which s/he must be available, and be able to present evidence of job search if asked.

Restrictions on active job search are permissible if the claimant can show reasonable prospects of obtaining employment regardless, or can show good cause for refusing certain types of employment (AOG 86427-31).

Whilst availability (which is a continuous state) can be 'deemed', which allows payment of benefit to continue while the Adjudication Officer is making a decision, active job search demands that claimants take certain actions each week and can demonstrate that they have done so when proof is required. These past actions cannot be deemed so that, once called into question, benefit is suspended. (UB Regs.1983 reg.12D and IS Regs.1987 reg.10A (4) explain instances in which active job search can be deemed, including the first and last weeks of unemployment, participation for up to five weeks on an employment or training programme for which an allowance is not payable, and/or a period of not more than eight weeks trying to establish self-employment).

If the claimant fails the "actively seeking work" test, benefit is disallowed for the period since the last signing-on day, usually one or two weeks. Even if the claimant is able to prove active job search at the next signing on day, s/he may have suffered four weeks without benefit, or on reduced rates of income support under the hardship rules (whereby claimants whose benefit has been suspended or disallowed on availability or "actively seeking work" grounds may be entitled to IS at a reduced rate if the Adjudication Officer is satisfied that unless IS is paid the claimant or a member of his/her family will suffer hardship) (IS Regs.1987 reg.8 (3) and 22). Claimants receiving reduced IS under the hardship rules do not need to actively seek work (*ibid* reg.10a (2)).

In these circumstances much reliance must be placed on the procedural fairness with which the rules are administered. Minister of State, Nicholas Scott, was at pains to reassure the Standing Committee that: "Only in the rare cases where a claimant states clearly that he has no intention of taking any steps to find employment will any question arise to be put to the AO about his entitlement to benefit" (Standing Committee F, 2nd February 1989, cols.260-1).

Where the correct procedures are being followed, a claimant will have received a warning letter; further advice from the counsellor as to what actions to take; an opportunity to disagree with the reasonableness of the steps suggested; and an actively seeking work review interview. If this procedure has been followed and the Claimant Adviser still feels that the claimant's active seeking is in doubt, then s/he will submit the case to an AO using the form UB 672, and should inform the claimant of the grounds for the suspension.

Good cause for refusal of employment

Claimants who are considered to be voluntarily unemployed under the Social Security Act 1975 S.20 can be disqualified for benefit for anything up to 6 months. The grounds for disqualification are virtually unchanged by the 1989 Act. Originally intended as a method by which to protect the National Insurance Fund from claims when unemployment has been brought on by the claimant's own actions, changes brought in by the 1989 Act are more readily understood in terms of Government's desire to move claimants off the unemployment register, with little or no guarantees as to the quality of employment they are expected to take up.

Before the 1989 Act claimants could defend their refusal or failure to apply for a job, or refusal to accept a job offered to them on the grounds that it was not suitable and/or that there was "good cause" for the refusal (SSA 1975 s20 (4)). This included provisions allowing claimants to refuse as unsuitable jobs in their occupation paying below that which they could have expected to be paid in their locality if they had still been employed, or below the "going rate" elsewhere. However, after the lapse of an interval since their last employment "which in the circumstances of the case is reasonable", claimants were expected to take work outside their usual occupation, provided the job offered paid the generally observed rate in that occupation.

The 1989 Act removes all references to the "suitability" of the employment and restricts the last remaining defence – "good cause" for refusing a job offer – by closely defining "good cause" in regulations (SSA 1989 s12 (1) and (3) and UB Regs.1983 reg.12E). The effect is to remove the previous requirement for officials to prove that the job offered was "suitable" and to require instead that a person should demonstrate that s/he has "good cause" for refusing it.

The claimant has "good cause" for refusing the job offer if it could lead to serious harm to health or excessive physical or mental stress; if s/he holds strong religious or conscientious objections; if s/he has household care responsibilities; if the travelling time involved is over an hour each way; if the expenses necessarily and exclusively incurred represent an "unreasonably high proportion of remuneration". The claimant also has "good cause" if the job is under 24 hours work per week; if it is not properly notified by the Employment Service or by a qualifying former employer; and if the offer is made within four weeks of vocational training lasting over two months in another occupation. (The good causes instanced in the regulations are not exhaustive so that principles from case law may still be applied).

Similarly, for the purposes of IS, prior to October 1989, a claimant was treated as not available for work if s/he refused suitable employment without good cause. Now the term "suitable" has been removed (IS Regs.1987 reg.10 (1)). However "good cause" is not defined in detail in the regulations. An IS claimant refusing employment without good cause will be treated as not available (and therefore not entitled to IS) for 26 weeks or for the period for which the opportunity is still open to her/him, whichever is the shorter. If the job is no longer available the claimant will be paid IS but it will be reduced by the voluntary unemployment deduction (*ibid.*, reg 22 (4)(c)(iii)).

It is worth noting that UB claimants can still cite "good cause" for their neglect to avail themselves of reasonable opportunities of employment (SSA 1975 s20 (1)(c)) whereas this defence has not been inserted for IS claimants even though the employment opportunity no longer has to be suitable (IS Regs.10 (1)(b)) – perhaps because IS claimants only need to be available for work which they can be reasonably expected to do.

A new S.20 (A) is inserted in the 1975 Social Security Act by S.12 (4) of the 1989 Act. It provides for exemptions from disqualification if the job offer refused arises from a vacancy due to industrial action; if the claimant has been unemployed for over 6 months and s/he turns the job down after a trial period of more than 6 weeks but less than 12; or if s/he refuses to "seek or accept during the permitted period any employment other than employment in his usual occupation at a level of remuneration not lower than he is accustomed to receive".

So, whilst S.20 (4) of the Act as amended states that in determining "good cause" "there shall be disregarded any matter relating to the level of remuneration in the employment in question", there is an exemption during the permitted period. The length of that period is between one and thirteen weeks, determined according to regulations with regard to the same factors determining the period in which a claimant can restrict her/his availability (UB Regs. reg.12F).

For IS claimants there is no reference to a period of up to 13 weeks in which employment can be refused on the grounds of occupation or employment, although they do have a period of up to 13 weeks in which to restrict their availability to conditions consistent with their usual occupation (IS Regs. reg.10 (1)(d)(iii)).

Prior to the 1989 Act occupational flexibility and pay flexibility down to the "going rate" were expected once a reasonable time had elapsed since the claimant's last spell in employment. The 1989 Act means that, once the permitted period has ended, full occupational and pay flexibility are expected – employment no longer has to be suitable. The only guarantee about the quality of the jobs which claimants are expected to take is that they are handled by the Employment Service.

The Adjudication Officers' Guidance makes it quite clear that claimants may be expected to take up employment after the permitted period, even though it could result in severe financial difficulties for themselves and their dependants. In the first place, the defence which arises from unduly high costs which are "necessarily and exclusively" incurred has been narrowly defined, and does not include child care costs or mortgage interest payments (AOG 89607 and HC Written Answers col.64, 18th December 1989). Secondly, matters to be disregarded after the permitted period include the fact that the wage offered is lower than the wage that the claimant previously received; or is insufficient to cover the claimant's financial commitments; or is lower than that received by most other employees in that occupation; or that it is less than the claimant received in benefit (AOG 89514).

The Guidance also makes it clear that reasons which are not good cause also include particularly high financial commitments; the fact that another member of the household has unusually high living expenses; or that the claimant or someone in his household would lose the right to other benefits available to the unemployed (AOG 89521).

The Secretary of State for Social Security, John Moore, clearly believed that the setting of a specific permitted period was more stringent than the "reasonableness" test that it replaced. During the Second Reading of the Bill he stated that "it would be quite wrong for unemployed people to be able to continue to restrict their search for jobs that are beyond the rates of pay that they can realistically now command" (*Hansard*, 10th January 1989, cols. 716-7). The problem of long-term unemployment was thus characterised as one of unreasonable wage expectations. The new legislation requires claimants to accept employment paying not only below the "going rate", but even below benefit levels. Minister Nicholas Scott admitted: "I cannot say that under no circumstances would a person be expected to take a job below the level of benefit that they were receiving out of work" (Standing Committee F, 2nd February 1989, cols. 249-50). In saying so the Minister seemed to signal a fundamental shift in public policy.

Summary

In general, the 1989 Act has narrowed the conditions governing entitlement to unemployment benefits. In particular benefit penalties may now be applied after a period of between one and thirteen weeks to those claimants who persist in restricting the work for which they are available on pay or occupational grounds, or refuse job offers on those grounds.

Claimants turning down vacancies which they consider 'unsuitable' are no longer protected in law from benefit withdrawal or reductions.

And finally, although existing legislation and Commissioners' decisions had determined that availability for work was an active not a passive state, an explicit requirement to seek work in each week, and retain proof of that search, was introduced for the first time since the 1920s.

Part 2
THE EFFECTS ON BENEFITS

4 The effects of the Social Security Act 1989: The statistics

In order to assess the effect of the October 1989 changes we asked the following questions:

1 Did the number of claims disallowed on the grounds of non-availability and restricted availability increase?

2 How many claims were disallowed on the grounds of the claimants' not actively seeking work?

3 Did the number of claims disqualified for refusal of employment and neglect to avail oneself of employment opportunities increase?

4 How many claims for hardship payments were made?

5 How many unemployed have been removed from the register as a result of the changes?

Trends in unemployment benefit decisions

To put the changes into context we have shown the general trends in the way decisions about unemployment benefit had been moving in recent years.

Claims for unemployment benefit or income support are made initially within the Employment Service. If a doubt arises about the claim it is referred to an Adjudication Officer who decides whether to allow the claim and whether to disqualify a claim. Table 4.1 shows the annual number of claims for unemployment benefit, with or without an accompanying claim for income support, and the percentage of these which were referred at the point of claim to an AO because a doubt had arisen about entitlement. These figures include both new claims and the repeat claims which those signing on are required to make, usually every two weeks.

Table 4.1
Number of new or renewal claims for unemployment benefit
and the percentage referred for adjudication

	Number of claims (million)	Percentage referred
1984	5.2	32
1985	5.3	32
1986	5.3	34
1897	4.8	39
1988	4.0	39
1989	3.4	35
1990	3.7	32
1992	4·7	34

All tables refer to Great Britain unless otherwise stated. Numbers rounded.

Source: Compiled from *Unemployment Benefit Statistics – Summary Tables*, 1990; DSS; tables 4 and 18.

The first point to note about these figures is the very large number of claims which are referred, around one in three of all claims. In 1990 these amounted to 1,173,700 claims for benefit being subject to suspension, delay or at worst eventual refusal.

The second point to note is that there is no marked increase in the percentage referred after the 1989 changes; indeed there is a fall from 35% of claims referred to 32%. The October 1989 changes did not therefore result in any general increase in claims being considered doubtful.

We then considered whether those claims that were referred for decision were treated differently after 1989.

Table 4.2
Number of fresh or renewal claims for UB referred to AOs
and percentage disallowed

	Number of claims referred (million)	Percentage disallowed
1984	1.5	67
1985	1.5	67
1986	1.6	66
1987	1.7	62
1988	1.4	60
1989	1.1	59
1990	1.1	64
1992	1·6	70

Numbers rounded. This table does not include claims reviewed after the initial stage.

Source: as above, table 18.

While the number of claims referred remained almost exactly the same in 1989 and 1990 (there were just 1,000 more claims in 1990) the percentage of claims disallowed rose quite sharply from 59% to 64%, reversing a general trend from 1985. This could indicate that the October 1989 changes had made it harder for a claim to succeed. In order to check this we need to disaggregate the total decisions and look in more detail at which particular decisions account for the increase in disallowances. The following two tables give the percentage of all disallowed and disqualified claims accounted for by the chosen categories and the numbers of such claims. They enable us to see if the overall increase in the percentage of claims disallowed or disqualified is related to changes in the conditions attached to the particular categories we are interested in and therefore whether the changes brought about by the 1989 Act have led to more disallowances and disqualifications.

Table 4.3
Percentage of all disallowances and disqualifications
by selected categories of decision

Decision in respect of	1989	1990	1992
Availability	6.5	3.8	2.6
Restricted availability	2.6	1.2	0.3
Actively seeking work	-	0.2	0.06
Leaving voluntarily	32	25	10.5
Misconduct	10	8	4.3
Refusal of employment etc.	1	0.6	0.14
Failure to attend restart	0.1	0.4	0.16
Total	52.2	39.2	18.06

Source: Compiled from *Annual Analysis of Decisions of AOs*, DSS, 1989 and 1990, table 1.

Table 4.4
Numbers of fresh or renewal claims referred and disallowed
or disqualified by selected categories

Decision in respect of	1989		1990		
	Referrals	Disallowed	Referrals	Disallowed	
Availability	56 73,766	41,365	44,441	26,250	59%
Restricted availability	30 53,968	16,326	25,307	7,993	31.6
Actively seeking work	236	86	3,481	1,219	35
Leaving voluntarily	56.6 355,855	201,633	309,726	174,514	56.3
Misconduct	42.7 152,435	65,151	130,737	53,467	41
Refusal of employment etc.	37.7 17,410	6,566	11,360	4,317	38
Failure to attend restart	8.2 813	717	4,392	2,621	59.7
Total	50.7 654,210	331,533	529,444	270,381	51

Source: As for table 4.3. (ASW figure for 1989 taken from *Quarterly Analysis of Decisions of AOs*, December 1989.)

Availability

Table 4.3 shows that for all but two categories of decision the percentage of disallowed and disqualified claims accounted for by the categories affected by the 1989 changes fell in the first year of the Act's implementation. Taking doubts about availability and restricted availability together, those disallowed because of doubtful availability fell from 6.5% and 2.6% to 3.8% and 1.2% between 1989 and 1990. As Table 4.4 shows, there was a large fall in the numbers of claims referred on grounds of doubtful availability from 127,734 in 1989 to 69,748, and a similar reduction in the numbers disallowed, from 57,691 to 34,243. This sharp downward trend follows an equally sharp fall in the numbers referred and disallowed in 1988, when the combined numbers of claims referred on grounds of doubtful availability and disallowed were 223,700 and 95,200 respectively.

The changes in 1989 did not therefore mean any increase in the numbers of claimants disallowed on grounds of doubtful availability; on the contrary, they resulted in 57,986 fewer claims being referred, a drop of 45%, and 23,448 fewer disallowed, a drop of 41%.

Actively seeking work

There was bound to be an increase in the numbers being referred and disallowed on the grounds of not actively seeking work because of course this category was only introduced in October 1989. But the number of claims affected is very small, only 3,481 referred and 1,219 disallowed; they in no way compensate for the large fall in the numbers disallowed on grounds of doubtful availability. However, this is not by any means the whole story.

It is not easy to establish the effect of the actively seeking work legislation for two reasons. The first is that the figures in respect of claimants for UB are confusing, and the second is that there are no figures at all for claimants who have no entitlement to UB but are claiming IS.

There are two different sets of figures relating to the outcome of claims from unemployed claimants in respect of actively seeking work, both supplied by the ES. The first is a set of tables sent from the Chief Executive of the ES on 3rd July 1990, the second a different set of tables also from the Chief Executive of the ES, on 14th February 1991, both in response to a parliamentary question from Paul Flynn M.P.. They relate to two different time periods and are summarised in Table 4.5.

Table 4.5
Actively seeking work

	Warning letters	Referred to AO	Allowed	Disallowed
9 Oct. 1989 to 25 May 1990	28,910	5,161	1,164	1,722
1 Sept. 1989 to 30 Sept. 1990	43,604	--	1,694	1,013

Source: Letter from Michael Fogden to Paul Flynn M.P., ref. 2235/90, 3/7/90 and ditto, ref. PQ649/91, 14/2/91.

28

There is a major discrepancy in the number of claims disallowed by AOs; if there were 1,722 disallowed up to May 1990 it is impossible that there were only 1,013 up to September. The second line of figures above are consistent with those published in the Quarterly Analysis of Decisions of AOs, but whether this makes them correct or not is unclear.

More important than these curiosities is the very large number of warning letters which the ES sent out, 43,604 in the first eleven months following the new regulations, i.e. about 1,000 every week. Even though relatively few of these ended up as disallowances it is likely that the effect of the letters will contribute to the sense which many claimants have that the ES has become less user friendly. The statistics on the warning letters are not published in the regular sources of information about claimants, so their effect is usually concealed.

Refusal of employment

Many of the fears of those opposed to the 1989 Act centred on the changes to the regulations about refusal of employment and the neglect to avail oneself of the opportunity for work. In the event these too have proved unfounded. As Table 4.3 shows, the percentage of claims disqualified for these reasons also fell in 1990. This group includes three similar categories: refusal of employment, neglect to avail oneself of a job opportunity and refusal or premature leaving of a training course. In 1988 the total numbers in these three categories referred for adjudication was 22,200, of which 9,300 were disqualified. As we can see from Table 4.4, the numbers of claims referred decreased to 17,410 in 1989 and continued down to 11,360 in 1990, while the numbers disqualified fell to 6,566 in 1989 and to 4,317 in 1990. Between 1989 and 1990 this represents a fall in referrals of 35% and in disqualifications of 34%.

In addition to the figures given in Table 4.4 a further 5,410 claimants in 1989 were referred to AOs for decisions in respect of contribution credits for refusal to accept employment or training, of whom 2,528 were disallowed. The corresponding figures for 1990 were 4,545 and 2,816 respectively, a slight increase on those disallowed.

Restart

Restart interviews are one of the main means by which the ES provides help for the long-term unemployed. They have two distinct functions, to offer a range of advice and opportunities to take up a job or one of the positive options offered such as Employment Training, jobclub, Enterprise Allowance etc., and at the same time they also serve as a control mechanism to check that claimants are still available for and actively seeking work.

Apart from disallowances for not actively seeking work the one category which has shown a large increase is the disallowances following failure to attend for interviews, which relate mostly to restart interviews. As we can see from Table 4.4, these have increased from only 813 referrals in 1989 to 4,392 in 1990, an increase of 540%. This is also well above the figure for 1988, when only 1,400 were referred. Similarly the numbers disallowed as a result of the referral have increased dramatically, from 717 in 1989 to 2,621 in 1990, an increase of 365%, and also well above the figure for 1988 which was just 1,000.

However, there is an even bigger mystery surrounding these figures than for those relating to actively seeking work. It is very probable that the figures published in the *Annual Analysis of Decisions of AOs* show only a very small proportion of all those disallowed benefit after failing to attend a restart interview. Figures given by the Chief Executive of the ES show that far more claimants are disallowed than appear in the official quarterly and annual statistics. It is not possible to make direct comparisons between 1990 and any previous years for most of the outcomes of restart interviews because from April 1990 the basis on which the statistics are collected was changed. Prior to April 1990 the statistics were for referrals to the various options in the restart menu; after that date they are for only those referrals which the claimants are known to have taken up. However, thanks to the information supplied by the Chief Executive it is possible to compare the numbers of claimants who were disallowed benefit for failure to attend their interview, and it is also possible to compare the numbers referred to the UBO because doubts arose about their availability, their job search or their willingness to take jobs offered to them. While we can compare these latter referrals it is not possible to say how many resulted in disallowance because no such information is available.

Table 4.6 gives the information covering four different time periods, the last two of which are directly comparable.

Table 4.6
Restart interviews: claims referred and disallowed for failure to attend and claims referred to UBO because of doubts about availability, actively seeking work and refusal of employment

	No.of restart interviews	Referred for FTA	Disallowed for FTA	Referred to UBO
1/10/87 to 30/6/89	6,321,223	844,186 (13%)	44,479 (0.7%)	197,484 (3%)
1/2/89 to 31/1/90	2,781,400	299,000 (11%)	26,800 (1%)	n/a
1/7/89 to 31/12/89	969,735	145,184 (15%)	13,375 (1.4%)	25,952 (2.4%)
1/7/90 to 31/12/90	894,044	n/a	21,083 (2.4%)	14,724 (1.6%)

Sources: Letter to Paul Flynn from Michael Fogden, 9/5/90; *Hansard*, 9/3/1990, col. 906; letter to Paul Flynn from Michael Fogden, 5/6/1990, and letter to Dave Nellist from Michael Fogden, 15/2/91.

The figures in brackets are the percentages of the total interviews, so that for example from October 1987 to June 1989 the 844,186 interviews which resulted in referrals to the AOs because the claimant failed to attend was 13% of all restart interviews, and similarly the 44,479 whose benefit was subsequently disallowed as a result of those referrals were 0.7% of all interviews. We can see that there has been a continuing rise in the percentage of those whose benefit has been disallowed because of failure to attend, from 0.7% in the 21 months up to June 1989, to 1.4% in the last six months of 1989 and 2.4% in the last six months of 1990. This no doubt reflects the change in procedure which was introduced in April 1990. Before then if a claimant failed to attend two interviews they were called in for an interview at a UBO when the consequences of further non-attendance would be explained and a third interview arranged. Benefit would only be suspended if the claimant failed to attend that interview. Since April 1990 benefit has been suspended if the claimant fails to attend the second interview and the claim is referred for adjudication.

Conversely however, the trend has been in the opposite direction in respect of referrals to UBOs because of doubts about claimants availability, actively seeking work or refusal of employment, which have fallen from 3% to 1.6%. Between the last six months of 1989 and the last six months of 1990 these fell from 2.4% of all interviews to 1.6%.

The mystery about these figures can be seen by comparing Table 4.6 with the figures in Table 4.4. According to the Chief Executive of the ES in the last six months of 1990 the number of claimants whose benefit was disallowed because of failure to attend their restart interview was 21,083. From the same sources we know that for the whole of 1990 the number disallowed for this reason was 37,601. Yet in the *Annual Analysis of Decisions of Adjudication Officers* for 1990 the total number disallowed for "failure to attend for interview, including restart", is given as 2,621. We cannot explain the discrepancy.

Income support only claimants

It is relatively straightforward to find out what happened to claims for UB because the figures are compiled quarterly and annually and these are the figures that have been used in the above tables. They relate to all claims for UB, whether accompanied by claims for IS or not, so some claims for IS will be included in the above tables. However, there are no equivalent figures for those who claim IS only. In a reply to a parliamentary question on 18th April 1991 Michael Jack, a Parliamentary Under-secretary of State for Social Security stated that "No information is available on... the proportion of income support claims which resulted in a disallowance."

This is a serious omission in the data because the large majority of claims from the unemployed are for IS only. The changes in social security legislation since 1979 have resulted in a very marked shift away from the contributory unemployment benefit to means-tested income support. Whereas in 1979/80 53% of those in receipt of unemployment related benefits were in receipt of UB and 43% relied on supplementary benefit, by 1988/89 the numbers were 33% and 67% respectively (*Hansard*, 4/4/90, written answer from Gillian Shephard, col. 685/6). On one day of the count in November 1990 only 22% of all claimants were in receipt of UB, while 62% were in receipt of IS; the remaining 16% had neither (*Analysis of Unemployment Benefit Statistics*, DSS, May 1991, table 8).

If the claimant is not entitled to UB but is entitled to IS the AO in the ES gives an "opinion" to the AO in the DSS as to whether the claimant fulfils the requirement to be available for and actively seeking work. Since there are no published statistics equivalent to those for UB, to understand what has happened to claimants for IS only we have to combine two separate tables from the *Quarterly Analysis of Decisions of*

AOs, each containing different data. One table contains data on the opinions offered by the ES on IS only cases where these opinions have been asked for by AOs in the DSS because the doubt about the claimants' entitlement has arisen within the DSS. These tables also include information about whether the opinions were favourable to the claimant or not. The other table contains opinions on IS only cases offered by the ES staff where the doubt has arisen within the ES, usually at the point of claim or at restart interviews. These tables do not include any information about whether the opinions were favourable. However, by combining both sets of data and by making the reasonable assumption that the distribution of favourable opinions is the same for both, (that is, whether the doubt arose originally in the ES or the DSS) we can make an informed estimate about the likely effect of the 1989 changes on IS only claimants.

Table 4.7
Opinions given by the ES on IS only cases, with estimates of percentage unfavourable to claimant in brackets

	1989		1990	
Total number of opinions given	96,810	(51%)	75,919	(51%)
Estimated number in respect of				
Availability	49,373	(57%)	37,200	(54%)
Restricted availability	42,596	(43%)	26,571	(47%)
Actively seeking work	(-)		8,351	(48%)

Source: *Quarterly Analysis of Decisions of AOs*, 1989 and 1990, tables 3 and 4. Numbers do not add up to 100% because there were a small number of other decisions which are not included here. See note at the end of the chapter for basis of calculations.

There is no way of knowing whether the DSS followed these opinions, so there is no way of knowing exactly what the benefit outcome was for the claimants. However it is safe to assume that in the vast majority of cases the DSS followed the opinion of the ES, since this is what the evidence from those working in the ES and DSS suggests and because the DSS would need some additional information in order to go against the ES opinion, so where the opinion was unfavourable it is more than likely that income support was disallowed.

Once again, the year on year trend is downwards, so it does not seem as though the 1989 Act resulted in increased disallowances for IS only claimants any more than for those with entitlement to UB as well.

However, what this table also shows is the very large number of claimants for IS only whose benefit was called into doubt. These numbers are in addition to the numbers given above for UB claimants. Taking both together we can now estimate the total numbers of claimants whose benefit was called into doubt and the numbers whose benefit was disallowed on the grounds of doubtful availability and not actively seeking work.

Table 4.8
Total number of UB and IS claimants whose benefit was referred to ES AOs,
in selected categories with estimated number disallowed

	1989		1990	
	Referred	Disallowed	Referred	Disallowed
Availability	123,139	69,508	81,641	46,338
Restricted availability	96,564	34,642	51,878	20,481
Actively seeking work	236	86	11,832	5,227
Total	219,939	104,236	145,351	72,046

Source: Tables 4.4 and 4.7 above.

This shows clearly the large drop between 1989 and 1990 in the numbers of claimants whose claims were referred to an AO, from nearly 220,000 to 145,000, a fall of 34%.

It also shows that almost exactly half (49.6%) of those whose claims are referred on these grounds do eventually have their claims allowed. In the meantime they will have been subjected to the anxiety about whether they will be paid, and most will have received either a reduced rate of benefit or none at all pending the decision of the AO. In addition to these claimants we saw in Table 4.4 that if we add in those claimants who were referred for decisions about leaving work voluntarily, misconduct, refusal of employment etc., and failure to attend restart interviews the percentage of those whose claims are subsequently allowed rises to just over 51%, making in 1990 a total of 270,381 claimants who were subjected to delays, anxieties and often financial hardship yet whose claims were judged to have been perfectly valid.

Hardship

It is in just such cases where financial hardship may arise, either while awaiting the outcome of a referral to an AO, or even when the decision is adverse to the claimant and he or she is disallowed benefit on the grounds of restricted or non-availability or for not actively seeking work, that the regulations allow for a hardship payment to be made. This is the ultimate safety net and should ensure that even those claimants who do not satisfy the availability or actively seeking work criteria have some money to fall back on. The two cases are dealt with under different but similar rules.

Availability

Under reg.8 (3) of the IS (Gen.) regs. claimants who fail the availability test can nevertheless still be awarded a payment of IS if the AO believes that they or any member of their family will suffer "hardship". The amount of IS is reduced by 40% of the claimant's personal applicable amount, or in certain prescribed exceptional circumstances, by 20%; the allowance for dependants is paid in full. Hardship is not defined and is at the discretion of the AO, and could be challenged on appeal. (This is a different "hardship" payment from that to 16/17 year olds under sec. 4(a) of the SSA 1986, which is a Secretary of State decision and not subject to appeal.)

In theory every time a claim is disallowed the AO should automatically consider whether a hardship payment is payable and if so, should make the payment. The revised AO guidance for September 1990 states that AOs must consider cases for hardship "even where the claimant refuses to comply with the requirement to be available without apparent justification", and that "it may be necessary for further enquiries to be made" before reaching a decision (AOG, Vol. 3, para 25300, amendment No.16, September 1990).

Actively seeking work

Reg. 10A (2) of the IS (Gen.) regs. makes similar provision to pay a reduced rate of IS to those who fail the actively seeking work test if the AO considers that hardship would otherwise result. Where a claimant is already in receipt of IS the AO should automatically consider the question of hardship and if it is payable should ensure that payments of benefit remain uninterrupted (Gillian Shephard, *Hansard*, 6/11/89, Written Answer, col.458). In November 1989 Gillian Shephard stated that claimants in receipt of UB only have to make a separate claim for IS before the AO can consider whether to make a hardship payment (*ibid.*). By February 1991 her successor Michael Jack stated that "a payment to avoid hardship will be automatically considered" for all claimants (*Hansard*, 21/2/91, written answer, col.260). The wording of the appropriate section of the AO Guide follows almost exactly that for availability cases quoted above (AOG Vol.3, para 25481).

The procedure which should obtain between the two departments was explained fully by Gillian Shephard in a parliamentary answer:

> When a doubt arises as to whether a claimant is actively seeking work UB is suspended for the weeks of doubt, usually the two weeks since the claimant was last paid. The case is then referred to an ES AO to make a decision on title to UB. If only IS is in payment he gives an opinion. If he decides that the claimant did not actively seek work, UB is disallowed. His decision/opinion is passed to the DSS AO to help him decide what IS should be paid. This happens for each fortnight which the claimant fails to fulfil the actively seeking work test.
>
> The DSS AO has to decide entitlement to IS, and, if awaiting the ES AO's decision/opinion, will assume it to be adverse to the claimant. IS will then be withdrawn until such time as he satisfies the AO that he is again actively seeking work. If, in the AO's opinion, hardship will result, IS reduced by 40% of the personal allowance element can be paid (*Hansard*, 6/6/90, col.637).

An IS claimant who fails the actively seeking work test should not have to make a fresh claim for IS. However, if no hardship payment is awarded he or she will have to make a fresh claim for IS once payment has been suspended for more than two weeks (Gillian Shephard, *Hansard*, 14/6/1990, written answer col.330).

The figures

In order to understand how well the safety provision of these hardship payments is working we need to set the number of payments in the context of the number of claims disallowed. This brings us back to the problem that there are no accurate figures for IS only claimants. We have therefore used our estimate of the total number of all claims, both UB and IS, as in Table 4.8 above.

Table 4.9
Number of hardship payments made and awards refused, 1990

	Claims disallowed	Hardship payments Made	Refused
Avail. and restr. avail.	66,819	2,164	1,147
Actively seeking work	5,227	644	282.

Source: Numbers of hardship payments, *Hansard* 6/6/1990, col.635/6; 1/11/1990, col.667/8; 21/2/1991, col.259/260.

There are two important points to make about these figures. The first is the very small number of hardship payments made in absolute terms, only 2,808 in the whole of the year, less than 4% of all claims disallowed.

The second point is the very small number of hardship claims considered. If claims for hardship are supposed to be considered automatically, why are there so few refused? If the claims were considered automatically there should be as many claims considered as there are disallowances, but this is manifestly not so. It may be that the refusals only refer to claims that have been initiated by the claimants themselves, in which case this too is a revealing figure since it would show how few claimants take advantage of the opportunity to claim, which is not surprising given the improbability of most claimants' knowing that the opportunity exists.

Even the above figures are an underestimate of how badly the hardship payments are working because they are related only to the number of claims which are eventually disallowed. Hardship payments could also be made pending the outcome of a decision, so a more realistic figure to take would be the number of claims referred for decision rather than those disallowed. However, since some of these referrals would not be eligible for hardship payments (for example referrals on grounds of availability where UB was already in payment), we could not know how many, so we have not used them. It nevertheless means that hardship payments are even less effective than Table 4.9 suggests.

At all events, it seems inconceivable that less than 3,000 claimants in the whole of the calendar year would have suffered hardship when their income support was withdrawn, so we can only conclude that this safety provision is an almost complete failure.

Reasons why UB is not in payment

The DSS annual analysis of unemployment benefit statistics provides information on why claimants fail to be entitled to UB. Table 4.10 gives the figures for the years 1985-1990.

Table 4.10
Reasons why claimants were not in receipt of UB.
Count taken on one day in November in each year

	1985	1986	1987	1988	1989	1990
Number of claimants(000s)	2,151	2,118	1,832	1,403	1,116	1,215
Percentage in each category						
UB exhausted	49	49	48	49	42	35
UB not yet determined	9.9	10.3	12.8	13.3	12.2	13.6
UB disallowed/disqu. for						
voluntary leaving	0.6	0.7	0.4	0.6	0.7	0.8
Misconduct	0.2	0.2	0.1	0.2	0.3	0.3
Contribution deficiency	37	36	34	31	37	42
Other reasons	3	4	5	6	7	8

Source: *Analysis of Unemployment Benefit Statistics*, DSS, May 1991, table 16.

This table gives some clues to the effects of recent social security changes. In 1990 there is a sharp fall in the number of those whose entitlement to UB was exhausted, following a similar fall in 1989. Similarly, there is a sharp rise in both these years in the numbers who fail to achieve entitlement because of deficiencies in their contribution record. This is presumably because of the 1988 changes to the contribution regulations which extended the qualifying period to two years. This has resulted in the changing pattern, clearly noticeable in Table 4.10, whereby claimants now more often fail to qualify for unemployment benefit in the first place, rather than exhaust their entitlement to it.

Two other points to note are the continual rise in the "other reasons", among which will be the failure to pass the availability tests, which have become much more stringent from 1985, and the generally steady increase of claims "not yet determined", which imply longer waiting times for claimants.

Contribution credits

The process of deciding on contribution credits is another part of the social security system steeped in mystery. When a claimant is disqualified from UB for any of the reasons mentioned in section 20 of the Social Security Act 1975, e.g. leaving work voluntarily, misconduct, refusal of employment etc., the disqualification also precludes the payment of contribution credits. When a claimant is disallowed UB on grounds of doubtful availability or actively seeking work the disallowance also precludes the award of credits. Both these cases are decided by ES AOs, and the claimant has a right of appeal in both. When however a claimant who is not entitled to UB fails the availability or actively seeking work tests the decision to stop the payment of credits is taken not by an AO but by a nominated officer in the local office of the DSS on behalf of the Secretary of State, and from this there is no right of appeal. The only way a claimant can dispute the ruling is to ask for an internal review at regional level or ultimately at the Head Office of the DSS (letter from Chief Executive of the ES to Clare Short M.P., ref. 1953/90, 18/6/1990).

One effect of this strange division of labour is that while there are published statistics on the numbers of decisions made by AOs on the disallowance of credits that are consequent upon the disqualification or disallowance of UB there are no equivalent figures on those disallowed by the Secretary of State and none are obtainable (*ibid.*). The picture that we have of the effect of the recent social security changes on the award of credits is therefore partial. Nevertheless, as can be seen in Table 4.11, there has been a very marked increase in the numbers of credit disallowances between 1989 and 1990, even without including those which were Secretary of State decisions.

Table 4.11
Decisions of ES AOs on contribution credits

	Total	1989 Allowed	1989 Disallowed	Total	1990 Allowed	1990 Disallowed
All questions	80862	34899	45963	130431	57203	73228
Leaving vol.	53670	20567	33103	89582	33980	55602
Misconduct	21156	12150	9006	36053	21422	14631
Neglect to avail	411	193	218	346	178	168
Refusal of employment	1615	648	967	1781	619	1162
Refusal or premature termination of training	3384	1171	2213	2418	932	1486
Refusal to carry out written recommendations	276	64	212	251	72	179
Restart	350	106	244	-	-	-

Source: *Annual Analysis of Decisions of AOs*, 1989 and 1990, table 2.

The number of disallowances jumped from 45,963 in 1989 to 73,228 in 1990, a rise in one year of 59%, accounted for by the rise in those disallowed by virtue of leaving voluntarily and through misconduct. This follows on a rise from the 35,200 disallowances in 1988, so that in the last two years the numbers of disallowances accounted for by AO decisions alone have more than doubled. The effects of this on claimants is to weaken their future entitlement to contributory benefits, so that we should expect to see even fewer claimants eligible for UB in the years to come.

Effect on the claimant count

Overall these measures are expected to reduce the roll of the unemployed by as many as 50,000 (John Moore, Secretary of State for Social Security, *Hansard*, 10/1/89, col.718.)

To see whether his prediction was accurate we need to know not only how many additional claimants were disallowed or disqualified from benefit in the year following the Act but also whether these disallowances and disqualifications result in the removal of the claimant from the register.

Table 4.12 compares the total number of all disallowances, disqualifications and adverse opinions of ES AOs between 1989 and 1990, showing the effect of the Act on total disallowances and disqualifications in its first year.

Table 4.12
Disallowances, disqualifications and adverse opinions

	1989	1990
Fresh or renewal UB claims	634,500	689,200
Contribution credits	46,000	73,200
Opinions required by DSS AOs	13,400	11,300
Total	693,900	773,700

Source: *Unemployment Benefit Statistics, Summary Tables*, 1990, table 18.

The figures in Table 4.12 do not include the numbers of adverse opinions given where the doubt has arisen within the ES, nor the number of disallowances on credits given by the Secretary of State. Nevertheless they show a sizeable increase between the two years, with almost 80,000 more claimants likely to have lost benefit or credits in 1990.

Since there was no increase in the number of claims disallowed in the main categories we have so far considered following the 1989 Act how can we then explain the fact that between 1989 and 1990 the proportion of claims referred to AOs which were disallowed rose from 59% to 64% (Table 4.1), which is reflected in the additional 80,000 disallowances etc. above? We know the rise was not occasioned by increases in disallowances on grounds of availability, refusal of employment, leaving work voluntarily or through misconduct so it follows that some other categories of decisions must have risen.

We have seen that there has been a sharp rise in the number of disallowances of credit contributions, which rose by over 27,000 in 1990 which contributed towards the increase in disallowances etc. The rest of the increase can be explained almost wholly by reference to one other change brought in as an amendment to the regulations which took effect on 19th December 1989 (reg.7(1)(0) of the SS(UB, S etc.) Regs.). Far and away the biggest rise has been in the disallowances consequent on the change to the "full extent normal" rule, (whereby claimants with part-time work could claim benefit for the days in the week when they were unemployed if

38

they were days on which they would normally expect to be employed.) The new rule introduced an automatic disallowance of unemployment benefit when part-time earnings reach the lower earnings limit, currently £52 per week. In 1989 12,583 claims were disallowed because they infringed the "full extent normal" rule; in 1990 this number fell to 3,866, but in addition to these there were another 109,997 claims disallowed because the claimant earned more than the lower earnings limit. In reply to a parliamentary question about the likely effect of the new rule Gillian Shephard estimated that around 5,000 people would lose entitlement to UB (*Hansard*, 16/1/90, col.162). In fact it effectively took over 100,000 off the unemployment register.

The effect of these additional 80,000 disallowances etc. on the claimant count is not easy to estimate because it is not clear how the count is made up. In answer to a parliamentary question asking how the official unemployment count was compiled the following reply was given:

> The unemployment count is based upon the administrative system for paying unemployment related benefits, that is, unemployment benefit, income support and national insurance credits. It relates to people claiming these benefits who say that on the day of the count they were unemployed and capable of, available for and actively seeking employment (*Hansard*, 27/3/90, col.153).

In reply to another question asking how many had been removed from the register as a result of actively seeking work disallowances and disqualifications for refusal of employment the further clarification was given:

> No-one is removed from the register simply because their unemployment benefit has been suspended, disallowed or they have been disqualified for not actively seeking employment, refusal of employment or for any other reason (letter from Deputy Chief Executive, ES, to Frank Field, ref. 0070/90, 8/6/90).

Still further clarification followed in response to another question, this time asking under what circumstances the disqualification, disallowance or suspension of a claim for UB and/or IS results in a person's removal from the register.

> The monthly count of the unemployment register relates to all people claiming UB, IS or national insurance credits at local offices of the ES including those who may not be entitled to receive benefits. A person is not included in the count if they voluntarily decide not to remain registered as unemployed.

> ES officials may advise claimants that there is no need for them to remain signing as unemployed if they are not receiving unemployment related benefits. For example, a person who may be disallowed UB for a lengthy period with no underlying entitlement to IS may be advised that nothing is gained by registering. At no time are claimants advised to cease signing where payment of benefit is only suspended pending an AO's decision (letter from Chief Executive, ES to Paul Flynn, ref. PQ616/91, 11/2/91).

It seems clear that if a claimant is merely suspended s/he remains on the register. In all other cases it seems to be a matter of the claimant's choice whether they are counted or not. There is little reason why someone who had no entitlement to benefits or credits would want to continue signing on, whether or not the ES officials so advised them. It is disingenuous therefore to claim that no-one is removed from the register following disqualification or disallowance since presumably the most likely outcome is that claimants in that position would cease to sign on. This seems all the more likely in view of the ES's internal policy to "do all they can to dissuade people from insisting upon registering" (letter from ES Area Office, Wakefield, to local managers, 5/9/89). With little reason to continue signing on the vast majority of the additional 80,000 disallowed claimants would probably have come off the unemployment count.

However, as we have seen, this fall in the numbers of unemployed on the register has not been for the reasons foreseen by the Secretary of State. He believed that the new measures to tighten the conditions for availability and to introduce measures to force claimants actively to seek work would account for the fall; there appears to have been no fall in the count arising from these changes. The fall in the claimant count was almost wholly due to the removal of 110,000 unemployed part-time workers from the register through the change to the "full extent normal" rules.

Conclusion

We are now able to answer the questions posed at the beginning of the chapter. In the year following the introduction of the 1989 Act;

1 The number of claims for UB and IS disallowed on the grounds of non- or restricted availability fell from about 104,000 to about 67,000 (Table 4.8).

2 The number of claims for UB and IS disallowed on the grounds of not actively seeking work was about 5,000 (Table 4.8).

3 The number of claims for UB and IS disqualified for refusal of employment or training and neglect to avail oneself of employment opportunities fell from 6,566 to 4,317 (Table 4.4).

Contrary to many people's expectations, there has been a sharp fall in the numbers of claimants being disallowed benefit on grounds of doubtful availability, and those disallowed for not actively seeking work have been very few and go hardly any way to making up for the fall in claims disallowed for doubtful availability. In other words the ES staff have not switched to using not actively seeking work as a substitute for doubtful availability to any great extent. Similarly, contrary to expectations, there has been a fall in the number of claims disallowed on grounds of refusal of employment and its related categories. Why there has not been the increase in disallowances that was widely predicted is discussed in the following chapters.

It is clear, however, that the policy change in April 1990 to disallow claimants who fail to attend restart interviews after only two warnings instead of three has resulted in more claimants losing benefit (Table 4.6).

There has also been a sharp rise in the number of claimants who have lost entitlement to contribution credits (Table 4.11).

4   In the calendar year 1990 only 2,808 hardship payments were made in respect of claims disallowed for both doubtful availability and failure actively to seek work (Table 4.11).

Since there were over 145,000 referrals to AOs on these grounds during 1990, of which over 72,000 were disallowed (Table 4.8) it is impossible to conclude anything other than that the safety-net of hardship payments is not working, leaving thousands of claimants and their families exposed to real financial hardship.

5   There appears to have been no fall in the claimant count arising directly from the 1989 changes to existing provisions governing availability, refusal of employment, leaving work voluntarily and misconduct. Nor from the new requirement to actively seek employment. In contrast, changes to the "full extent normal" rule have resulted in over 110,000 being removed from the register, their earnings taking them above the weekly earnings qualifications for unemployment benefit.

Note on the deficiency of the published statistics

The statistics

In attempting to use the published data on the outcomes of claims for UB and IS we came across three different sorts of problems;

- the unavailability of some essential information;
- the near-unintelligibility of the published information;
- the discrepancies between different official statistics which supposedly related to the same topic.

Unavailability of published statistics

By far the biggest problem is the total lack of useful data relating to IS claims. There are no figures for IS only claims equivalent to the analysis of AO decisions for UB. Since the vast majority of claims from unemployed people are for IS only this is a very serious omission. There are figures in the *Quarterly Analysis of Decisions of AOs* relating to the opinions given by UB AOs on IS only cases, but these are not disaggregated into the different reasons for the decision and there is no way of knowing whether the opinion was followed or not by the DSS. In short, we have no way of knowing exactly how many IS cases are disallowed benefit because of non-availability, failure actively to seek work, or for any other reason.

Similarly, while the statistics relating to disallowances of contribution credits for those claiming UB are published those relating to disallowances of credits for those claiming IS only are not. For the same reasons as above, this leaves a serious gap in our understanding of the effects of the recent changes at a time when there was a very large increase in the number of credit disallowances for UB claimants, which jumped from around 46,000 disallowances in 1989 to over 73,000 in 1990.

With the computerisation of the local offices the publication of these data in a comprehensible form ought not to present insurmountable difficulties.

There are no disaggregated figures available on the outcome of appeals against disallowances and disqualifications, either for UB or IS cases. There is therefore no way of knowing how many cases of which kind were overturned or confirmed on appeal. This information is available in each local area so it ought not to be too difficult to make it available nationally.

The unintelligibility of the published data

The main statistics we relied on were those in the *Quarterly and Annual Analyses of Decisions of Adjudication Officers*. These documents present their data in the most economical fashion which assumes that the user has full knowledge of the meanings of the headings used and exactly which information is included in each heading. There are no explanations of any kind, so for example it is assumed that the reader would know the meaning of "renewal claims", "reviewed claims", "UBO limited decisions" etc. It is further assumed that the reader would know whether Table 1, which gives information on all UB claims, includes claims for IS or not; in Table 2, relating to contribution credits why that particular set of data was given and none on, for example, matters to do with availability for work or actively seeking work, and for Tables 3 and 4, which are both about the opinions given by the AOs in the ES to those in the DSS, what the difference is between the two tables and why one is disaggregated and the other not. In our opinion the figures as published are virtually unusable without further clarification from the statisticians who compile them. It ought not to be very difficult to include in the booklet a brief explanation of exactly what the statistics include and what they mean.

Discrepancies

As we showed in Table 4.5, the Chief Executive of the ES gave two answers to PQs about the number of disallowances for not actively seeking work which were plainly incompatible. He claims that the number of disallowances from October 1989 to May 1990 was larger than that for the whole year from September 1989 to September 1990, which of course is impossible.

Even more confusing is the discrepancy between the published data on disallowances following failure to attend for restart interviews. The figure given in the *Annual Analysis of Decisions of Adjudication Officers* for 1990 for these disallowances is 2,621. In answer to a PQ the Chief Executive of the ES gave the number for the same period as 37,601 (see Table 4.6). This throws considerable doubt on the accuracy of one or other's figures; if the Chief Executive is right it shows that the published official statistics are under-reporting these disallowances by a multiple of 14!

Note on Tables 7 and 8: estimates of IS only cases

In the absence of published figures on disallowances from benefit in respect of claims for income support we have made our calculations on the basis of the opinions given by the AOs in the ES to their counterparts in the DSS.

It is important to distinguish between ES decisions and ES opinions. The ES AOs give decisions on matters which arise in connection with claims for unemployment benefit and on certain matters which may lead to disqualification under section 20 of the SSA 1975 (see below) on claims for IS. They give opinions on other matters, mostly to do with availability and actively seeking work, on claims which are only for IS. These may be given at the request of AOs in the DSS or on the initiative of the ES AOs. It is these opinions which form the basis of our calculations about IS only claims.

The published statistics on ES AOs opinions on IS only cases are incomplete. There are two relevant tables in the *Unemployment Benefit Statistics: Quarterly Analysis of Decisions of Adjudication Officers*, namely tables 3 and 4.

Table 3 gives information on the opinions of ES AOs required by DSS AOs; these all relate to requests for opinions which have originated within the DSS when doubts have arisen about claimants' entitlement. These opinions are presented according to the different headings to which the opinion relates; the vast majority of which are about availability and restricted availability; for example in 1990 48% were about availability and 35% were about restricted availability, with a further 10% about actively seeking work, a total of 93%. (Nearly all the rest are about leaving voluntarily, misconduct and refusal of employment etc.) These tables also state whether the opinion was favourable or unfavourable to the claimant. It is therefore possible to tell both the percentage of opinions which relate to each type of issue and the percentage of decisions in each category which were unfavourable to the claimants. So for example we can tell from these tables that in 1990, out of the total of 21,758 opinions given, 10,553, or 48% were to do with availability, of which 5739, or 54%, were unfavourable to the claimants.

Table 4 provides information on all the other opinions given by the ES AOs to the DSS (letter from David Gent, DSS, to Alex Bryson, 15 May 1991). These relate to claims where the doubt had arisen within the ES, either at initial claim or restart. These opinions are in addition to the opinions given in table 3, and in addition to the decisions given in table 1 of the *Quarterly Analysis of Decisions of AOs* (David Gent, DSS, personal communication, 29/7/91). However, they are not disaggregated in any way; the only information contained in the table is the number of opinions. There is no reason to think that the distribution of such opinions between the different headings, and the percentage which are unfavourable to claimants will be very different from the distribution in table 3. Where the issue which is in doubt is anything which falls to be disqualified under sec. 20 of the SSA 1975 (principally leaving voluntarily without just cause or through misconduct, refusal of employment or neglect to avail oneself of employment) an ES AO can give a decision, not simply an opinion even in the case of IS only claimants. That is why the vast majority of claims referred to the ES for opinion relate only to availability and actively seeking work (David Gent, personal communication, and David Dunsford, DSS, personal communication).

We have therefore assumed that the distribution both of headings on which the opinion has been given and the distribution of unfavourable opinions for table 4 is the same as that for table 3. We have then added together both sets of opinions in tables 3 and 4 to give an annual total, and distributed the headings and unfavourable opinions on the same basis as for table 3.

Unfortunately, information on opinions on actively seeking work claims for the first quarter of 1990 is inexplicably omitted from the relevant *Quarterly Analysis of Decisions of AOs*. To arrive at an estimate of the likely number we have assumed that it would have been the average of the other three quarters. It does however make this figure more likely to error, which is unfortunate as this estimated figure is then used as the basis of the numbers estimated above. Nevertheless, it is still likely to be reasonably accurate, and in the absence of any other published information, it is the best estimate we can make.

There are no published statistics on the outcome within the DSS of opinions given on IS only cases by the ES; there is no way of knowing whether the DSS upheld the opinion or not. In a letter from William Smith to Alex Bryson he stated:

> There is no guarantee that such opinions result in adjudication officer decisions in the DSS. For example, fresh evidence received after a request for an opinion can persuade the DSS AO that a disallowance is inappropriate. To include opinions together with the numbers who have had their benefit entitlement suspended or withdrawn would give an incorrect impression because it does not follow that an opinion results in the loss or reduction of income support (letter from William Smith to Alex Bryson, 13th June 1991).

This may be true enough to warrant a reluctance to simply add them to the decisions recorded in table 1 of this source for the purposes of compiling the official statistics. In the absence of any other information we feel justified in using them as if the adverse opinion resulted in an adverse decision for the purposes of compiling our estimates because all our anecdotal evidence suggests that DSS AOs rarely depart from the ES opinion in practice.

5 Policies for the unemployed: The New Framework

We are going towards a minimal, basic service (member of staff, Brighton jobcentre).

The Employment Service has been re-organised in order to increase efficiency, to improve the service to the unemployed to help them to find work or training and to enable the staff better to police entitlement to benefit.

The New Framework, announced by Michael Howard in April 1990, is made up of five interconnected parts:

- Back to Work Plans, giving individual guidance for each client, agreed between claimant and adviser and recorded at the end of advisory interviews, and introduced in all regions in May 1990.

- Routine checks done as part of the "active signing" process. These are done by the Signing Clerks, who check on the progress of the "back to work plans", and help to identify those who will need more detailed help from an adviser. They were introduced in the vast majority of offices by December 1990.

- The merging of the roles of Restart Counsellors and Claimant Advisers to provide more continuity of contact for individual claimants: the "caseloading" approach. The process was begun in April 1990 and by December over 90% of advisers had the dual role.

- More systematic follow-up of those who do not take up places on employment and training programmes. The aim, according to the Chief Executive of the ES, is to refer those who did not attend back to the Claimant Adviser "so that more can be done to identify and remove barriers to returning to work" (letter to Paul Flynn M.P., ref. PQ 617/91, 11/2/91). This began in April 1990.

- More attention to those unemployed for over two years, including the requirement to attend restart courses. This process began in January 1991.

While the ministerial language and that of the Chief Executive of the ES, from whose letter to Paul Flynn M.P. the above summary is taken, is couched in terms of the help and guidance given to the claimant, the accompanying internal management documents lay much more stress on the policing aspects of these changes. In the draft guidance to ES staff issued to implement the New Framework there are constant references to the need to ensure that the control procedures are rigorously enforced. For example, active signing is justified because "entitlement to benefits, particularly availability and actively seeking employment is not being reinforced" and the Signing Clerks are told that their job is only to provide Claimant Advisers with information about whether the claimant attended their appointment or started the appropriate menu item by the agreed date (*New Framework for Advising Claimants, Active Signing Guidance*, Claimant Services Branch, September 1991, paras.2 and 7). Indeed they are specifically prohibited from giving the claimant advice on how to seek work, thus underlining their control function (*ibid.*, para. 20). The role of the Claimant Adviser at the 13 week review is to help the claimant to find work or training but also "to check that claimants continue to meet the requirement to be available for and actively seeking work" (*New Framework, 13 Week Reviews*, NF/90/29, para. 3). Those who have been unemployed for over two years will be reminded of the need to actively seek work because "advisers should remember that a check on actively seeking employment criteria is a thread common to all of our interviews and is a vital part of the Back to Work Process" (*New Framework, "Target Caseload"*, NF/90/30, para.4). With the very long term unemployed, those out of work for 30 months or more, advisers are told "at all times doubts about availability/actively seeking should be rigorously pursued" (*ES Framework for Customer Management Guidance*, August 1990, para. 15). The "caseloading" system is clearly seen as one of follow-up for the purposes of control at least as much as help; those who are singled out for caseloading are those who fail to start a job or training or those who have agreed to attend but about whom the adviser has doubts, or those who drop out within three weeks of starting on ET or attending a jobclub. Any claimant who has been unemployed for between six months and two years who declines all offers is to be "caseloaded" (*ibid.*, paras. 17 and 19). In an internal letter to all local ES managers an Area Manager in Yorkshire described the concept of caseloading more bluntly, but, in the light of the spirit of the management guidance, probably more accurately when he claimed that:

> There is much to be said for counsellors following up their own cases at all stages – that gives clients much less opportunity to 'wriggle off the hook' (letter to all managers from Area Office, Wakefield, 5/9/89).

The New Framework: a view from the inside

As the Operations Manager for one of the regions in the survey proudly claimed in one of our interviews, the new style Employment Service has a motto cleverly derived

46

from an acronym, – SMART – though he spoiled the effect by not being able to remember what came after "specific, measurable and accountable". This section is an account of how those who work inside the Employment Service and in the DSS[1] view the recent changes in their working conditions.

Under pressure

The biggest single point that the staff in all regions made was that there were too few staff to do the job properly, and that alongside cuts in staff resources there was a rise in the number of claimants. The new regulations concerning active signing, actively seeking work and availability had also generated more work within the service and more paperwork, for which no extra staff had been given. Taken together it meant that the New Framework was not being properly implemented.

Among the points made by the staff were:

- Actual job losses and cuts in complement, e.g. Hove DSS complement reduced from 184 to 84 in recent years with the resulting closure of specialist sections and the Haywards Heath DSS office cut by half in just one year (worker in Hove DSS).

- Staffing level stayed constant (or even reduced) but number of claimants increased, e.g. in the ES in Sussex and the DSS in St Helens. The staffing shortfall might eventually be made good, though not in numbers sufficient to satisfy local staff.

- The volume of work puts staff under great pressure; for example the volume of telephone enquiries in one DSS office was sometimes incessant. The local paper had tried all day to get through on the 'phone and had failed, giving them a story which made the front page.

- The administrative burden imposed by the new forms was "colossal":

  They have created more paper, created more work, but they are not giving us the extra staff to deal with it" (worker in UBO, Hammersmith).

- The high staff turnover in London resulted in poor quality service to claimants.

- When the ES was restructured the London offices lost a lot of staff who were redeployed to the north of England. The effect in London was that offices had to be staffed by casuals and transfers between offices, again lowering the quality of local knowledge and quality of service to claimants.

- Less qualified staff were 'acting up', e.g. administrative officers doing interviews because of a shortage of executive officers, and restart interviews being done by jobcentre staff with little knowledge of benefits, which must call into question the quality of advice to claimants.

- Computerisation in the DSS gave rise to many difficulties: There are massive arrears building up even in quiet offices which have never had arrears before (worker in Hove DSS).

On top of the pressure of work staff mentioned other factors which had resulted in a lowering of the quality of their working conditions. Priorities were seen to be constantly changing, from restart to new claims, from long-term unemployed to fresh claims, from the paying of benefit to job placement. One of the main effects of the reorganised service has been that budgets in the ES follow the number of unemployed claimants dealt with, resulting in management pressure to discourage the offering of help to casual callers who are in work and merely want to change jobs. These people are generally easier to help than long-term claimants, and provided much needed morale boosts to the jobcentre staff. In future their numbers will dwindle as they find the staff with no time to help them. By contrast, the fraud sections attract above average funds, so managers have an incentive to boost their work.

A curious by-product of the money following the claimants may be that, because the budget is calculated on a complex formula based on both the number of claimants and the turnover, the more successful the jobcentre staff are in placing claimants in work or other "positive outcomes" such as training, the fewer claimants they will have on their books and so the less money their office will attract. Moreover, as a member of the St Helens jobcentre explained, the drive to get a positive outcome meant that staff were under pressure to send less than suitable applicants for job interviews, which put their relationship with employers in jeopardy.

Our interviews with staff who work in the ES and DSS suggest that the result of the recent organisational and legal changes has been to lower staff morale, leaving them with a sense of frustration and sometimes anger. Staff in one DSS office said "morale is at an all time low", a view supported by one of the full-time chairmen of the appeals tribunals in Wales who thought the DSS was "demoralised and disoriented". In one jobcentre morale was said to be "low", with a rider that staff turnover was such that the staff would have changed in the time it took a case to be dealt with on appeal. Linking the low morale specifically to the reorganisation, one member of the St Helens jobcentre commented:

> There have always been targets of one form or another so when they brought these ones in there were the same old moans – 'how do they expect us to do it and when?' The difference was that middle management don't care about us any more. There is no job satisfaction anymore, just travel to work, help with jobsearch.

That management was uncaring was also voiced in one of the DSS offices, though this time for what they were felt to be doing to services for the claimants. A working party on organisational change concerned with centralising the DSS services as part of the move to agency status was described by a staff member of the Brighton DSS as "essentially a cost-cutting exercise. The phone service is being reduced, visits are being stopped; they don't give a damn".

The mood of many of the staff is caught in this comment by a member of the Brighton jobcentre referring to the direction in which the ES is seen to be going:

We are going towards a minimal, basic service. In the last six months fresh claims have reduced the services we can provide; we have cut down to the priorities of a minimum service. We are all getting a lot of stress. The benefits side will be much the same because it has to be.

Effects on procedures

The effect of staff working under pressure is that in many instances the measures embodied in the New Framework are not being implemented. The administrative burdens of the new rules and regulations were such that staff thought that it was simply unrealistic to follow them. As a manager of the Hammersmith jobcentre put it:

> If you were rigid and rigorous it would take up too much time. If I filled in a 195 every time someone refused to go to an interview or did not turn up I'd be all day at it.

Similar comments were made about most aspects of the new procedures; the following are the main points made by staff of the offices interviewed.

- They were expected to take 40 minutes over the new claims interviews but could only take about 20, making it less likely that new claimants receive all the advice and guidance which the new framework suggests they need. "We still check availability, but there is no real job search advice" (Brighton jobcentre).

- As a result of the shortened new claimant interview some offices were not doing a proper "back to work plan".

- Review interviews after 13 weeks were often not being done. As one staff member of a jobcentre put it: "The biggest priority is paying benefit on time. We put resources into that so we can't spend time on New Claimant Advisors mucking about on this 13 week stuff" (Brighton jobcentre). The only follow-up for many claimants is the restart interview at about 26 weeks.

- The penalties for refusal of employment were almost never considered until the restart interview.

- "Active signing", i.e. the checking by the benefit clerks that claimants have been actively seeking work, is often not done, and was seen as unrealistic given the large numbers signing on.

- "Permitted periods" are often not given, and when they are it is often impossible to arrange a review interview at the end of them.

- Only one of the areas had begun the system of "caseloading", i.e. trying to keep a claimant linked to one counsellor.

- In some areas it is difficult to know whether a claimant who has gone to Employment Training or a jobclub has dropped out, making it impossible to apply any benefit sanctions.

In other words, as a supervisor of the Hove unemployment benefit office put it, "We are not putting the legislation into practice." The New Framework was still a new idea, and one of the areas thought that they would be implementing more of it in future, but it was generally the case that it was being very patchily implemented.

One particularly interesting insight into the effect which administrative procedures can have on Employment Service staff behaviour and eventually therefore on benefit outcomes can be seen in the difference in the administrative burdens of disallowing benefit on grounds of restricted availability and of not actively seeking work. To disallow a claim on grounds of not actively seeking work involves far more work on the part of the staff; warning letters have to be sent, and the claimant has to be reviewed every two weeks once the disallowance takes effect. To avoid what is seen as unnecessary work staff often prefer to disallow a claim on grounds of restricted availability instead, since this involves no warning letters and no review. From the claimant's point of view this probably means a longer period of time on reduced or no benefit as it is likely to take longer to get reinstated when the disallowance is on grounds of restricted availability.

Effects of agency targets

One of the main effects of the way in which budgets are allocated to jobcentres is that the service will eventually become solely for the use of claimants; its role as a general employment placing agency will disappear. In evaluating the work of the centres there is a clear hierarchy; placing the long-term unemployed is rated most highly, followed by placing other claimants. Placing non-claimants is not counted at all for the purposes of determining staffing levels. Staff are therefore now actively discouraged from helping non-claimants and have withdrawn services from them. As the manager of the Hammersmith jobcentre explained:

> In future, jobcentre staff will be determined by the local unemployment benefit register. It shouldn't be like that because it shouldn't be dealing only with the unemployed but also providing a service for employers.

He might have added that it should also be for those in employment who wish to change jobs, or for other non-claimants, such as women returning to work.

The effects of this can clearly already be seen, as the following comment from a jobcentre staff member shows:

> From April 1990 each individual office has its own budget. Not surprisingly it is not enough. The budget on staffing depends on the number of claimants. We are trying to discourage others from using the jobcentre. We used to have a book of local authority jobs in the county councils and the local health authority; we kept their lists on the boards. We had a problem of people coming in, using the book and leaving without us getting any recognition. All that has been withdrawn now. Extra services like counselling and the book were used by non-claimants; we don't get extra staff for providing for them so it is cost efficient to provide just the basic services (Brighton jobcentre).

The probable effects of this radical change in the role of the jobcentres will be that the service will, like all services for claimants only, become a second class, second-rate, stigmatised service. Employers may well find that it is not worth their while notifying vacancies if they know that they will only be seen by the unemployed, thus reducing the effectiveness of the jobcentres as placing agencies still further. Already jobcentres are not allowed to compete with private employment agencies, as one of their staff explained:

> We are not allowed to compete with private agencies. If it's a really good job we are supposed to not take it but to say to the employer 'Put it in an agency'. People use them (jobcentres) because they are cheap (Fulham jobcentre).

Given that one of the major complaints about jobcentres is that they seldom have any jobs to offer, this emphasis away from being a general employment agency can only lead to a further deterioration in the quality of service for both claimants and non-claimants.

The introduction of performance related pay in jobcentres and benefit offices from April 1990 is likely to influence the behaviour of staff, with potentially unfortunate effects for claimants. Performance is taken on the quality of work over a year, and placing claimants in positive outcomes is not meant to be an overriding consideration, though jobcentre staff believed it will be. There are some indications that this is already having an impact and that claimants are being put under more pressure as a result. Staff in the Employment Service mentioned that one reason why there had been an increase in disallowances on grounds of restricted availability for claimants who were not available to work on Saturdays was "to get the quota up". They went on to add "personal performance indicators are having their impact, especially on New Claimant Advisors" (Brixton UBO/jobcentre).

According to a worker in the St. Helens jobcentre, staff are now told to "encourage people off the register", which is why it was important to "get the quota up". Indeed, one jobcentre said that they now keep statistics on those that they persuade not to pursue a claim at reception or the new claims interview; they even have a term for them, "non-pursuers". Staff at two different jobcentres who discussed this issue were clearly embarrassed at this policy and both declared that they personally would never seek to discourage anyone from claiming.

It is our impression that staff in the Employment Service whom we spoke to were very sympathetic to claimants and did not seek to harass them. Indeed, many had been claimants themselves. As a member of the Brighton jobcentre put it, "all these things that come in on paper would be a hell of a lot worse if it wasn't for the people who worked there". But it is a matter of priority for the management of the ES to meet the performance targets which they have set in the Performance Agreement with the Department of Employment, so the pressure will be on the staff to get enough "positive" outcomes, including deterring claimants from registering for benefit. In addition to internal management controls, if individual pay is linked to either preventing people from claiming or to "positive" placements, it will become increasingly difficult even for sympathetic staff to refrain from putting considerable pressure on claimants either not to claim or to take up a training option which they do not really want or need. As these comments from jobcentre staff show, this process has already begun. Mr X said:

if fraud don't get you they'll do you on the legislation. There's no way that you can't take up anything, unless you sign off – which a lot of people do (Fulham jobcentre).

We check up on take up of Employment Training, Enterprise Allowance Scheme and all other positive options. The Section Manager will want to know why the claimant did not pursue an option, so he is called in for interview the next time he signs on, or if he's only been a few days on the option and left the New Claims Adviser will ask why (St. Helens UBO). [ET and EAS and other positive options are not compulsory, and claimants should be perfectly free not to pursue them; the only exception is a specific job offer.]

Ms.Y said that after restart there was continual follow-up. It was possible for a claimant to have to see the Restart Counsellor every two weeks before signing on. She explained that:

this [was] the easiest way for a counsellor to earn a credit if the claimant signs off. It's like bullying to get them off the register. Each counsellor has a personal target based on his caseload; if someone looks easy they all go for him (Fulham jobcentre).

This is likely to be what the future holds for claimants, however well-intentioned the staff may be.

The New Framework: effects on claimants

The stuff that's done officially, warning letters and so on, are only the tip of the iceberg (member of staff, Brixton UBO).

The effect on claimants of the pursuit of agency targets is likely to be that they will feel even more harassed than they already do now when claiming benefit. This, combined with the requirement to show that they are now actively seeking work, is likely to increase the sense that signing on takes place within an environment where staff are more concerned with their own needs than with those of the claimant, and where policing the claimant is likely to take precedence over assistance with job placement. While these are important outcomes of recent organisational and legislative changes they are not the only ones.

There was a general recognition among staff that things had got tougher for claimants. Some thought it was the new claimants who were bearing the brunt of the changes because the emphasis was to prevent their becoming long-term unemployed, others thought it was at restart that the full effects were felt. For new claimants, form filling was described as a "minefield" which they had to negotiate carefully to avoid being disallowed on grounds of restricted availability. Some staff even felt that the experience of signing on now was so intimidating that some were deterred from making a claim at all, especially if they left their last job voluntarily, though they may still have been eligible for full or partial benefit. Even though in general the actively seeking work requirements were not being strictly implemented they still, in the words of one jobcentre worker, "panicked" some claimants, especially "middle-aged women".

Among the more specific effects on claimants mentioned by Employment Service staff were:

- Staff shortages in London jobcentres meant that some offices closed an hour earlier.

- Staff shortages meant that telephone calls took a long time to answer and some claimants would not have been able to get through at all.

- Staff shortages meant that new claims interviews could often take anything up to two weeks to arrange, with the result that claimants were not able to claim either for unemployment benefit or for income support. As these benefits are then paid two weeks in arrears this means claimants are initially without money for anything up to four weeks. Those suffering hardship may have been given an emergency payment, but by no means always.

- The emphasis now on only dealing with claimants at jobcentres means that those using the service are more likely to be asked whether they are claimants. Claimants may therefore be deterred from calling in to jobcentres on spec in case they are offered jobs by the staff, refusal of which could entail benefit penalties.

- The payment that claimants could get after they had begun work but before their first pay day was abolished in 1988. This may now deter some claimants from taking a job, as they would now have to last a month before getting any money.

- The actively seeking work requirement means that claimants over 50 who had been allowed to sign on quarterly are now required to sign on on the same basis as other claimants, which is a significant deterioration in their claiming conditions.

- The changes in the contribution qualification conditions for unemployment benefit, specifically the doubling of the qualifying period from one year to two, had significantly reduced the numbers of unemployed who could now qualify for unemployment benefit.

While all these changes meant that in general things had got worse for claimants, it was also the view of many staff that the effects of the benefit sanctions were only felt by claimants who were either foolish or honest. Streetwise claimants would have little difficulty in answering the availability questions so as to avoid disallowance, nor was it difficult to show that one had been actively seeking work, whether one had or not, and to engineer refusals of employment in such a way that one could avoid benefit penalties. As a staff member of the St. Helens jobcentre said, "the hard core are very aware". Thus the very people the measures were designed to catch, the persistently "workshy", had little difficulty in avoiding the sanctions, while the vast bulk of the unemployed were both harassed by them and even actively encouraged by the regulations to be dishonest in order to avoid the sanctions.

With the increasing complexity of the regulations it is not surprising that those whose first language is not English experience particular difficulties in claiming. As advice workers in London and Newport put it:

> People who can't speak English well are coming a cropper. They have difficulties form-filling; it's like doing an exam (Hammersmith Unemployed Centre).

> There are considerable problems for ethnic minorities claiming benefits generally – filling in forms, medical examinations for women. A woman recently went down to the DSS with a sick note, didn't get herself understood and left without making a claim (Newport Mind).

These comments were echoed by those working within the ES:

> The process of signing on now involves much more than ever before and if you've got social problems or literacy difficulties it's an alien thing; it frightens them (Fulham jobcentre).

A problem sometimes arose with claimants from ethnic minorities who had only ever worked in restaurants and who not unnaturally restricted their choice of jobs to restaurant work, but were then disallowed benefit on grounds of restricted availability.

The penalties for failing the new tests are real, and literally tens of thousands of claimants lose benefit each year as a result of failing them. What is less obvious, but felt by some staff to be no less real, is the effect on claimants of the climate created by the new insistence on policing the workshy. As one of them put it:

> The stuff that's done officially, warning letters and so on, are only the tip of the iceberg. To be told that you won't get your benefit if you don't attend restart or whatever, these local office practices don't appear in the statistics (Brixton UBO).

The effects of both the formal penalties and these informal office practices are at worst to create a climate of intimidation, and at best to leave claimants feeling that the experience of claiming benefit is likely to be fraught with difficulties to overcome rather than one where help and guidance is offered.

The Regional Chairman of the Social Security Appeals Tribunal for the area covering St Helens said that appellants often stated that they wished the DSS and ES were there to guide them through the mazes of social security rather than catch them out. In his opinion it raised the issue of how appropriate it was to try to offer advice and counselling in the same environment and using the same advisers as were responsible for imposing benefit penalties. In his view, these developments in the ES were "on the wrong lines". This point was confirmed by the comments of a Newport Careers Officer, who, because his role was simply to offer advice outside the formal system, felt he could work productively with his claimants. The separation of counselling and policing points the way to how the ES could be made more responsive to claimant need.

Those who offer claimants advice and assistance outside the Employment Service generally thought both that the new regulations were being sympathetically enforced and that, despite this, claimants nevertheless reported to them that they were feeling more intimidated when claiming.

In Newport neither the local M.P., Paul Flynn, nor the Newport Resource Centre, a local advice agency, had had many claimants coming for help with claiming, while the CAB had not noticed any increase in their usual steady stream of people needing such advice. The M.P. thought that both the ES and DSS had been "fairly gentle" with claimants.

In Brighton the picture was rather more varied. The CAB had had no-one needing help with actively seeking work, and the volunteers who worked for them had had no problems satisfying the ES staff that they were meeting the requirements. There had been no increase in referrals about availability and refusal of employment, but there had been an increase in claimants coming for help over the disqualification for leaving work voluntarily. In the opinion of a member of staff working there the pressure that the ES staff were under meant that claimants were being "let off lightly".

In contrast the Brighton Unemployed Centre had had a constant stream of enquiries from people "panicked" by the actively seeking work requirements, though none had so far been disallowed or even had a warning letter. This centre had, however, experienced difficulty in keeping as many of its volunteers who were claiming now that they had to show that they were actively seeking work. This centre had not noticed any increase in enquiries over refusal of employment, but had noticed that disqualifications for leaving work voluntarily had "massively increased".

Despite the absence of any general increase in requests for help from claimants using this centre the worker there felt that claimants were nevertheless under considerable pressure now to leave the register. "The main problem is people being hassled into taking work or just leaving the register." The problem was that there were so few jobs that the only way off the register was in to ET or EAS. When his centre had made a documentary on ET early in 1989 they had shown that "everyone felt pressured into leaving the register." Because of staff shortages in the ES it was new claimants who were under most pressure as these were more hopeful prospects than the long-term unemployed; hence the new claims interviews "put people under a lot of stress".

Another Brighton agency, Claim It, also reported little change since October 1989, apart from an increase in people wanting advice on actively seeking work. This agency believed that pressure was put on claimants in respect of actively seeking work at restart, which had changed its focus from being helpful to claimants to benefit control. For this agency also, the biggest single issue was the numbers being disqualified for leaving work voluntarily.

In a fourth advice centre, Brighton Advice, the most noticeable effect of the changes had been that they had lost most of their volunteers, who now had to be actively seeking work so could not continue working for them. They had also noticed an increase in disallowals for restricted availability. They had not noticed any increase in disallowances for refusal of employment, but thought this was because claimants were being intimidated into taking such jobs as they were offered, as had happened to one of their volunteers, and because there were so few jobs to offer. In general it was their opinion that "the changes have been effective in stopping people claiming in the first place".

In St. Helens the Merseyside Unemployed Centre felt that the prevailing level of unemployment effectively militated against implementation of the new legislation, which was only being used against those who had made no effort at all to find work. Nevertheless, they believed that the actively seeking work requirements had had an impact and were pressurising claimants into taking one of the training options, even though there were no prospects of work afterwards. Because people had had their expectations lowered over the years they were now more acquiescent and would take up options without the full weight of the regulations having to be invoked. People now accepted that claiming involved "jumping through hoops", so actual suspensions of benefit were rare. In the eyes of this centre, the new regulations were part of a long-term strategy to use the unemployed to force down wages, use the legislation to force people into low paid work, and to keep them there through the discipline of the disqualification for leaving voluntarily.

In London the Hammersmith Information Centre reported that the changes had not yet taken effect. They had seen no-one whose benefit had been stopped because of failure actively to seek work, nor for any of the other possible reasons. "It doesn't seem that they are particularly diligent in enforcing ASW." Another London centre had not had any referrals from people whose money had been stopped for failing actively to seek work, but they had seen a number of claimants who had been very worried by the new requirements and who had felt very pressurised into taking other options such as the Enterprise Allowance Scheme. Staff in this centre also believed that the ES were not properly implementing the regulations because of staff shortages and also because ES staff thought they were unworkable:

> I don't think they are implementing the Act. It's to do with staff time and resources. Some perhaps think it's a waste of time. Certainly at our meeting with managers we said the actively seeking work rules are ridiculous and they nodded, didn't dissent (Hammersmith Unemployed Centre).

Nevertheless, despite this, advisers still felt that the climate had become more hostile. When asked if he had noticed any changes since the Act the advice worker in the Hammersmith Unemployed Centre replied:

> It's the whole atmosphere and how people perceive restart. It makes it so difficult, daunting; people feel under pressure...

> The interviewers think they are helping, but claimants come to us feeling very upset and pressurised...

> People are prepared to stop claiming and take any job, including casual work. People go on to ET or EAS as a way out.

In this centre once again it was the voluntary unemployment deduction that was seen as the biggest problem.

The Shepherd's Bush Advice Centre reiterated that they had seen no actively seeking work disallowals and believed that the ES staff were not enforcing it; and they too felt that the voluntary unemployment deduction was the biggest issue.

Two other points were made by advice centre workers. They felt that the sanctions would generally fail against the very kind of claimant at whom they were targeted because experienced claimants "know exactly what they ought to be saying; they can't be getting the ones they want off the register", while at the same time causing anxiety for other claimants (Claim It, Brighton).

Most centres saw the long-term unemployed as a real problem for the ES which they had dealt with by what several of them called "recycling". They had been on the various training options and still failed to find work, or had taken one under duress and quickly left it again and were coming back again and again to the despair of the ES, who had nothing left to offer them. Advice workers also pointed out that to a certain extent this process accounted for the fall in the official numbers of long-term unemployed, because once they had taken one of the "positive options" they re-appeared in the statistics as a new claim, even though they had never had a real job.

Restart

Restart is the name given to the review interview which is supposed to take place about six months after the claimant first signs on and subsequently at six month periods. The aims of the review are to offer advice, guidance and motivation to help the claimant back into work or training, and to carry out the checks that the claimant is properly available for work and actively seeking it. Since the review interviews, which some claimants are supposed to have at the end of their permitted period or after thirteen weeks (whichever is the shorter), often do not happen, the restart interview can be the first review the claimant has.

Evidence from within the ES and from claimants' advice agencies strongly suggests that restart has become a less positive, more coercive experience for claimants. The advice agencies make the point generally, as these two comments from Brighton and London show:

> Most people who are refused benefit due to actively seeking work are refused at restart. Before, restart was more positive, with advice. If you were questioned about looking for work it was because they were going to give you help.. it was not so inquisitorial. The jobcentre people were aware of that shift, that it wasn't just the positive, supportive thing they saw it as before (Claim It, Brighton).

> It's the whole atmosphere and how people perceive restart. It makes it so difficult, daunting; people feel under pressure (Hammersmith Unemployed Centre).

Those in the ES can point to specific practices which have made restart more challenging for claimants. They now only get two warnings to attend instead of three, and when they come they are likely to find themselves for the first time since they have been on benefit faced with specific offers of jobs, refusal of which may lead to their benefit being suspended. They are also more likely to have their actively seeking work behaviour seriously questioned, and to be offered other "positive" options such as ET or jobclub. The flavour of the restart experience is captured in these descriptions by a worker in the Fulham jobcentre:

> Refusal of employment only really occurs at restart. If they turn down a job it is assumed that they already have one, so they pass it to Fraud. If not, they do them on actively seeking work. They are issued with a warning letter and called back in four to six weeks. If they say they are still doing nothing they are done. But that's not many, it depends on the counsellors.

After restart there was continual follow-up. It was possible for a claimant to have to see the Restart Counsellor every two weeks before s/he signs on. She explained that this was the easiest way for a counsellor to earn " a credit if they sign off. It's like bullying to get them off the register. Each counsellor has a personal target based on his caseload. If someone looks easy they all go for him."

One of the possible effects of this harassing of claimants was in evidence in this jobcentre. Some were recruited directly into the ES from their restart interviews, but then

> some people who come to work for us after restart stay for a day, then don't come back, don't even bother to sign on again, they're too scared.

When this happened it would presumably be seen as a "positive" outcome and count towards a credit, as the former claimant could be counted either as having found work or as having stopped signing on. For the claimant the outcome would be less "positive"; they would not only have lost the benefit and then lost the job but, if they had overcome their fear and signed on, they would have also been subject to the voluntary unemployment deduction.

For many claimants the sanctions take effect without their having the interview. The most common sanction is the disallowance of benefit which follows on the failure to attend the interview after the second invitation. In the eyes of the ES this shows the success of restart, indeed, it is even a reason for its popularity, as the Regional Director of the ES in London and the South East explained:

> Restart revealed to all but the politically committed that there was widespread abuse of the social security system. It led to major behavioural changes, yet it is still popular.

From this perspective, failure to attend must mean that the claimant has no need of benefit. While this may be true in many cases it is not always so. We were given examples of claimants mistakenly being asked to attend two interviews at different places on the same day and being suspended for not attending both, of warning letters not having been received, and of suspended claimants later providing good reasons why they missed the interviews.

One way in which several of the areas had markedly improved attendance at restart interviews was to schedule them on the same day and in the same office as the claimants' benefit was paid.

One problem for the ES is the increasing number of claimants who have been through all the options the service can offer but who remain unemployed:

Now on restart we get those who've done ET, EAS... We think "What are we going to do now?" We can't do anything with them. Long term sickness benefits have shot up because of this (Fulham jobcentre).

The "recycled" unemployed thus become the disabled unemployed.

The figures on the outcomes of restart interviews lend credence to the claimants' views that the interviews were often less than helpful. Table 5.1 gives the outcomes of restart interviews for the last nine months of 1990.

Table 5.1
Outcome of Restart, 1 April to 31 Dec. 1990

Number of interviews	1,329,907	(100%)
Restart course	23,340	(1.8%)
Jobclub	40,165	(3.0%)
Job placing	15,122	(1.1%)
Ent. Allow. Scheme	6,430	(0.5%)
Employment Training	56,617	(4.3%)
Moved to other benefit	22,660	(1.7%)
Total of positive outcomes	164,334	(12.4%)
Disallowances, FTA	31,679	(2.4%)
Referral to UBO re	24,146	(1.8%)
Availability, ASW, and R.E.		

Source: Letter to Dave Nellist M.P. from Michael Fogden, Chief Executive of the ES, 15/2/91, ref. PQ667/1991.

We can see from Table 5.1 that only 12.4% of all restart interviews end with some kind of positive option taken up. It may be that many other claimants do begin jobs or training as an indirect result of their interviews, but there is no information on this. The hard information we have confirms the evidence given to us by the claimants we interviewed that for the vast majority of claimants, seven out of eight, the interview leads to no positive outcome.

A minuscule proportion of interviews, only 1.1%, resulted in the outcome that most claimants want, namely a job. As a means of helping the long-term unemployed back into work it is clearly extremely ineffective. Once claimants are invited to the interview they have over twice as much chance of losing their benefit through failing to attend than of getting a job through the interview, (2.4% as against 1.1%) and if they do attend they still have a greater chance of being referred to the UBO for doubts about their benefit entitlement (1.8%) than they have of getting a job. This too confirms the impression that many of our respondents had that restart is often not just a waste of time but a risky waste of time.

In the covering letter with the tables from which Table 5.1 was compiled Michael Fogden states that "In the nine months to the end of December we have placed 165,400 long term unemployed people into jobs." The total numbers placed in jobs as a result of restart interviews is only 15,122. This means that the ES placed ten times as many long-term unemployed claimants into jobs without restart interviews as it did with them.

Restart courses

Restart courses are short courses, normally lasting about a week, or two weeks in the case of those with special needs such as literacy or language difficulties, which aim to help the long-term unemployed to rebuild their confidence and motivation, reassess their skills etc. as a prelude to helping them back into work.

From December 17 1990 people who have been unemployed for two years or more who refuse the offer of a place on an approved training scheme during their restart interview have been "asked" to attend a restart course. The request is backed by the possibility that benefit will be disallowed if the claimant refuses to attend. Announcing his intention to introduce the possibility of disallowance for refusal to take these courses Michael Howard said that the long-term unemployed "clearly have much to gain from such a course" *(Hansard,* 11/5/90. col.270). They now have much to lose as well. There is little doubt that the figures for disallowances following failure to attend restart interviews, including those disallowed for failure to attend the courses, will continue on its upward trend next year.

The New Framework: the views of the claimants

> If the jobs ain't there you won't find them, will you? (a claimant from the Newport sample).

The Employment Service Office (it may be a jobcentre, a UBO, or an of ice integrating the two) is one of the main agencies through which the Government's policies for the unemployed are implemented. Claimants go there to register their claims for benefit, to be helped with "back to work plans", to be offered jobs or training or assistance in their jobsearch activities, to be advised about rel;vant benefits with which to top up their wages, to be given their permitted period within which to search for work in their usual occupation, to have their availability and capability for work assessed, to have checks done to see whether the reason they left their last job will incur any benefit penalties and whether their jobsearch activities have been "active" enough. Three months later they may be required to return to the jobcentre for their follow up interview and three months after that for their restart interview, where much the same mixture of advice, assistance and policing are offered, though with more emphasis on the need for the claimant to make an explicit jobsearch or training plan.

The most noticeable feature of the jobcentre is the uneasy mixture of assistance and benefit control. There is no doubt how the claimants view the balance between the two; with few exceptions those in our sample saw the help as being at best well-intentioned but useless since what they wanted above all was a decent job and this was the one thing the jobcentre could not provide, at worst insensitive and degrading. Either way, it was insignificant compared to the ever present reality of the controls which could lead to loss of benefit. Even where these were not being actively enforced the threat of them far outweighed any potential benefits the jobcentre had to offer, especially at the restart stage.

Very few of the claimants could recall being offered a job at a jobcentre, whether at the initial new claimant interview or at restart. (Hardly any in our sample could recall having had a follow-up interview after three months.) While a few had found jobs through the self-service cards, most did not expect to find a job by loo،ing at the cards since it was their common experience that the jobs had already been taken. In any case, such jobs as there were were usually low paid and unattractive. When better jobs were on offer claimants often found they lacked the necessary qualifications. The following comments from Brighton claimants are characteristic of the widely held views of the claimants in our sample in all four regions:

> The jobcentre is virtually useless... There's lots of boards with hotel waitress, bar work, the rest of it you might as well forget. There's nothing there I don't think for anybody. The thing is, any decent jobs in there you find have already been seen by like fifty other people so there's no chance of you getting one anyway.

> Last summer I went in there, I applied, well I went up to them with three jobs because you have to take the numbers down and go up to them. They phoned up all of them and the jobs were gone. That's the problem with the place; they're not efficient to know that the job's gone so 90% of the jobs that you see up there aren't actually existing any more.

Several claimants had been offered training under the Employment Training scheme, but almost without exception the offer was vitiated by being linked to threats, real or imagined, of benefit loss if the offers were not accepted. This led to the widely held belief that the offer had far more to do with reducing the number of unemployed on the register than with the training needs of the claimant. The quality of the training was generally held to be poor; "slave labour" was a term used by several claimants. The following comments about Employment Training from claimants from each of the regions were typical:

> To me it's just something to get you off their figures when they stick 'em on the telly and they say unemployment's gone down by x amount (St Helens).

> I was on this ET. I got on it for a year and I think it's a waste of time myself, 'cos they're not organised, 'cos when they actually place you up in the jobs there's no actual official trainer. We were painting the old ladies flats at C... There was no official painter and decorator qualified to tell us what to do (Newport).

> I think they're just trying to scare you, to scare you on to it, because you could think like 'Oh well, I'd rather have the extra tenner than nothing at all' (Hammersmith).

> I ended up feeling that all they wanted to do was to get me off the unemployment figures... The last thing that occurred to me was that she actually wanted to help me find some sort of training which, you know, would be of any assistance in the future and I must admit I came away from there and I looked at all these forms that I'd filled in and I thought well what a complete and utter waste of time (Brighton).

61

Claimants could see the potential of and would welcome a good training scheme. One felt that she was missing out on the potential help the jobcentre had to offer because, having dependent children and being a lone parent, she was not required to be available for work and so was not included in the jobcentre's control mechanisms. She felt she was left to vegetate at home when she would much prefer to have been called in for interview and have an interest taken in her. Others had tried to use the training, only to find that the reality was less than ideal. One wanted to take a course in weight-training and was mystified to find herself offered a course in child care, another wanted a course on car mechanics and was sent on a plumbing course. A third wanted to take an HGV driving course and recalled his experience when he finally tracked down the trainer to whom he was directed:

> The chap there said when we'd had the interview 'Well, yes I do agree that all I can offer you is a minimum of six months basically slave labour working for the council and a possibility once you've taken your HGV test and passing. If you don't then you've got to do another six months', and I came away from that feeling that the whole thing had been a complete and utter waste of time; everybody's time (Brighton).

With no jobs to offer and training seen mostly as poor quality and a means of bringing down the claimant count the jobcentre has an uphill struggle to present itself in a positive way to claimants. The helpful advice embodied in the much publicised "back to work plans" had either gone unnoticed by the claimants or, where it had been offered, had made little impression. All those who could remember having done a plan said the advice consisted of being told to look in the papers for vacancies, ask friends, or ring round likely employers, advice dismissed by one Brighton claimant as "stunningly obvious". Nor could any claimant remember being given advice about in-work benefits in any detail. Most claimed not to have been told about them at all, while one of the few who was said he was told he could get housing benefit to top up his wages but was not told how much. No-one had been given a clear statement about the financial consequences of taking a particular job, though this may of course have been due to the fact that no-one had been offered a job.

The negative perception of jobcentres and unemployment benefit offices had been reinforced since the new Act because of a combination of factors. There was a strong belief that the ES staff were only interested in getting the number of unemployed down by any means, regardless of the claimant's wishes, and there was now a greater emphasis on asking inquisitorial questions designed to catch claimants out and stop their benefit. While this was particularly true of restart interviews it also held for new claims. When going to the jobcentre claimants anticipated trouble, not help, and were ready for it.

Views about the way the staff treated claimants varied, as one would expect. Some staff were seen as helpful and interested in the claimant as a person, others as decidedly not so. Two claimants who were helped on to a training course that they had wanted and one who was helped in to an Enterprise Allowance Scheme had found their visit to the jobcentre worthwhile. For the majority it had been not only a pointless visit in that nothing of value had come from it but often a belittling or degrading experience because of the questioning. Sometimes claimants felt intimidated and pushed in to options they did not want because their benefit was at stake. That claimants often felt embattled in one way or another can be seen from the following comments:

> The only trouble is they ask you that many questions and repeat themselves over and over again. No, what I mean, some of the questions... and so that's why people... I never signed on for six months and I wasn't even working. I said 'Sod it, I can't be bothered' (St Helens).

> It's all these forms. If you've got somebody who's not very bright, you got these forms like, two inches thick, and you think 'Oh my God have I got to fill all them in?' And some of the questions, you don't understand them, you just can't.. you need a dictionary to understand it (St Helens).

> It's their attitude; 'Oh you're here again! You're poncing. Oh not another one!' (Hammersmith).

> I mean after filling in the B1 and everything all the information was written there anyway and this girl just sat there firing out all these questions like, 'Why did you leave your last job? Why didn't you look for something else?' I'd answered everything, you know, and still, it was intimidating (Hammersmith).

> I get the impression I'm sure everyone else agrees that they're really only interested in processing you as quickly as possible. If you don't quite fit the category they want they'll try and squeeze and push so that you do actually fit into it (Hammersmith).

> They're not really interested in you per se at all; you're just another statistic, another piece of work they don't want to do (Hammersmith).

While some claimants felt very negatively towards the staff in the jobcentres and UBOs, others were ready to concede that the staff too were under great pressure which prevented their being as helpful as they might have been. Staff were seen to have very little time for each claimant, so that it was very difficult to cultivate the personal touch they would all have liked, and some were aware that the jobcentre was poorly equipped to find jobs as only the low paid jobs were placed there.

It is against this background, with claimants generally feeling that jobcentres are heavily biased towards the control of benefits rather than offering positive assistance, that we can now turn to the way in which those controls are experienced by the claimants, and how they try to counter them.

Awareness of benefit penalties

Claimants were well aware that their benefit could be stopped, so they knew that if they were caught out by the staff at the jobcentre or benefit office they stood to lose their money. It was this which heightened their awareness of the controls. However they were less clear about exactly which penalties were attached to which behaviour, which gave their dealings with the authorities an air of unpredictability and uncertainty.

Some claimants were aware that refusal to take a job that was on offer could result in loss of benefit, and it was widely, though erroneously, believed that you had three chances before benefit was stopped. However, as none had had jobs offered them this was all rather speculative. Nevertheless, had one of them been offered a job and refused it he or she could have lost benefit through this mistaken belief. It was seen by claimants as reasonable that such a penalty should exist, though some felt that it could be used to force claimants to take very low paid jobs against their will. There was, however, a simple way round the problem, as one pointed out:

> I think I would probably play the game and go along to the interview but if I didn't particularly want the job then I would know ways and means of blowing it (Brighton).

This vagueness about penalties extended to actively seeking work. Most claimants were aware that failure to show active job searching meant loss of benefit, but few knew for how long it would last. Nearly all the claimants in our sample knew that they now had to show that they had been actively seeking work. For some it was a reality because they had been asked to prove that they had been, for others it had made no appreciable difference as it had not been enforced. None thought it would help them find a job; most had simple ways round the requirements. All four groups agreed that while staff in the jobcentres and benefit offices had told them that they could now be required to show proof of their active jobsearching none had been pressed to do so. Some had not been asked to account for themselves at all, some had been called in for interviews where they had been questioned about their efforts to find work but had quickly satisfied their questioner, but none had been threatened with loss of benefit.

The requirement was seen as contributing to the general sense that there was more pressure since 1989 to get a job. The following comment is one which was echoed by other claimants:

> Well it's just, well just all these little things like you're going to have to come back in three months time and you should be actively seeking work. You may be asked at any time. I think somebody actually said to me 'You can be asked at any time to prove that you are actively seeking work, that includes newspaper cuttings, signing on at job agencies' and they didn't just say at a restart interview, they did say at any time (Brighton).

However claimants also agreed that it was not very helpful to have this additional pressure put on them since there were so few jobs around to be had. As one Newport claimant succinctly put it, "If the jobs ain't there you won't find them will you?"

Even though the requirement was not being very rigorously implemented claimants still felt obliged to go through the motions of keeping records of their jobsearching as an insurance. "I did it to cover myself in case they asked because I didn't want any hassle with my money" (Newport). When they found that they weren't being asked to show the records they had kept they soon stopped keeping them. Several claimants reported having stopped in this way, which is potentially risky because if they were then required to produce proof of their efforts they would have none.

One of the claimants had found the need to keep written records of his activities too daunting and when the staff he had approached proved to be less than helpful he simply gave up, which again could potentially have put his benefit in jeopardy.

The requirement was generally seen as a tiresome hurdle to be overcome, involving unnecessary extra work simply in order to qualify for benefit rather than as an aid to finding work:

> All it is is messing you about, making you go out of the house, walk around these places on the bike or in the car, going round them all, get all your 'noes', send 'em in, and that's all they're doing, messing you about. They're not giving you nothing, they're not offering you nothing (Newport).

In response to what was felt to be an unreasonable and pointless burden claimants had found their own remedies. While some had filled in their record sheets to cover themselves, others claimed to have simply made up what they felt the benefit staff wanted to hear. Some claimed to have made the whole thing up just before signing on, others said they got their friends to sign as if they were employers saying that the claimant had applied to them for a job. Such cheating was seen to be wholly justified:

> Well it's not exactly difficult to cheat the system anyway. Just go for jobs you know you're not qualified for. What's the point of it, it's all a joke anyway isn't it? (Newport).

Sometimes claimants clearly felt a sense of anger at being asked to look for jobs when they felt none were there, and showed it in the way they set about providing their evidence:

> I've just sent a load of letters off to totally different things and just say 'Well there you are, there's twenty letters I've just sent off, I'm looking for work.' Even though you might not really want any of the jobs just fill in a letter and send it off, don't take any notice of how you've written or anything, just throw it in an envelope, take 'em in all sealed and stamped and say 'There you are, there's twenty letters, I'm going to post them now' and say 'How can you take the benefit now when there's twenty letters there for twenty jobs?' (St Helens).

The relaxed way in which the requirement had been implemented so far encouraged claimants not to take it very seriously. Benefit staff seemed not to be very eager to enforce this particular rule; one claimant reported that his benefit officer had told him that he was not there to stop his benefit but to help him find work. But while benefit staff were generally seen as being fairly easy-going on this issue there was also a belief that it was all a game of bluff and that it would be very difficult to enforce in any case, given the lack of jobs:

> There's 2 to 3 million unemployed and so they're not going to stop everyone's benefit, and anyone can get letters from a job, anyone, it's so easy. It don't mean that you're going to get that job but you can easily get proof of jobs, even getting last week's *Gazette* and bringing it in (Hammersmith).

The impression we were left with from the interviews with claimants was that the actively seeking work requirement was an irritant which contributed to their sense of being pressurised not into useful job searching activities but into either the pointless recording of fruitless efforts at chasing non-existent jobs or into the fabrication of evidence which was felt to be more than justified by the futility of the regulations. Far from enabling claimants back into work it contributed to their sense of frustration and annoyance and actively encouraged them to be dishonest. That it was all as yet only a mild irritation was because the staff of the Employment Service had generally had the good sense to moderate the requirement in the light of the lack of available jobs.

Liaison between the Employment Service and DSS

> DSS and DE legislation is so interconnected yet you are getting different applications and different laws (full-time chairman, Social Security Appeals Tribunals, St Helens).

Staff members in both the ES and the DSS referred to the poor liaison between the two agencies, and the failure to set up effective co-ordinating machinery. There were a number of aspects to this, mostly with adverse consequences for claimants.

A recurrent issue is the delay in payment of income support because the ES won't accept a claim until after a new claims interview. As a staff member in the Hove DSS office explained:

> The main problem has been with fresh claims interviews; it's a real hassle. The person will get a B1 [an income support claim form] but won't have a fresh claim interview for a couple of weeks so we've had to do hardship payments. Claims used to be dealt with straightaway; they aren't now. It's to do with the changes now that it's the ES.

Many claimants would not be eligible for hardship payments and so just have to wait. Even when claimants are eligible some offices would make hardship payments "only if the claimant insisted", and staff readily conceded that most claimants do not (St Helens DSS). In other offices they refer claimants in this position to the hazards of the social fund instead of making a hardship payment. This means that, even if the claimant is successful in getting a payment, it will take time and will often be in the form of a loan.

In one area, liaison between the two offices is such that even when the DSS is willing to accept a claim and authorise payment the UBO refuses to put it into effect:

> At the end of the first two weeks we send down instructions to the UBO to pay, having received the first B1. If they haven't had a fresh claims interview they'll send the order book back saying they haven't claimed. They are not treating the first B1 as the actual claim until they've had a claim interview (Hove DSS).

One way in which the lack of co-ordination could work to the claimants' benefit was mentioned by two different offices (Hove DSS and Brixton UBO). It concerned the inability of the UBO computer to allow for the classification of suspension on grounds of failure actively to seek work or refusal of employment in claims that were already in progress. We were told that the results of this technical hitch were "either their income support is not touched or they lose it all". Both outcomes are contrary to the legislation; one would pay more money to claimants than their entitlement and one less.

Even without computer bugs wrong payments are made simply because of poor inter-departmental liaison. A staff member at the Brixton Jobcentre said that through lack of communication between the two departments "there were a number of claimants who were indefinitely suspended, so are not getting credits, but are getting their full income support." This was simply because the ES had not informed the DSS that the claimants had been suspended or asked them to stop payments. Conversely there were also other cases known to him where the DSS had stopped payment even though no decision to suspend or disallow benefit had been made within the unemployment benefit office. While each department was able to cope with work that fell within its domain he felt that "when anything overlaps DSS and DE they just forget about it; even if the DE makes a proper submission the DS may just ignore it".

In other words, purely because of poor liaison between the two departments, some claimants wrongfully continue to receive benefits when they should not and others have their benefits wrongfully stopped.

The lack of co-ordination could also affect claimants adversely at the appeal stage in respect of appeals against disqualifications of unemployment benefit or deductions in income support. Where claimants had been disqualified from unemployment benefit on any of the usual grounds, i.e. leaving employment without just cause, being sacked for misconduct, refusal of employment etc., the consequences would be that they lost entitlement to unemployment benefit for up to 26 weeks and simultaneously, if they were eligible for income support, this would in most cases be paid at a reduced rate. Where claimants were not eligible for unemployment benefit but were eligible for income support, this would be paid at a reduced rate if the DSS were advised by the ES that the claimant would have been so disqualified on one of these grounds if they had been eligible for unemployment benefit. In other words, decisions about whether to penalise claimants on one of these grounds is always taken in effect, if not in law, by the staff in the Employment Service because they have the relevant experience and expertise.

When lodging an appeal against one of these decisions it is essential that the appeal is lodged with *both* departments where income support is at issue as well as unemployment benefit. If the appeal is lodged against only the income support decision it is almost certainly bound to fail because all that the DSS has to show is that the claimant has been disqualified by the ES, regardless of the reasonableness of the decision, or, if no decision had yet been taken, that "a question as to disqualification" arises (Regulation 22(4)(c) Income Support (General) Regulations). Since it is the ES who makes the decision on which all else turns it is to them that the appeal must also be made.

As the full-time chairman of the Social Security Tribunals in St Helens pointed out, the lack of co-ordination between the two departments means that the obvious rerouting of appeals from the DSS to the DE in these instances does not always happen. He claimed there was

> a big waste of money occurring taking these appeals because we know they'll lose from the start, and that they should get the DSS to transmit the appeal to the DE so that it results in an appeal against both departments.... It hasn't worked totally smoothly because of lack of co-ordination between DSS and DE.

Waste of public money is one consequence; wasted time, wasted journeys, unnecessary frustration and still more delays in having an appeal or even the loss of the opportunity to appeal through too long a time delay and therefore the loss of the chance to recover lost benefit are the consequences for the claimants.

The dependence of the DSS on the ES in matters concerning decisions about whether to disallow benefit or to disqualify claimants was seen as problematic by staff in both departments and by those on appeals tribunals. The practice is for the ES to make decisions about whether claimants are available for work or have brought themselves within a disqualification when the claim is for unemployment benefit, and for the ES to pass an "opinion" to the DSS on these matters when the claim is for income support. This "opinion" is invariably accepted by the DSS unless they have additional contradictory information. The effect of this is that it is the ES that makes decisions about claimants' availability for work even where the claim is for income support only. An unemployment benefit officer in the Hammersmith UBO was highly critical of the dependence of the DSS on the ES for decisions about availability even in cases where the claim was solely for IS. She explained that

> if a person trying to make a new claim was believed to be non-available or restricting availability it is written on the back of the B1 and it never gets off the ground.

The significance of this is that it is quite possible that many claimants for IS are being disallowed at the new claim stage by ES staff using regulations applicable to unemployment benefit even though the rules applicable to IS are less stringent. To qualify as available for work under the unemployment benefit regulations the claimant must usually be available for 6 days in each week (Unemployment, Sickness and Invalidity Benefit Regulations, 1983 7B); to qualify as available for work under the income support regulations it is necessary to be available for only 24 hours in each week (Income support (General) Regs. 7(1)(c)). It is quite probable that many claimants could fail the UB test while passing the IS test, yet they might still be disallowed income support. There is some evidence that this is in fact happening; a member of staff in the London South Regional Office of the Social Security Appeals Tribunals said that they had dealt with an appellant who had been disallowed IS on grounds of restricted availability when she had been available for 30 hours. If her interpretation of the regulations is correct it is likely that many claimants are currently being wrongfully denied IS on these grounds.

A secondary consequence of the DSS's dependence on the decisions (or opinions) of the ES is that inevitably the decision making process is slowed down. By the time a claim for IS has been referred from the ES to the Adjudication Officer in the ES, the decision sent back from the Adjudication Officer to the ES and then forwarded to the DSS it was not unusual in one southern region for six weeks to have elapsed, during which time the claimant would have been without benefit and even without a decision against which to appeal. In London the delay could be far longer, with many cases taking as long as six months.

The confusion arising from two different sets of laws and regulations was commented on by a full-time SSAT chairman in St Helens:

> DSS and DE legislation is so interconnected yet you are getting different applications and different laws. For the citizen they should not be different. Why does UB have a different organisation? It doesn't need a different law from IS. The two laws cause confusion.

He went on to voice the fear that the law was becoming so sophisticated because it was being used as "a tool for political policy". The examples he gave to illustrate the point were drawn from problems arising through different interpretations of clauses relating to the severe disability premium, but he could just as well have cited the regulations on availability for work. Where the possibility for such confusion exists it is all the more imperative to have good liaison between the two agencies, but good liaison seems not to be the general rule.

Note

1. During the research the DSS was gearing up to the launch of its Benefit Agency. Administrators of DSS benefits in local and regional offices acquired 'agency status' in April 1991.

    Although not directly affected by the Employment Service's New Framework and Active Signing, they were undergoing changes similar to those experienced by the DE as it prepared its offices for agency status in April 1990 – office reorganisation, integration and closure; pressures to cut staffing complements and adjustments to new performance targets. DSS staff were also having to cope with a huge computerisation programme. And, of course, they had to be conversant with the 1989 Act insofar as it affected claimants of income support.

6 The quality of decisions in the Employment Service

Much room for improvement (*Annual Report of the Chief Adjudication Officer*, 1989/90)

Given the opaque complexities of the social security regulations and the fact that they are often changing, it is a miracle that so many decisions are made within a reasonable time and are correct in fact and law. But it is by now well established in the annual laments of the Chief Adjudication Officer that many decisions are either based on poor information, an inadequate understanding of the law, or show poor judgement.

In addition to the poor quality of much adjudication there is considerable evidence to call in to question the judgements made by the counsellors and other staff in the ES, who refer many claims for adjudication only to have them allowed by the AOs. The importance of this for the claimants is that in many cases their benefit is either reduced or stopped altogether pending the final decision; they are guilty until proved innocent, which can often have very considerable financial consequences for them. Whether claims are suspended pending a final decision is yet another area of complexity, as Table 6.1 shows.

When UB is suspended on grounds of availability or actively seeking work claimants should automatically be told that they may be able to apply for income support on hardship grounds under regulation 8(3) of the Income Support (General) Regulations.

It is clear from Table 6.1 that it is essential that decisions are reached quickly in all these cases; for those suspended for refusal of employment, leaving voluntarily or misconduct they will receive either nothing at all if they are ineligible for income support, and at best a reduced rate of income support if they are eligible. For those making a fresh claim who are suspended on grounds of doubtful availability or not actively seeking work they will receive nothing at all unless they are awarded a

Table 6.1
Benefit position on doubtful claims referred to ES AOs

Doubt arises in connection with	UB only	UB + IS	IS only
Avail./rest. avail. (Fresh claim)	Suspend	Suspend	Suspend
Avail./rest. avail. (Continuing claim)	Do not suspend	Do not suspend	Suspend
Actively seeking work	Suspend	Suspend UB	Suspend
Refusal of employment	Suspend	Suspend UB	See note
Leaving voluntarily	Suspend	Suspend UB	Paid with 40% deduction
Misconduct	Suspend	Suspend UB	Paid with 40% deduction

Note: Refusal of Employment; no income support is paid while the vacancy remains open; income support is paid subject to the 40% deduction once the vacancy ceases to remain open.

hardship payment, which is very rarely. The length of time waiting for a final decision from the AO is therefore very important. It is also very important for the claimants that their claims should only be suspended if there is a real chance that they are not entitled.

Time taken to reach a decision

As we have already seen, about one in three of all claims for unemployment benefit raise sufficient doubt in the minds of staff in the ES taking the claim to warrant referral to an AO for decision. This means that ES staff refer well over a million claims for adjudication every year; in 1989 it was 1,177,900 and in 1990 it was 1,173,700 (*UB Statistics, Annual Analysis*, 1990, table 18). The practice of keeping information on the time taken to process the decisions was discontinued in April 1990 so the latest figures available are for the quarter ending 31 March 1990 and are based on a 5% sample of referrals.

Table 6.2
Percentage of referrals to AO decided within four weeks

Availability	90%
Restricted availability	89%
Refusal of employment	85%

(Letter from Michael Fogden, ES, to Paul Flynn, ref. 1885/90, 7/6/1990.)

While these figures are quite impressive, they nevertheless mean that, grossed up to the likely effects over a year, 7,000 claimants had to wait for over a month to find out if they had lost benefit because of doubts about availability, to which must be added about the same number again who were only claiming IS, while nearly 2,000 had to wait over a month in respect of refusal of employment. These times are from the time the referral reached the AO, which could be some considerable time after the initial claim.

The number of those referred for doubts about actively seeking work in the sample were very small; taking the only data available and combining the six months up to the end of March 1990 there were 65 cases in all; of these only 3 took over a month to decide.

The impressiveness of the speed with which claims are decided according to the official statistics does not, however, accord with the evidence given to us by those who work in the ES or in advice agencies, at least as far as London is concerned. The AO is supposed to reach a decision "so far as practicable" within 14 days (Social Security Act 1975, section 99). Despite this legal requirement, which has since been watered down by case law to exonerate AOs who failed to meet the target because of heavy workloads, there were many comments made to us about the undue delays which the decision-making process could take. Delays could occur between the submission of the claim from the benefit office to the Adjudication Officer, and from the AO back to the benefit office.

We were given evidence that in London the delays in the process had worsened. An appeals submissions officer in the Brixton UBO said that whereas the target that had originally been set was eight weeks for the resolution of a claim this had been changed to eight weeks just to get the claim to the AO. He said that normally it took four to six weeks between the suspension of the claim and the submission of the papers to the AO.

Once in the hands of the AO the target of 14 days to reach a decision could become very much longer. This problem was particularly acute in income support cases, where adjudication decisions are normally taken by DSS officers who must await opinions from ES AOs. The appeals submissions officer at the Hammersmith DSS office said that delays in adjudication were "extreme", with many cases taking as long as six months. One reason given was that there were simply not enough AOs within the ES. In the DSS in his area they aimed to adjudicate within 21 days (despite the legal requirement to do so in 14). The adjudication of IS was about to be moved to Wigan, which the DSS officer saw would give rise to problems since staff in Wigan were unlikely to have the local knowledge which should inform decisions about availability and voluntary unemployment.

One reason for the delay in adjudication in cases of voluntary unemployment was that the AOs needed to get the evidence from the claimant's employer. They allowed a month for the employer to reply before sending a reminder, which in the view of a worker in a St Helens UBO was too long.

The problem for the claimant in the delays in the adjudication process is that until a decision is reached there is nothing against which to appeal; meanwhile benefit is paid either at a reduced rate or not at all. As the regional chairman of the SSATs covering St Helens observed, such delays "represent human suffering".

Once an appeal is lodged it takes an average of about six months to reach a tribunal hearing (*Hansard*, 18/2/91, col. 26). The President of the Social Security Appeals Tribunals in an interview with us accepted that the turnaround time for processing appeals was "far too long" and one of his top priorities was to reduce the delay. He said the two main reasons for the time taken were simple inefficiency and the long delays between a claimant's appeal and the receipt of the submission from the AOs in the ES or DSS. He knew of cases where tribunals had had to wait two years for the AO's submission, (though these were not in cases relating to unemployment benefit).

One way of shortening the delay is to ask the AO to review the decision before it reaches the tribunal. Workers in Claim It, Brighton, thought that the quality of decisions made by the AOs was falling as their volume of work increased. This meant that it was not difficult to get them to change their decision on review by presenting them with new evidence. Another Brighton agency, Brighton Advice, agreed that it was not difficult to change decisions before they reached the tribunal; once at the tribunal they reckoned to win 80% of the voluntary unemployment cases they represented and all of those to do with availability and actively seeking work, which is a reflection on the poor quality of the original decisions.

If the claimant lost the appeal and then appealed to the Commissioner he or she would have to wait on average a further 404 days (*Hansard*, 18/4/90, col. 839). For the few claimants who go this far it is surely a case of justice delayed being justice denied.

Quality of referrals to Adjudication Officers

Table 6.3 shows the outcome of claims referred from the ES to the ES AOs.

Table 6.3
Outcome of fresh or renewal claims referred to ES AOs. Number of referrals and percentage allowed

	1989 referrals	% allowed	1990 referrals	% allowed
All referrals, of which	1,079,100	41	1,079,700	36
Availability	73,766	44	44,441	41
Restricted availability	53,968	70	25,307	68
Actively seeking work	236	64	3,481	65
Leaving voluntarily	355,855	44	309,726	44
Misconduct	152,435	57	130,737	59
Refusal of employment etc.	17,410	62	11,360	62
Failure to attend restart	813	12	4,392	40
Total	654,210	49	529,444	49

Source: *UB Statistics; Annual Analysis of AO Decisions*, 1989 and 1990, Table 1.
(ASW figure for 1989 taken from *Quarterly Analysis of Decisions of AOs*, December 1989.)

It gives an indication of the relative difficulty which the staff taking the claims in the ES have in judging whether or not the claim should be allowed. The number of claims referred to AOs which the AOs subsequently decide to allow as valid claims indicates the degree of difficulty the staff making the referral had in judging the validity of the claim; the more claims the AOs allow the poorer the initial judgement of the referrer in doubting the validity of the claim. We can see that the particular set of claims which are of interest to this report generally give rise to more difficulties at the point of claim than most claims; whereas in 1989 41% of all claims referred to AOs were subsequently allowed as valid 49% of the group of claims in Table 6.3 were allowed; in 1990 the discrepancy had widened from 36% of all claims to 49% of our selected categories. In other words, in 1990, whereas about one in three of the doubts raised by ES staff about all fresh and renewal claims for UB proved to be unfounded, this proportion was one in two of their doubts about availability, actively seeking work etc.

A closer look at Table 6.3 reveals the particular problems with which the ES staff have the greatest difficulty. The highest proportion of referrals allowed by the AOs were those in respect of restricted availability, actively seeking work and refusal of employment, all of which were allowed by AOs in over 60% of cases. In other words, roughly two out of every three cases referred to AOs in these categories were not only "guilty until proved innocent" but were treated as guilty despite being innocent because they suffered benefit loss while the issue was being decided in their favour. The money lost was then made up because the award would be backdated to the date of claim, but in the meantime they may well have undergone considerable financial difficulty as well as anxiety. The number of claimants affected each year is very high; in 1990 there were over 270,000 in the categories shown in Table 6.3.

With regard to cases where doubts arose about availability, restricted availability and actively seeking work we must add to the numbers in Table 6.3 all those whose claim was for IS only. During 1990 these amounted to approximately an additional 72,000 claims referred to ES Adjudication Officers for their opinions on entitlement, roughly 50% of which were favourable to the claimant. This adds another 36,000 claimants to the above 270,000 who lost money unnecessarily.

It might be thought unfair to use the number of claims subsequently allowed by AOs as a measure of poor judgement on the part of the staff in the ES who make the initial referral. There is however other evidence to suggest that the quality of the initial referral is often inadequate. A paper on the subject of "Deficient References to Sector Adjudication Officers" in August 1990 sent from a London Regional Adjudication Manager to all area managers begins:

> For some considerable time, the subject of deficient references to the AO has been a bone of contention to Area and Sector Adjudication staff alike (letter from Regional Adjudication Manager (Northern District) to E.S. Area Managers, 21/8/90).

In an attempt to improve the quality of the submissions from the ES staff to the AOs the letter draws the attention of area managers in the ES to a long list of matters which constitute "important, regularly occurring deficiencies in submissions". Deficient submissions are, the letter explains, those where essential evidence or information which is available to, or is obtainable by, the UBO is not forwarded to the AO, and includes those where there is "omission of details in spaces provided on forms requiring completion by the claimant or local office". There follows a list of 71 items, which, we are reminded, "is not exhaustive but highlights continuous errors".

Those which relate to the headings with which we are particularly concerned make alarming reading. Among the 17 items on "availability" are reminders that a) availability should be "deemed" when a doubt is raised on a case where UB is already in payment; b) that the relevant section of the UB672 giving details of why the doubt has arisen should be completed and c) that the details about the claimant's availability (e.g. hours, rate of pay etc. etc.) should be completed. If ES staff are regularly failing to deem availability in cases where UB is already in payment many claimants will have their benefit suspended wrongly, and if the details about why the doubts arose or the details about claimants' availability are regularly left off the submissions to the AO it can only result in yet more delays before the details are provided. It also shows a strange notion of adjudication to think that AOs could make a decision in the absence of such information.

With regard to actively seeking work, the six points mentioned are more or less a description of how to refer a claim where doubts about jobsearch arise. They include a reminder of all the documentation needed, which is considerable and gives some idea about why staff in the ES may be reluctant to use these regulations when they can refer on simple grounds of availability instead. The following is the first of the six points:

> All submissions should include UB671 or UB671R; UB671S; UB671W; UB672; any written evidence of the claimant's jobsearch activity; the counsellor's written statements of what was discussed at the interview; the counsellor's opinion of the claimant's job search activity, using their knowledge of the local labour market.

Other points mentioned are that the claimant's answers as to what they have done to look for work must be recorded, the steps the claimant is advised to take to find work must be specific, reasonable, and most likely to lead to offers of jobs, and the specific "fortnightly" period of the suspension should be referred to. (It is of course possible for the claimant to have failed the test in one week only, though the reference to "fortnightly" might suggest otherwise.) If all these points are regularly left out of the submissions it calls into question whether the ES staff doing the claimant interviews have grasped the significance of the regulations. That such guidance should be necessary lends credence to the comments of the workers in the Hammersmith UBO and the Fulham jobcentre who said that they had had no training in the actively seeking work regulations, and that they had either not received the official circular with guidance on how to implement the new regulations or if they had they had simply not had the time to read it.

On refusal of employment there are five points mentioned, most to do with ensuring the recording of relevant dates but one reminds the counsellor about the importance of the "permitted period", which again suggests that this important safeguard may be often overlooked.

Quality of adjudication

The most authoritative accounts of the quality of adjudication in both the DSS and the ES are the Annual Reports of the Chief Adjudication Officer. In the one for 1989/90, he once again makes his familiar judgement that as far as adjudication on income support was concerned the "overall standards remained disappointing", while with regard to the ES he states the "the standards of adjudication were again unsatisfactory", giving as the main reasons that the decisions were based on insufficient evidence (*Annual Report of the Chief Adjudication Officer*, 1989/90, paras. 1.9 and 1.12).

For the purposes of compiling his report a sample of the decisions of ES AOs was monitored. Regard was had to whether the decisions were based on sufficient evidence, whether the findings of fact were correct, whether the law had been correctly applied and whether the decision had been accurately recorded. Table 6.4 gives his findings in respect of selected categories of claims for UB. Table 6.5 gives the same information but with the numbers in each column expressed as a percentage of the decisions before the AO.

Table 6.4
Reasons for deficient decisions by AOs, selected categories

	All decisions	Leave vol.	Misc.	Avail.	Rest/avail.
Decisions before AO	3291	1083	462	226	129
Insufficient evidence	1214	546	187	60	47
Wrong finding of fact	152	44	10	21	13
Incorrect law	130	19	10	33	10
Not properly recorded	512	70	28	85	26
Others	180	38	10	22	8
Total comments	2188	717	245	221	104

Source: *Annual Report of the Chief Adjudication Officer*, 1989/90, Appendix 15.

Table 6.5
Reasons for deficient decisions by AOs
as percentages of all decisions before the AOs

	All decisions	Leave vol.	Misc.	Avail.	Rest/avail.
Decisions before AO	100%	100%	100%	100%	100%
Insufficient evidence	37%	50%	40%	26%	36%
Wrong finding of fact	5%	4%	2%	9%	10%
Incorrect law	4%	2%	2%	14%	8%
Not properly recorded	15%	6%	6%	38%	20%
Others	5%	4%	2%	10%	6%
Total comments	66%	66%	53%	98%	80%

Source: *Ibid.*

Where a decision is found to be deficient a "comment" is made; these comments are what are recorded in Tables 6.4 and 6.5. A decision may attract one or more comments, so it does not necessarily mean that 2,188 of all the decisions monitored were deficient; it means that there were 2,188 comments raised on the 3,294 decisions. We can see from these two tables that whereas all the decisions monitored had a total of 2,188 comments raised on them, a ratio of 66 comments per 100 decisions, the decisions on availability and restricted availability had a far higher ratio of comments, 98 per 100 and 80 per hundred respectively. With regard to decisions about availability, a quarter were based on insufficient evidence and 14% had an incorrect application of the law, a far higher percentage than any of the other categories. With regard to restricted availability, over one in three decisions were based on insufficient evidence. Despite these extraordinarily large ratios of comments to decisions the Chief Adjudication Officer commented that AOs had "appeared to cope well" with the 1989 changes to UB law. He seems to have based this conclusion on the fact that his office "received very few requests for guidance on how the new legislation should be applied" (*ibid.*, para.4.18). In the light of the extensive deficiencies found through the monitoring process it would perhaps have been better if they had made more requests for guidance.

In respect of the other categories of decision the CAO said:

> Over a third of misconduct decisions examined and half of "leaving voluntarily" decisions were deficient in this respect [insufficient evidence to support the decision]. This is a major weakness, with obvious risks of injustice to claimants (*ibid.*, para.4.9).

It is clear from the results of the monitoring process that the CAO's judgement that the standard of adjudication in the ES was "unsatisfactory" with "much room for improvement" is well founded (*ibid.*, para. 4.8).

A contributory reason why the standard is low is touched on in the *Report*. In 1989/90 absences of AOs were covered by upgrading clerical staff rather than by building in an allowance of extra AOs as had happened previously. The CAO comments:

> This will mean that a significant number of decisions will be taken by temporary AOs rather than by full-time experienced AOs. This can only have a negative effect on the standards of adjudication (*ibid.*, para. 4.5).

He therefore recommends that the ES reconsiders the way AO absences are covered.

The main recommendation he makes in respect of the overall poor standards of adjudication is that the ES and the Benefits Agency set performance targets for adjudication:

> It cannot be right that so many AO decisions are taken on insufficient evidence or by applying the law incorrectly – frequent findings in this and previous reports...Too often time is wasted reviewing and revising a decision on account of a piece of information which ought to have been sought before the claim was originally decided. Too often time is wasted on an appeal to an appeal tribunal when the original decision was clearly wrong and ought to have been revised (*ibid.* para.1.15).

Appeals

The CAO's comments on the quality of submissions from the DSS and ES to appeals tribunals makes equally dismal reading. On IS cases he reports that the standard of appeal submissions "has declined" since his previous report and is now "unsatisfactory" (*ibid.*, paras. 5.4 and 5.5).

The most common failing was absent or deficient argument; matters raised by the appellant were often ignored. AOs also supported incorrect decisions and frequently omitted to cite and record the relevant legislation and caselaw accurately (*ibid.*, para. 5.4).

Ironically, one reason was that many AOs used the specimen submissions supplied by the CAO's office, but with a "tendency to make the appeal fit the specimen rather than adapt the specimen to suit the appeal", which contributed to the errors.

Table 6.6 gives the relevant information on IS appeals.

Table 6.6
Information extracted from local office appeals records; income support

Appeals received in previous six months	4474	(100%)
Decision reviewed and revised by AO	1066	(24%)
Appeal withdrawn by claimant	431	(10%)
Appeal disallowed by SSAT	692	(15%)
Appeal allowed by SSAT	328	(7%)
Appeals outstanding	1957	(44%)

Source: *Ibid.*, Appendix 17.

About a quarter of all appeals never reached the tribunal because the decision was revised by the AO. This is presumably an indication of poor preparatory work or poor judgement in the original decision, where insufficient evidence would often have been the cause.

With regard to the ES the CAO commented that there had been "no improvement in the standard of submissions during the year". Table 6.7 gives the numbers of comments raised by the ES appeals submissions.

Table 6.7 shows that on average each submission had deficiencies in about 2.5 of the headings listed. In almost half the submissions the arguments supporting the decision were absent or deficient, while in 57 out of the 172 submissions the decision which was the subject of the appeal was, in the judgement of the monitoring team, incorrect!

The President of the SSATs, Judge Holden, invited to comment on the quality of appeals submissions, stated that there is "criticism again this year of the failure to justify a particular period of disqualification for misconduct or leaving work voluntarily", which confirms the evidence of our respondents on advice agencies (*ibid.*, para. 5.37).

Table 6.7
Examination of written submissions to appeals;
unemployment benefit

Number of submissions examined	172
Number of comments raised	440
Number of comments because decision under appeal incorrect	57
Review appropriate but not made	11
Summary of facts incomplete or inaccurate	65
Statute law inaccurately or incompletely stated	47
Caselaw irrelevant or inaccurate	45
Grounds for appeal insufficiently covered	36
Argument absent or deficient	80
Other deficiencies in submission	99

Source: *Ibid.*, Appendix 23.

In general it seems that the quality of submissions to AOs from ES office staff is often poor, as is the quality of the subsequent adjudication by AOs. We would wish to support the CAO's call for the setting of adjudication targets by the ES and the Benefits Agency, since, as the CAO remarked, in the matter of the quality of adjudication there is "much room for improvement".

7 The policies in action: How the regulations are applied in practice

One of the main benefits of this research has been the opportunity to use a wealth of individual case material supplied by benefit advice agencies, and in particular by many CABx all over the country. Using those case examples and more general comments from those involved in day-to-day work with claimants we can see how the new regulations have worked in practice. In this chapter we explain what the regulations are and how they have been implemented. This takes us into the area of the intricate relationship between unemployment benefit and income support and the consequences of the poor liaison between the two departments. We can see that regulations are often wrongly applied and are open to widely different interpretations, making the claiming of benefits often an unpredictable and even risky experience. The chapter is arranged into sections covering the main topics and claimant groups affected by the legislation; taken together they provide an insight into the process of claiming benefits which it is not otherwise possible to obtain.

Availability and restricted availability

In 1984 there was a big fuss about whether unemployed people could sit on SSATs. It was decided that they could since SSAT panels were supposed to be representative of the region's population at large. However it had led to some people having their benefits stopped for not being available for work (Regional Chair of SSAT, Merseyside).

The regulations

With certain exceptions, most claimants for either UB or IS must demonstrate that they are available for work. Precisely what this means is laid down in regulations.

Although there are many similarities in the regulations for UB and IS there are also some important differences between them.

To prove availability for IS purposes the claimant has to meet the requirements laid down in Regulations 7 to 10 of the Income Support (General) Regulations 1987 and subsequent amendments, which, in a much simplified form, lay down the following conditions. Claimants must be available to take up work which they can reasonably be expected to do and be prepared to work for at least 24 hours a week. (There are other conditions relating to disability and part-time students which will be dealt with later.) They must also conform to the general conditions governing availability laid down for UB claimants.

Some claimants for IS are specifically exempt from the need to be available; the important groups for the purposes of this section are lone parents or carers generally where the person cared for is in receipt of attendance allowance, pregnant women where the pregnancy makes her incapable of work or for 11 weeks before the expected birth, people over 50 who have not worked for the previous 10 years and who have no prospect of employment, (i.e. mainly women whose marriages have ended through death or divorce or whose dependent children have grown up, or people coming out of long-term residential care), or those over 60.

The conditions which have to be met to prove availability for UB purposes are laid down in Regulations 7-12 of the Social Security (Unemployment, Sickness and Invalidity Benefit) Regulations 1983 with subsequent amendments, and modified by Commissioners' Decisions. In simplified form these conditions are that the claimants must be willing to accept work at once (or in some cases within 24 hours) and that they have a reasonable prospect of obtaining work under the conditions they specify. Regulation 7B says that if you impose any restrictions on the "nature, hours, rate of remuneration, locality or other conditions of employment" you are prepared to accept you will only be considered to be available provided you can show that you still have a "reasonable prospect" of getting a job, or that the restrictions are reasonable in view of your physical or mental condition. This regulation also allows a period of grace (the "permitted period") of up to 13 weeks within which you may impose restrictions that are consistent with those in your usual occupation (e.g. you could ask for the normal rate of wages even if that were high).

The reality: illustrative cases; "bogus restrictions"

From the cases which come to the attention of advice agencies we can have some idea about how these regulations are being interpreted by staff in the ES and DSS and the likely problems this raises for claimants.

Hours

The following cases were all reported by various advice agencies;

1   A woman working part-time for a Social Services Dept. and receiving IS on top of her wages was required to be available for work when her youngest child reached the age of 16. Her benefit was suspended because her conditions of

employment required her to give a week's notice. She had told the UBO that she had a week's holiday which could be used as notice, and that in any case she would be prepared to break her terms of contract if necessary if a job was offered. (Cleveland County Council Welfare Rights Service, 24/4/90)

2   A man who was available for full time work told the UBO that he was hoping at some future time to obtain custody of his two children, and at that time he would restrict the number of hours he would work. He was judged to be unavailable; the decision was reversed when the advice agency intervened on his behalf. (Catford Centre for the Unemployed, 11/12/89)

3   A married man with 3 children, unemployed for most of the last 5 years, failed the availability test and was refused the full rate of IS because he had to attend the hospital one day a week for tests to ascertain his suitability to be a kidney donor for his brother. (Cleveland County Council Welfare Rights Service, 24/4/90)

4   A woman applied for IS and UB and said that she was available from 10am to 3pm each day, a total of 30 hours. Benefit was suspended and the matter referred to the AO for decision. (Outcome unknown.) She told the advice worker that she had put those hours as they were her preferred hours, in view of her children, but that she would work during any daylight hours. She said that the significance of her restrictions was lost on her and she would have told the UBO of her wider availability if they had asked. (Chelsea CAB 20/4/90)

5   A 19 year old woman made redundant applied for benefit when 4 months pregnant. Staff at the UBO offered her an appointment on a day when she was due to attend ante-natal clinic, and when she asked if they could change it they took this as evidence that she was not available for work and refused her claim. The decision was reversed when the agency contacted the UBO manager, who said that they were "having to tighten up a bit". (York CAB, 9/10/89)

6   A 59 year old woman who had worked as a clerical worker for 45 years Mondays to Fridays stated on her availability form that she was looking for work Mondays to Fridays, 9.00am to 5.00pm. The AO decided that she was not available as she had not included Saturdays. The woman told the advice agency that she would have been prepared to work Saturdays had a job been available. (Brighton CAB, 9/10/89)

In addition to these cases from the advice agencies there are two more, the first from *The Guardian* (9/2/91), the second is one which went to appeal before an SSAT in Oxford in January 1990.

7   An Asian man who had been made redundant signed on in December 1990 and said he was prepared to work from 9.00am to 5.00pm every day except Saturdays. Despite the fact that he was a machinist in the leather trade, where the normal working week was Monday to Friday, he was suspended from benefit for thirteen weeks.

8   A woman caring for a child was looking for full-time work in a factory, as a childminder, or in a shop. She was prepared to work from Monday to Saturday, but because of her child-minding arrangements was not prepared to start work before 9.00am. The local jobcentre stated that work in such occupations was only available to a very limited extent because of her unavailability before 9.00am. The Adjudication Officer referred the matter to the SSAT for a decision.

The tribunal found in the appellant's favour on the grounds that the restrictions she had placed on her hours were reasonable, given her circumstances, and not every member of staff needed to be in a shop at 9.00am.

Discussion

There are a number of points which arise from these cases. Taken together they give a flavour of the strictness with which the regulations are often applied. The first point to note therefore is that it is by no means a formality to pass the availability tests.

The first case illustrates the point that to be available one must be available at once. There is no provision in the regulations for allowing a claimant to work out a week's notice, even though she would then have been willing to take a full time job in preference to her current part-time one. It also illustrates the difficulty of deciding when someone is or is not available; she said she was willing to leave her job at once, yet this was not accepted.

It also raises a difference in the treatment of those on IS and UB. Where someone is already in receipt of UB and a doubt arises about their availability they continue to receive benefit until a final decision is made by the AO (Reg.12A, SS (Unemployment, Sickness etc.) Regulations). There does not seem to be any similar provision for those on IS, so that when the doubt arose as to this claimant's availability her benefit was suspended immediately. There can be no justification for such different treatment.

In the case of the man hoping to have custody of his children, he was in fact available at once, though he may not have been in the future. There is no provision in the regulations to judge people's future availability and the decision to disallow his benefit was wrong, as was subsequently admitted. This claimant went to an advice centre; most do not.

The cases of the brother of the kidney patient and the pregnant woman both illustrate the harshness with which the regulation can sometimes be applied. They also show how different standards are applied to those out of work and those in it, since it is more than likely that, if they had been in work, both would have been given time off to go to the hospital or to the ante-natal clinic. As they are out of work, their need to attend the appointments is taken as evidence that they are not available.

In the case of the brother of the kidney patient it was possible to get round the disallowance by getting his partner to take over the claim for IS.

The woman who said she was available from 10.00am to 3.00pm illustrates the way in which poor counselling by ES staff results in unnecessary loss of benefit for claimants. Had she had the significance of her restriction pointed out to her at the time she would have given different answers which may well have resulted in a different outcome. It also illustrates the problem of ES staff having to decide about IS claimants. The woman was available for 30 hours, more than the minimum 24 required for IS purposes, but she must also satisfy the ES staff that she can get a job within the restrictions she has set. The staff in the ES may or may not take into account the fact that she only needs to find work for 24 hours to satisfy DSS requirements.

The woman who offered to work full time but to limit her starting time to 9.00am once again shows the strictness with which the regulations can be applied, as few would disagree with the finding of the appeal tribunal which held the questioning of the woman's availability to be unreasonable. It provides another reminder that claimants often have good reason to feel that their benefit is unfairly withheld.

As for the 59 year old who had worked for 45 years from Mondays to Fridays it seems incomprehensible that anyone should think it limited her job prospects as a clerical worker to say that she was only available from 9.00am to 5.00pm five days a week. It is even more unreasonable, given that she was only six months off retirement. It will come as no surprise to know that she won her appeal against this bizarre decision.

The case quoted in *The Guardian* raises three issues. First, the restrictions the claimant placed on the hours could not reasonably be said to hinder his prospects of getting the sort of work he normally did as these were the hours normally worked in the trade. Second, he should in any event be given a permitted period of anything up to 13 weeks in which to look for work in his normal occupation, which seems not to have happened. Third, even if he was deemed to be not available, there is no provision in the regulations to stop his benefit for three months. If the restrictions he has put on the job have made him unavailable he should be disallowed benefit until such time as he changes the restrictions and makes himself available again; a three month, or any other prospective period of disqualification, is illegal. This must raise the question of how many other claimants have had their benefit wrongfully stopped.

Wages

Even before the 1989 changes some UBOs had refused to allow claimants to say that they would accept "any reasonable wage" and had insisted on a named figure. There is considerable evidence to show that when a figure was named this could be used as a reason for disallowing benefit on the grounds the wage expected was too high. The following cases illustrate some of the problems that this policy, now universally followed by benefit offices, causes claimants.

At the simplest level, in many cases benefit is disallowed because the AO decides that the amount of wages asked for places undue restrictions on the chances of the claimant finding work. This is probably the commonest way in which claimants are affected, yet it is very clear from our evidence that there are three major problems with this simple procedure. First, such a decision is a matter of judgement and very much open to differing opinion. We have several examples of claimants appealing against such a decision and the SSAT upholding the appeal simply on the grounds that they do not think the amount of wages is unnecessarily restrictive. There must be many occasions when such an appeal would succeed but where no appeal is lodged.

Second, it is also clear that when claimants are forced to name a figure they often say what they would like to have, not what they in fact would actually settle for. We have several examples of claimants naming a figure, then being disallowed, and only then realising the significance of the figure they gave. Had it been properly explained to them that by naming such a high figure they were jeopardising their benefit they would certainly have changed their demand.

Third, it is also clear that the figure named is often just something plucked out of the air with no real significance for the claimant's jobsearching behaviour because even when they have stated a figure on their UB671 they look for jobs paying less. The following judgement of a social security appeal tribunal in an appeal against disallowance of benefit on the grounds of high wage expectations illustrates all three points above:

> We accept the appellant's view that a request for £200 per week wage initially when he filled in his first UBO form was not unreasonable. We accept his evidence that he was given this as an indication of what he would want and that having recently been in prison he was not very much in touch with wage levels. We do not think in view of the nature of the work which he was looking for (which was on some occasions motorway construction or road construction)... that this was in any way an unreasonable figure.
>
> We note also and accept the appellant's evidence that he did subsequently amend that figure and would have been prepared to take work at something less (Oxford SSAT, 4/12/89).

This case also incidentally contained another example of a wrongly imposed penalty. When the DE found the claimant to be unavailable they stated that he was "not available for employment from the date of the decision for an indefinite period". This was communicated to the DSS who stopped his money "indefinitely". There is no provision in the regulations for any such forward disallowance; the correct procedure is to disallow the claim on the day and until such time as a fresh claim is made which does meet the availability criteria, which is very different from "indefinitely". The SSAT observed that as a result of this wrong decision the appellant was excluded from benefit for a considerable period of time.

In another case a man stated at his restart interview that he wanted £130 net per week. Subsequently his benefit was suspended because of this, then reinstated two months later after he went to an advice agency who advised him to change the figure to £100, and also to appeal against the disallowance. As a father of four he would have been entitled to claim family credit, which would have made a significant difference to his weekly income, but he said that he was not given this advice at restart (Droylsden CAB, 15/11/89).

The following case from an advice agency illustrates again the different treatment of UB and IS cases:

> Client claimed IS since last October. Without warning a letter came instead of Giro saying he had placed too many restrictions on availability for work. They informed him (and us) it was just concerning too high a wage level; they were quite satisfied he was actively seeking work. He completed a new form and IS resumed, leaving two

weeks without payment. He was given no warning that he might have to reconsider wage level question. We advised an appeal (Lichfield CAB, 6/7/89).

If he had been getting unemployment benefit the benefit would not have been suspended pending a decision by the AO, and it is quite possible that this would have given the claimant time to find out more about the reason for the doubt about his availability and to resolve it without losing any benefit. The difference in treatment seems quite unnecessarily arbitrary. This case also illustrates the precarious nature of life on benefit; instead of the usual girocheque the claimant received a letter saying his benefit had been stopped! At the very least there is a case for sending such claimants warning letters and inviting them for interview to discuss the issues rather than peremptorily disallowing benefit.

It is quite clear that many claimants have their benefit stopped just because they have put down an expected wage which is considered too high, yet this wage figure is more often than not a pure fiction. Because of poor advice claimants do not realise the crucial significance of the figure they give and most would happily change it rather than lose benefit. In any event it is all hypothetical, since they will often also look for jobs below the wage stated, and are in any case seldom offered jobs by the jobcentres at any wage, let alone one they may have stipulated. The new practice of insisting on a figure and not allowing claimants to say they will work for the going rate for the job has merely created a new set of completely artificial barriers between the claimant and benefit. This not only results in many claimants losing money for quite spurious reasons, but as the next example shows, can mean a good deal of being messed about for no good reason. This is part of the statement of an appellant who won an appeal against a decision to disallow benefit on the grounds that he had asked for too high a wage.

I then proceeded to Crown House where I sign once a fortnight and asked to see the supervisor. She came out to see me and she stated that "I'm sorry Mr M. to tell you that your money has been stopped as from today, 30/1/90". I asked her who had stopped the money and she answered DSS.

So I went over to DSS and the young lady who interviewed me did not know anything about it but she went to make enquiries for me and came back with the answer that it had been stopped my Mrs R. (his Restart Counsellor at the UBO) and that the Adjudication Officer at Crown House had imposed the suspension. I then asked for a B1 form, in order to make a claim for my wife and two children but the DSS just replied that it was just a waste of time as all benefits had been stopped.

Friday 2nd Feb. 1990 again I went to the DSS to see if I could get any money for my wife and two children as we were penniless, and the young lady I saw got in touch with the DE and came back with the answer that if I retracted my statement about the wage I wanted they would give me a crisis loan, which I would have to pay back.

During my suspension I went to the DE at Crown House to see what was going on about my claim as I had no notification how long my suspension was going to last; I asked them about my appeal form and they said they had sent it over to the DSS, so off I went to the DSS to see when my money was going to be put right etc. as I was on a reduced rate of benefit and also to ask had they received my appeal form from the DE. They replied "No", so off I went again to the DE Crown House, where... they checked again and said "I'm sorry Mr M. your appeal form has been lost but we will send another one over to them".

All through this carry on I find that all the departments have been blaming each other for the suspension and none of them know why as they keep changing their reasons for stopping it in the first place with no notification whatsoever (Cleveland Social Security Appeal Tribunal, 3/5/90).

This claimant speaks well enough for himself to need no further comment on the frustrations he went through. (It is worth noting, however, that the hapless official in the DSS was blamed for stopping the appellant's money when in fact the DSS were acting on instructions from the UBO. DSS staff in our interviews complained that this unfair shifting of the blame on to them by their colleagues was not uncommon.) Suffice to add that, once again, a wrong penalty was imposed, since he should have been automatically considered for a hardship payment and not offered a repayable crisis loan, and his suspension should have been lifted as soon as he changed the wages figure. As we now know, he won his appeal both because the figure he gave was considered reasonable by the SSAT and because he had been prepared to take jobs below it. One could scarcely have a clearer example of the futility of this regulation and of the needless frustration and hardship it causes.

During the "permitted period" claimants are expressly allowed to confine their job searches to jobs which pay the level of wages in their usual occupation (Social Security Act 1975 20A 1 (b)). We have evidence to show not only that this is not always honoured by the ES but that they may even defend such dubious behaviour when challenged. A claimant who signed on at Westminster ES in March 1990 was given a permitted period of 13 weeks and simultaneously disallowed benefit because of "the limitations you have put on the type of job you have said you will take"! The man was an advertising copywriter, a specialist occupation, and this was clearly accepted by the ES otherwise they would not have allowed him a 13 week permitted period. It makes no sense at all to both allow him a permitted period and to disallow benefit because he has restricted the type of work to his normal occupation. When this was pointed out to the ES manager he stated in a letter that it is possible for a claimant to be deemed to be unavailable during their permitted period because "it does not remove the question of how available that job is, how qualified they are to do the job, how available for work they are at the time, or other possible restrictions concerning wages or hours" (Charing Cross CAB, 11/4/90). Once a permitted period has been granted it certainly ought to remove the questions mentioned by the manager; if those questions arise at the interview they could prevent the granting of a permitted period, but once a permitted period has been granted it implies that the job sought is available, and that the claimant is qualified to do it at the usual rate of pay and usual hours. It is expressly stated in section 20A(1)(b) of the Act that a claimant shall not be disqualified from receiving unemployment benefit during the permitted period if he restricts his jobsearch to "employment in his usual occupation at a level of remuneration not lower than he is accustomed to receive". To take the view the manager does is to negate the principle of a permitted period, and is another cause for concern that claimants may be having their benefit stopped wrongly.

Nature of work

Just as claimants are no longer able to say they will work for "the going rate" they are now no longer allowed to say they will take "any" type of work; they are now required, in practice though not by law, to name specific occupations. As with wages, this can be simply yet another means of disallowing benefit for spurious reasons as the following example from an advice agency shows.

> Our client said he was looking for any kind of work, but was told he must be more specific. Having been a taxi-driver for many years he specified "taxi-driving" and left it at that. He was subsequently denied benefit because he was alleged to have placed unreasonable restrictions. In fact, as he'd attempted to say on the form, he would have been willing to accept any job. Form UB671 is very misleading; it can be taken as only seeking a general picture of the claimant's availability but in fact persuades the claimant to indicate what are often bogus restrictions (Spen Valley CAB, 21/2/89).

The claimant appealed and won.

Locality

While we did not come across any problems with claimants being expected to travel unreasonable distances to work it does seem possible that claimants in rural areas may have additional problems proving their availability,

> Client is married with 7 children who lives in a rural area. Nearest public transport is 4 miles away and UBO is 8 miles away. The client is long term unemployed and has exhausted his own means of transport, funds and borrowing capacity to provide transport.

> UBO are exerting a lot of pressure on client to withdraw his claim. They are apparently demanding that he obtain transport and threatening to withdraw his benefit saying that he is not available for work if he cannot get there.... The client is constantly being told he should not be signing on because he is not available due to his transport situation (Boothferry CAB, 27/9/90).

As the Regional Chair of SSAT in Cardiff said:

> If you choose to live in the country you don't get sympathy usually, you need to take the consequences. You can't complain that you need to walk ten miles to work if you have chosen to live there in the first place.

This hard line may be less reasonable if public transport services have been withdrawn or curtailed after the claimant had chosen to live in the country.

The effects on claimants

Sometimes claimants who are found to be not available for work are steered towards other more appropriate benefits, such as sickness benefit or income support if, for example, they have to restrict their hours of work because they are caring for a sick dependant. If, however, they are not eligible for any other benefit, they lose entitlement to both UB and IS for as long as their availability remains in doubt. They receive no money unless they can qualify for a hardship payment of IS.

Being disallowed on grounds of doubtful availability has worse consequences for the claimant than being disallowed for not actively seeking work, as this, while carrying the same benefit penalties, is automatically reviewed after two weeks and the claimant could in the meantime have re-earned entitlement by being more active in their jobsearching. However, the administrative burden on ES staff is less when disallowing someone on grounds of doubtful availability because it does not entail warning letters and reviews, consequently it is possible that some claimants are being disallowed on this ground when they should be disallowed for not actively seeking work, as was suggested to us by staff in two ES offices in London.

There was general agreement that since 1989 the regulations in respect of restricted availability were being more tightly enforced. In particular claimants were being made to be far more specific in their answers to the questions on the UB671. Answers as to wage rates had to be specific; "the going rate" or "the average" were not acceptable, and in some offices would certainly have been grounds for suspension of benefit. Similarly claimants had to specify which sort of jobs they were seeking, and had to be precise about the hours they were available each day of the week; it was not even permitted to say "any".

The insistence on specificity means that it is easier to decide whether someone is or is not available, and so opens the way to disallowing more claims if that is what the staff choose to do. In response to this tightening up several of the workers in advice agencies for the unemployed reported that they advised claimants never to admit to any restrictions when answering the questions. This is only a risky strategy when staff have jobs to offer claimants which might test the truth of their statements, but they seldom had. It is also less risky than it should be because so few offices have any real systematic follow-up after the initial claim until the restart interview six months later.

That the UB671 is seen as simply another obstacle to be surmounted on the bumpy road to benefits is nicely illustrated by the comments of the regional SSAT chairman for the area covering St Helens:

> People will say what they think they need to say to get the benefit, so when you ask them "Why did you sign that?" they look at you as if you are stupid and say "You don't get the bloody money if you don't sign it".

The effect of the tighter questioning is to encourage some claimants into dishonesty; they know that if they say they are not prepared to work for a wage which the new client adviser thinks is acceptable they will not get benefit, so they agree to whatever is suggested, whatever they may think privately. It cannot but help to make claiming a demeaning process for many people.

As to whether the changes in the regulations have resulted in more people being disallowed opinion was divided, with some ES staff and claimants' advisors saying that there had been no discernible change and some reporting increases since 1989. Those that reported no change said this was because there had been a high level of activity on restricted availability even before the changes in the regulations, which had merely reflected common practice rather than changed anything. It did not seem to be the case that the opportunity to push claimants into very low paid jobs on pain of losing benefit built in to the new regulations had in fact resulted in a significant increase in claimants being pushed off the register. Partly this was because claimants knew how to answer the questions, partly because of the reluctance of ES staff to hound the claimants, and partly because of a lack of implementation of the review procedures which are designed to give teeth to the regulations.

ES staff generally advise claimants to alter their expectations, especially over pay, when filling in the availability questionnaire so as to avoid the possibility of suspension. As a supervisor in the Hove UBO explained:

> Where the claimant was being unreasonable, in most cases you'd talk to them. 9 times out of 10 you can get them to alter the amount. It's the same with hours.

Or again, from a staff member of the Brighton jobcentre:

> A lot of it is playing the system. If someone makes themselves unavailable it forces us to act; we have no choice if they refuse to change it, even if you've said "Do you realise what this means?" We aren't bastards and let them sign their own death warrant; we tell them and ask them what they want to do.

A similar procedure was adopted by advice agencies; for example in one Brighton centre their advice was to "tell the client to grovel and to agree to anything so it scotches things at the beginning." If it was too late for that because the claimant had already filled in the form they got the claimant to write in saying that they had reconsidered their position and to give different answers, which usually resulted in the suspension being lifted. This is clearly a much better strategy than waiting for the AO to make a decision and then to appeal.

There was therefore a general belief that only claimants who were too honest, or not smart enough to take the advice of the ES staff, or who were for other reasons deliberately sticking to their restrictions who had their benefit suspended.

There was also another view which reflected less well on ES staff. It was the view of a staff member in the Brixton UBO that there had been an increase in the number of cases of restricted availability, many of them for refusal to agree to work on Saturdays. The reason given for this was the need of the staff to raise the numbers of those they prevented from making a claim which helped them to reach their own performance indicators.

Brighton Advice thought that suspensions for restricted availability had definitely increased in volume and they had found it very difficult to get the office or AOs to revise the decisions before the appeal stage. The Brighton CAB also met with this reluctance to review these particular decisions before appeal.

In the other two regions SSAT full-time chairmen had a less benign view of how some ES staff conducted new claims interviews. One in Newport thought there were often "misunderstandings":

> There's a difference between what I'd like to have and an absolute acceptable minimum. Adjudication Officers often say "he asked for £200; I checked with the jobcentre and there weren't any jobs at that rate so I disqualified him".

The St Helens SSAT chair went further, suggesting an even more sinister approach to claimants:

> I do get the feeling that there is entrapment. People don't recognise the significance of what they are saying. For example they may be asked: "What do you want to be?" "A crane driver, that's what I am, a crane driver." "But you can't be; what else do you want to be?" Well, I've been on £250 so I'd like £200". The Claimant Adviser is silent, then decides to disqualify him.

Advice centres had several tales to tell of claimants who had been disallowed on grounds of restricted availability which they thought very unreasonable. Newport CAB had won an appeal against disallowance when the claimant had specified that she was prepared to work from 9.00am to 6.00pm at clerical work after the AO had argued that there were few clerical jobs available at such hours in the area; Brighton Advice reported that another had been suspended despite the total of their hours adding up to 40; and

> the most ridiculous one was a Brighton woman who worked at Burgess Hill before she had a baby then she had the baby and was told she was placing unreasonable restrictions because she had been prepared to work out of Brighton before.

Perhaps the last word on enforcing these regulations should be left to the regional chair of SSAT in Merseyside:

> In 1984 there was a big fuss about whether unemployed people could sit on SSATs. It was decided that they could since SSAT panels were supposed to be representative of the region's population at large. However it had led to some people having their benefits stopped for not being available for work.

Actively seeking work

> You might just as well ask them to do three pirouettes before handing over their giro. It's just setting up hurdles (Regional Chair of SSAT, Merseyside).

The regulations: unemployment benefit

The conditions governing whether or not a claimant has met the requirement to be "actively seeking employment" are set out in regulations 12B-D of the Social Security (Unemployment, Sickness and Invalidity Benefit) Regulations 1983 as amended.

These state that the claimant must take "such of the steps which are reasonable in his case as offer him the best prospect of receiving offers of employment". This is the touchstone, and provided claimants can show that what they have done meets this criterion they should be accepted as actively seeking work.

The regulations go on to say that in determining whether the claimant's jobsearching meets this criterion the following must be taken into account; the claimant's skills, qualifications, abilities and physical or mental limitations; the time since he was last in employment and his work experience; the steps which he has taken to find work and the availability and location of job vacancies. There are more detailed conditions regarding people engaged in various activities such as being a lifeboatman or doing voluntary work, or being a part-time student or trainee, and allowances should be made for homeless people who are having to spend time looking for accommodation.

The regulations also provide a list of possible steps which claimants should take, which include job applications direct to employers, looking for information about vacancies from advertisements and job agencies, and registering with agencies. (Interestingly, it does not include visiting jobcentres.) This list is not exhaustive, and provided the steps taken meet the criterion laid down above they should suffice.

The regulations also provide for "deeming" that claimants are actively seeking work without their having to prove it. This means that claimants do not have to prove that they are actively seeking in the first week of their claim or the last week before they begin work, with certain other allowances for specified people such as lifeboatmen, the blind and people on part-time training courses. All claimants are allowed two weeks grace in the year when they need not look for work, provided they notify the UBO in advance and will be away from home for at least one day in each week (in effect, when on holiday).

The regulations: income support

Regulation 10A (3) of the Income Support (General) Regulations 1987 as amended provides that the test for actively seeking work for IS claimants shall be the same as that for UB claimants, so here at least the two sets of regulations are identical.

The penalties

There are however differences in the penalties depending on whether the claim is for UB or IS.

For UB claimants, failure to satisfy the regulations means that benefit is suspended immediately and the case is referred to the AO for a decision. Benefit can only be disallowed for the one or two weeks in which the claimant failed to satisfy the conditions; after that he may re-apply and requalify for benefit if he can show that he has in the meantime actively sought work. Unless he can successfully appeal against the decision, the benefit is entirely lost.

For IS claimants there is provision under regulation 10A(2) to make a payment of IS, subject to a deduction of (usually) 40% of the claimant's personal allowance, even if the claimant fails the actively seeking work test, if in the opinion of the AO the claimant or a member of his family would otherwise suffer hardship. If the AO is not satisfied that hardship would result, then an IS claimant would also lose all benefit for the week or fortnight concerned.

The practice

There was a clear consensus in each of the regions that the actively seeking work regulations were not being very rigorously applied. Hardly anyone, whether in the ES, DSS or advice agencies had come across any examples of claimants' having their benefit stopped as a result of falling foul of them. In the words of the Merseyside regional chair of the SSAT, it has been a "dead duck".

This view was confirmed by His Honour Judge Holden, President of the then Social Security Appeals Tribunals, who said in interview with us that the Adjudication Officers and departments were not enforcing the actively seeking work legislation, adding "there is no doubt about it".

In seeking to explain why this might be he said that the regulations were being enforced sympathetically by the AOs and that this was no bad thing as being unemployed was a debilitating experience. He also thought that the complexity of the regulations encouraged AOs to "let things through", and that the knowledge that appeals tribunals would be likely to overturn any decisions where there was any possibility of finding for the claimant probably also acted as a deterrent to AOs.

The evidence we have from the advice centres confirms that the regulations on actively seeking employment are not being unreasonably enforced. A number of agencies commented that they had hardly dealt with any cases where this was an issue, and one even gave as the reason that they knew that their local ES staff disapproved of the policy and thought it inappropriate. While many said that claimants had had no difficulty in satisfying staff of their active searching, some added that nevertheless staff often drew claimants' attention to the new regulations so that they were now perceived as a lurking threat, even if as yet largely unactivated.

There were of course some examples of the regulations being applied in a heavy handed fashion. In one case in London a man aged over 50 was told at his restart interview that he had to apply for about 50 jobs in the next three weeks or his benefit would be stopped, which had not unnaturally created "great anxiety" (Charing Cross CAB, 8/3/90). In Reading, a 59 year old woman who had been on supplementary benefit and income support for about ten years was told to find a job or risk losing her benefit 5 months before her sixtieth birthday (Reading CAB, 12/2/90). These insensitive applications of the regulations were, however, very rare.

Some advice agencies were themselves directly affected by the new rules when their volunteer staff had to prove their active jobsearching. Brighton Advice lost most of its volunteers once the new rules had come in:

> ASW has had a major impact on the volunteers here. We used to have a large number of unemployed but they have dried up now. One of them wanted to do law but he was being hassled, despite this work being relevant to his future experience. Now he is working in a cafe.

From Northern Ireland there was an example less of harshness than of failure to give proper advice. A 47 year old woman told the UBO that she could not look for work as she helped her mother to look after her 89 year old grandmother who was in receipt of the attendance allowance. She was told her benefit would stop if she did not bring proof of looking for work; until the local CAB intervened she was not told she could qualify for invalid care allowance, which would exempt her from the need to be available for work (Glengormley CAB, 16/10/89).

One case illustrates how it is sometimes a matter of chance which regulation is used to stop benefit. A young mother wanted to return to work a matter of months after having her first baby. She applied for a job but was not given it because, although the woman was satisfied with her child care arrangements her prospective employer was not. The claimant was disallowed unemployment benefit because, as the letter from the UBO stated, she had "failed to avail herself of a reasonable opportunity and was therefore not considered to be actively seeking work as she had made this conditional". This claimant was stopped benefit for not actively seeking work, but she could just as easily have been stopped for failure to avail herself of a job or for having placed restrictions on her availability. Each of these reasons for disallowing benefit carries a different penalty, the first a one or two week suspension, the second a possible 26 week suspension while the third could be any period until she satisfies the UBO that she is once again available for work. (In fact she very soon afterwards got a job in a supermarket, which casts doubt on the wisdom of calling her wish to find work in question at all.) (Waterlooville CAB, 18/12/89)

The possibility of different time limits on the penalties can be a cause of confusion, not just for claimants but also for staff in the ES and claimant advisers. In one case a claimant was suspended on grounds of not actively seeking employment; the period ran from the three weeks before the date of his suspension and continued for another two weeks, until his next signing day. The most he should have been suspended for is two weeks (Oldbury CAB, 5/4/90). In another, an advice agency recorded that when a man had been suspended for not actively seeking work he was not able to receive any benefit other than a hardship payment until the appeal was heard. In fact he should have been able to requalify for benefit after a maximum of two weeks (Thurrock CAB, 2/2/90).

As with availability, there may be particular problems for those living in rural areas when in comes to proving active job searching. In one case in Scotland a woman had her benefit stopped on the grounds that she was not actively seeking work. She lived in a rural area and it was winter, and in her view there was no point in looking for work as there would be none (Stirling CAB, 14/5/90). Since the unemployed often have very little money finding the fares to pursue work outside their immediate locality is a constant problem even for those living in towns, and it is likely to be aggravated by living in a rural area.

It is not only those who want to draw benefit who have to actively seek work. A correspondent to *The Guardian* pointed out soon after the new regulations came into force that her 56 year old husband, who had taken early retirement as a teacher in the early 1980s when local authorities were desperate to reduce their workforce, had up till October 1989 been receiving national insurance contribution credits in return for signing on. From October onwards he was told that he now also had to prove that he was actively seeking work in order to qualify for the credits. Her letter ended:

> Why should he be forced to apply for other work just as we have settled into our reconstructed lives? Why should he be browbeaten into signing off and paying voluntary contributions out of his very modest (taxed) pension?

> In 1983 he was required to leave work. Now he is required to find something else – or else! I find it difficult to express adequately my sense of outrage and frustrations at this state harassment (*The Guardian*, 10/10/89).

Several reasons were given for the lack of enforcement. It is easier for the staff to use the restricted availability regulations to achieve the same end as these do not involve as much administrative work and are thought to be easier to make stick at appeal. The correct application of an ASW disallowal involves sending out warning letters and following up the suspension by fortnightly reviews; neither of these applies to suspension for restricted availability. The cost to the claimant is that very often the suspension will last longer, as would any subsequent disallowal.

There is evidence that, even when claimants are thought not to be actively seeking work, ES staff use the availability regulations rather than those relating to actively seeking work. In a submission to an appeal tribunal in Oxford an AO stated that the appellant had "not applied for any vacancies" in a particular seven week period. Despite the comments from an officer in the local jobcentre that the office work the appellant was seeking was available "to a very limited extent" and that her expectations for office work were "reasonable", the AO decided to disallow her benefit. However, he did so on the grounds of her restricted availability, not on the grounds of failure actively to seek work, which was the basis of his case (Oxford SSAT, 20/9/90).

The reason why he was able to do so, and why the appeal tribunal upheld his decision, is that it has long been held that availability is more than just a passive state and implies some activity on the part of the claimant (R(U)5/80). It was this long-standing principle which led many to argue during the passage of the 1989 Social Security Bill that there was no need for the actively seeking work regulations at all since the availability regulations, as interpreted by the Commissioners, already assumed the concept of active jobsearch behaviour. It seems from this example, and from the general lack of use of the actively seeking work regulations, that AOs are continuing to use the principle of active availability and are using failure actively to seek work to underpin their decisions on availability.

Another reason for the non-implementation cited by workers in both the ES and DSS was the lack of relevant training:

> We can't implement it [ASW]. There is no training... You don't get [the circular] or if you do there's no time to read it (Fulham jobcentre worker).

> We've been given no training at all, only the amendments to the regulations with briefings; they come down from London. The only thing we get locally is if there are cock-ups locally we'll get a memo from the local UBO manager (Brighton DSS worker).

Lack of extra resources to do the extra work involved in the administrative procedures was given as another reason.

A more general reason for the lack of enforcement was that staff often did not like the regulations, particularly as they knew they were so few jobs about. Commenting on the 1989 changes a Fulham unemployment benefit officer said:

> It would have been fine to introduce them when the register was falling and there were lots of jobs, but there are no bloody jobs.

In similar vein, the Hammersmith jobcentre manager said:

> No one wants to stop someone's benefit. They can bring in all the laws they like, but if you don't want to do it...

Given that there is so much discretion left to the individual officers the enforcement of these regulations is likely to be very patchy.

Even though sanctions were rarely imposed it did not mean that the ASW requirements had had no effect on claimants. Several advice workers commented on the worsening of the atmosphere they had brought about. In the Hammersmith Unemployed Centre an advice worker said the whole atmosphere had become more "difficult and daunting" and claimants came to the centre feeling "very upset and pressurised" as a result of the new emphasis on ASW interviews. In the Brighton Unemployed Centre the advice worker said:

> The real problem is confusion on then actively seeking work forms. People panic – they come to us all the time.

Another was clear that the effects had been significant:

> There are people doing pointless things to find employment because they know it is necessary. I think it has definitely changed people's attitudes, especially young students who wanted to stay on benefit. There's a realisation that you can't stay on benefit without doing a lot. For others who were generally looking anyway I think it can make them feel quite bad (Brighton Claim It).

Whether the legislation was deterring those it was intended to weed out is debatable. According to the Regional Chair of SSATs in Cardiff it would:

> I believe the (post 1989) system will take people off the books, that is one of the objectives. There are some who are dodgers, others who are reluctant; it will begin to operate first on the dodgers and after that on the reluctant.

This was not the view of others who commented on this. It was more generally believed that, as an advice worker in the Hammersmith Unemployed Centre put it, "you have to be daft to fall foul of the rules". Another said:

> People know exactly what they ought to be saying; the ES can't be getting the ones they want off the register.

According to this more generally held view, the "dodgers" would be the last to be affected, not the first.

In the opinion of the London Regional Director of the ES the ASW requirements were a useful means of helping the unemployed back in to work:

> The dependency culture is real. We try to show that it is in their interests to get a job... The changes in legislation are a valuable tool, an extra stimulus, in a friendly way for the most part.

This benign view is not shared by most advice workers, nor by the claimants themselves. They are more likely to agree with the view of Merseyside regional SSAT chairman:

Personally I don't think it is reasonable to expect someone to go to the jobcentre every week. You might just as well ask them to do three pirouettes before handing over their giro. It's just setting up hurdles.

Part-time students: the 21 hour rule

> This ridiculous catch-22 situation (Cleveland County Council Welfare Rights Service advice worker).

Claimants who have been unemployed for at least 3 months and who then take up a course of study which does not exceed 21 hours per week may qualify for IS provided they are prepared to leave the course immediately if a suitable employment vacancy becomes available (IS Gen.Regs. reg.9(1)(c)). However they are still required actively to seek work and the same test is applied to part-time students as for all claimants whether the claim is for IS or UB (IS Gen.Regs. 10A(3)). The conditions of the test are set out in regulation 12B of the SS (U,S, etc.) Regs.

The AO guide allows part-time students some latitude in their jobsearch to take account of the time they spend studying. Regulation 12B(2)(e) of the Social Security (Unemployment, Sickness etc.) Regulations states that in determining whether a claimant has fulfilled the actively seeking work requirement regard must be had to any time spent on any course of vocational training or study. The AO guide adds:

> Reg 12B (2)(e) recognises that a claimant who takes part in one or more of various activities while he is unemployed does not have as much time available to him to seek employment as do other claimants. Although he must take such steps as are reasonable in his case a claimant is not expected to give up these other activities so that he can devote more of his time to seeking employment. Instead the time he spends engaged in the activities must be taken into account in deciding what steps it was reasonable for him to take in any week (AOG Vol. 10 86466).

This sensible policy is not always carried out in practice. Advice agencies provided evidence of ways in which the requirement to be available for and actively seeking work was preventing claimants from pursuing courses of part-time study, even where these would have ultimately improved their job prospects. As Norwich City Council point out in their paper on *Norwich at Work* (Norwich City Council, July 1990) this even extends to disallowing benefit for HGV trainees taking a two week course which would markedly improve their value in the labour market. When the country so desperately needs skilled labour this rule is often seen by those in advice agencies as being completely counter-productive if enforced unsympathetically. The following is a case from Cleveland:

> Ms G., aged 28, recently made unemployed, does a 5 hour a week course at night. Suspended from benefit because a) she paid for the course herself and b) it leads to a career qualification. She informed the UBO that she was available for and actively seeking work and had made 16 job applications in one week (Cleveland Welfare Rights Service, 24/4/90).

Paying for the course herself meant that she would be reluctant to give it up if a job was offered to her which prevented her studying. This led the advice worker to comment:

> From a policy point of view it seems senseless that in a Britain devoid of certain skills claimants who try to improve their chances of employment are faced with the brick wall of availability and ASW. Perhaps your report could highlight this ridiculous catch-22 situation (*ibid.*).

In similar vein, Walthamstow CAB reported a case of a man who in June 1989 at his restart interview was told that the A level course he planned to take would not jeopardise his entitlement to the income support he was getting. He began the course in September 1989, taking three A levels and studying less than 21 hours a week. In December 1989, after the new ASW requirements, he was told he would have to be actively seeking work and was referred to an Employment Training course. The ET course would be at a lower level than his A level courses and would last as long. The bureau reported that "this all seems ridiculous to our client". In their view taking the A level courses was certainly improving his longer-term job prospects, especially as he was registered as dyslexic (Walthamstow CAB, 8/12/89).

We have examples of two men being disallowed benefit while on part-time training schemes which would have helped them qualify as draughtsman and one of a young man who managed to gain a place on a two-day a week signwriting course against considerable opposition, only to have his benefit disallowed for not being available for work (Cheadle CAB, 14/11/89 and Wigan CAB, 31/5/89).

The Newport CAB reported that their "biggest problem" with respect to the October 1989 changes was young people found to be unavailable for work when attending part-time courses of training or education, though this was seen to be more of a problem with education authorities misdesignating their courses as "full-time" than with the insensitive application of the regulations by the ES.

A Newport DSS worker said that they occasionally "had a purge" on part-time students:

> They use restricted availability, sending out the DE questionnaire and suspending them all until they are happy with the answers. Last year they suspended them en bloc.

Similar purges may have happened to some extent in Brighton; an advice worker in the Unemployed Centre reported that they had recently had three people in in the same week with problems related to showing that they were actively seeking work while studying under the 21-hour rule. The worker commented that "it is hard to show that you are actively seeking work if you are on a college course".

A worker in Claim It in Brighton said that claimants were now less able to use their benefit to subsidise their studies. If they were not eligible for an education or training grant this meant that they now had fewer opportunities to improve their basic education or skills while waiting for a job to come up.

This reduction of opportunities was seen as a major problem by one of the planners in the Hammersmith and Fulham Economic Development Unit, whose attempts to provide training for the unemployed had been hindered by the requirement that their trainees should be actively seeking work. Given the numbers of women wanting to return to work who may need some retraining to make them more employable this worker thought that the pressures now being put on the women to be actively seeking work, which jeopardised their commitment to the training courses, was "ludicrous". She thought that the requirements to be actively seeking work were being enforced inconsistently by the local ES offices with the result that there were different interpretations as to how much and what sort of allowances to make for those on part-time courses, making the outcome of claims unpredictable. She also thought that whereas part-time students had always been required to be available for wor k and ready to drop their studies in order to take up employment this was now being enforced much more rigorously. She gave an example of three women on a new technology course who had recently been pressured into taking full-time work which they had not wanted. (If they had been on their course for more than two months, and if it had been recognised as training, they should not be expected to take jobs outside the area of their training for four weeks.)

The borough for which she worked, Hammersmith, had been given a £100,000 grant by the Dept. of the Environment which had been distributed to local voluntary agencies to provide vocational training courses. A condition of the funding was that the programmes had to have a 70% success rate in placing trainees in employment or further training. Despite this, the local ES refused to accept participation in the courses as counting as actively seeking work. She said that in order for the ES to recognise courses as counting towards actively seeking work they had to be based in an educational establishment. The borough was about to establish a training centre with £500,000 provided from industry. As the centre was not an educational establishment there was now doubt about whether those participating would be exempt from the requirement to be actively seeking work; if they were not this could undermine the effectiveness of the courses. The poor co-operation between the departments of Employment and the Environment meant this was still a grey area which needed to be resolved.

Concern had been expressed to the local ES in Hammersmith and Fulham that part-time students had been deliberately placed in difficulties by being called for their restart interviews during their examinations. The manager of the ES had given a written assurance that this was not intended and that anyone so called could easily defer their interview. At the same time he had outlined the general policy they followed in dealing with part-time students in which he makes it clear that pursuing a course of part-time study cannot, by itself, be regarded as actively seeking work, nor as "good cause" for refusing a job offer should one arise. While each case would be treated sympathetically on its merits, he could give no guarantee that a student might not be compelled to leave a course in order to take up a job offer.

One way in which colleges in London had attempted to meet the need for students to be actively seeking work had been to take steps to ensure that students could engage in job searching whilst at college, by, for example, establishing a "Job Mart" or by appointing a tutor with responsibility for job placement; in short, by establishing a sort of unofficial jobcentre at the college.

Similar problems are met by those who are not studying but who are carrying out other worthwhile activities covered by Regulation 12B. The most bizarre example of this we came across was in Hastings, where a scheme was set up and funded by the DSS Consortium for Opportunities for Volunteering who had given the grant on condition that those running the scheme used volunteers. The scheme was specifically to provide second-hand furniture very cheaply to people on benefit. With total disregard for the irony of the situation the local ES made it "virtually impossible since 9th October 1989 to employ volunteers because of the 'actively seeking work' rule"! (Hastings and Rother CAB, 23/11/89).

On the margins of capability

IVB or not IVB? – that is the question.

For many unemployed claimants the issue whether to claim as capable for work or incapable is problematic. It has consequences which affect the type and amount of benefits and the conditions attached to the receipt of the benefits. Claimants who are capable of work may receive unemployment benefit and possibly income support provided they meet the conditions of being available and actively seeking work, and through income support they may also receive grants and loans from the social fund and have most of their housing costs met. Claimants who are incapable of work do not have to be available for or actively seeking work, and may qualify for invalidity benefit. This is paid at a higher rate than unemployment benefit, but claimants are then less likely to qualify for income support and its associated benefits, and have their invalidity benefit taken into account for housing benefit purposes, which may considerably reduce its value. The decision as to whether a claimant is or is not capable for work rests initially in the Employment Service with the AO and in the DSS with one of their medical officers.

Agency policies

Swings and Roundabouts (Newport DSS officer).

What is clear from this research project is that each of the two departments has an interest in pushing claimants on to the other; the ES may deal with its long-term unemployed who have been through all the other options by finding them to be incapable of work and redirecting them towards the DSS and invalidity benefit, while the DSS reclassifies its disabled claimants as fit for light work and redirects them to the ES. That this traffic does in fact take place is very clear from many sources. The following comments were repeated in similar form in each of the four areas:

> More claimants are being sent to the DSS Regional Medical Officers... more found fit for work than ever before. It's swings and roundabouts because whilst people are going from sick to unemployment from the RMO, if the UBO is doing its job others will go the other way (Newport DSS).

> They (UBO and jobcentre staff) agreed that there was a lot of flux between invalidity benefit and unemployment benefit with the DSS and DE working in opposite directions (Hammersmith and Fulham jobcentre).

It is possible for this to happen quite properly as claimants themselves move in and out of degrees of incapacity. However, we were given the impression that decisions were often being taken in response to departmental directives or out of exasperation with claimants for whom one could offer no more "positive" options. There was little doubt that the DSS had had a purge of its disabled claimants since all areas agreed that there had been a surge in cases where previously disabled claimants were being suddenly found fit for light work. Reasons given were that the Audit Commission had drawn attention to the numbers on invalidity benefit and suggested that many should be capable of some work which galvanised the DSS into reviewing all its disability cases, and in one area, Newport, to the appointment of a new and "over-zealous" RMO. Sometimes there appeared to be no discernible reasons, as the worker in an advice agency for the disabled in Newport said:

> The invalidity benefit sweep-out has begun ... This time of year, the new civil service in-take, I don't know whether it's poor training but there have been a large number of invalidity benefit rejections for apparently no reason... a new broom (Newport Action Aid for the Disabled).

Evidence that the decisions were not always soundly based came from advice agencies who claimed a high success rate in appeals. An advice worker in Claim It, Brighton, commented:

> The quality of decision making on "fit for light work" is very poor, and therefore we usually win tribunals in that area. For example, last week we had a man who couldn't sit down yet a telephonist's job was cited at the tribunal.

There is therefore the Kafkaesque situation of workers in the DSS trying to remove claimants from invalidity benefit while at the same time their counterparts in the ES are moving them back on to it. The Disablement Resettlement Officers in the jobcentres have their job placement targets to meet so they try to push the less promising claimants on to other benefits, notably invalidity benefit, to improve their chances of meeting them. Meanwhile the DSS may be sending along to the jobcentres claimants whom they have removed from invalidity benefit but who may be wholly unsuitable for work, as the following example from London shows:

> There have recently been problems with DSS finding people who have been on invalidity benefit "fit for work" and sending them along to the jobcentre. One case the day before a man aged 59 came in barely able to walk with two sticks. DSS had told him he had to sign on, even though when he is 60 he will receive automatic credits (worker in Hammersmith and Fulham jobcentre).

Sometimes it is possible for advice workers to negotiate a sensible compromise with the ES who will agree to accept claimants who have recently been deprived of their invalidity benefit as available for work even when this is doubtful. As a result of the 1989 changes, however, this was seen as now being increasingly difficult to do as the ES had tightened up their definition of availability.

One consequence of the push in to work of claimants who may not be fully ready is that they may take a job but soon leave it and so fall foul of the voluntary unemployment deduction. This was referred to as one of the "most prominent" issues by the Shepherd's Bush Advice Centre.

Advice workers commented on the unrealistic list of standard jobs which the DSS used when defining light work. It was this list (car park attendant, cinema usherette, lift attendant, cashier and hotel receptionist) which usually helped the claimant, when represented, to win the appeal, since often they were unsuitable for the particular claimant or they did not exist in the area.

Advice agencies agreed that it was usually better to opt for a disability benefit than for unemployment benefit as this avoided all the requirements to be available for and actively seeking work. For this reason they advised claimants to appeal against decisions finding them fit for light work. Nevertheless they had some misgivings about doing so as many claimants did not like to think of themselves as incapable of work; indeed some advisers said they thought that some claimants persisted in signing on as capable when they clearly were not and would have been better served claiming a disability benefit. None suggested the opposite, that there were many claimants who were capable who were looking to sign on as incapable.

This pressure on those with disabilities to opt for disability benefit rather than make themselves liable to the rigours of the availability and actively seeking work regulations is an unfortunate consequence of the 1989 Act. Ironically, the Act has had the opposite effect of that intended by the Minister for Social Security when he refused to exempt the older unemployed and those with disabilities from the requirement actively to seek work. Such exemption, he claimed, "would encourage them to write themselves off" (House of Commons Standing Committee F, cols.235-6, 31st January 1989), In fact, despite their wish to remain in the labour market, many claimants with disabilities are now seeing the advantages of claiming disability benefits rather than claiming as unemployed.

It is possible for claimants to fall between the criteria of both departments and to be found fit for light work by the DSS but not available for work by the ES. There was some evidence that this was happening. In fact there are three different tests for the claimant to negotiate since in addition to these two it is also possible to be found not sufficiently incapacitated to qualify for invalidity benefit but nevertheless incapacitated enough for sickness benefit. Advice workers in Newport and Brighton reported cases of claimants falling between the various categories. In Newport the claimants who could not satisfy the invalidity benefit test could still get sickness benefit; workers in Brighton Advice claimed to win every appeal they took on this issue. As with most benefits, advisers felt that many claimants who could have been helped by appealing failed to do so.

As a result of the different tests and the lack of co-ordination between the two departments, advice agencies sometimes find themselves arguing to the DSS that a claimant is incapable of work and should be allowed invalidity benefit, while at the same time they are arguing about the same person to the ES that s/he is capable for the purposes of unemployment benefit and income support. Once a claimant has been judged to be capable and removed from invalidity benefit there is no guarantee that the ES will accept that s/he is available for work. Advice workers in both Newport and Brighton referred to this as a growing cause of appeal.

The issue also arises when an incapable claimant is persuaded to try their hand at ET. As one disability adviser put it:

We do have problems with some jobcentres – not Newport – particularly around ET. People were told that they could earn an extra tenner so they moved off invalidity benefit to do ET. The trouble is that the second you say you're capable of doing something you've had it (Newport Action Aid for the Disabled).

What this means is that taking the ET course would amount to an admission of being capable for work, thus jeopardising the invalidity benefit. There is therefore a disincentive for disabled people to take up offers of training.

Issues for the claimants

There are many people who are on the borderline of being capable for work. Such claimants must take several different considerations into account when deciding whether to seek unemployment or sickness benefits. Being incapable avoids the need to be actively seeking work and will probably result in a higher rate of benefit. The downside is that claimants have to accept that they are sick or disabled which many would prefer not to do. The higher rate of benefit may be a blessing but it can also be a drawback if it takes the claimant above the IS level so that they lose entitlement to housing costs, especially where these include mortgages.

From the cases which came before the advice agencies the following issues arose.

Disputes about incapacity   When claimants have been in receipt of sickness or invalidity benefit and are then found fit for work regulation 8(2) of the Income Support (General) Regulations provides that pending the outcome of an appeal they may continue to receive income support without the need to sign on as available for work providing their GP continues to certify that they are incapable of work. Evidence from the advice agencies is that this is not always known by the DSS, who continue to require such claimants to sign on. It was suggested that this may be because the Adjudication Officers' Guide makes no reference to this regulation in the section dealing with this situation (AOG, para. 98815) (Botanic CAB, 3/10/89). The following are typical of cases known to advice agencies:

> Two clients signing on under protest, one for severe depression and one with severe back problems, have been told by the DSS that they must show evidence of actively seeking work even though they claim they are unfit for same.

> Both are awaiting their appeals and have now medicals in to support same which appear to verify their complaints (Banbridge CAB, 31/10/89).

On the face of it, both are covered by the exclusion in reg. 8 and should not have had to prove availability.

Pending the outcome of an appeal their IS is subject to the 40% deduction (IS (Gen.) Regs. 22 (5)). If they are one of a couple a simple way round this deduction is for the partner to become the claimant (Belfast Law Centre, 19/12/89).

The decision about whether someone is eligible for IVB is made at the IVB branch. However, the decision about whether someone is incapable of work is made by the AO in the local office, and is a separate decision from that relating to eligibility for IVB. Where claimants wish to contest a decision that they are capable for work the

AO should be asked to consider the matter under para. 5 of Schedule 1 of the IS (General) Regulations which allows the AO to determine that the claimant is incapable of work. This will avoid the claimant's being required to be actively seeking work while they are claiming that they are incapable (Belfast Law Centre, 19/12/89).

It is also possible to be considered as available for work even when in receipt of medical certificates, which, while it means that the claimant is subject to the requirement actively to seek work, does have the advantage of removing the 40% deduction from any IS in payment pending the outcome of an appeal. Thus the potential for confusion between the ES and the DSS in deciding what should happen to claimants who are caught on the margins of being capable for work is considerable. One such case has been fully written up in an article by a CAB worker in Cannock. It concerned a man on IVB who was appealing against being found fit for work. The UBO refused to allow him to sign on as available for work so the DSS reduced his personal allowance by 40% under regulations 8(2) and 22(5) of the IS (Gen.) Regs. The CAB argued that he was available for work, despite the continued production of medical certificates from his doctor, and cited regulation 12B(2)(a) of the Social Security (Unemployment, Sickness etc.) Regulations, which provides that the steps which a claimant must take in order to prove that he is actively seeking work shall be "reasonable" taking into account his "physical or mental limitations". They eventually got the UBO to accept this argument, thus removing the 40% deduction of his IS, but not before it had taken "approximately ten hours, 15 phone calls and a visit to the UBO" to sort it out (Lisa Miles, Cannock CAB, March 1990).

Incapacity and restricted availability The law and regulations are such that there is likely to be considerable room for different interpretations about when the restrictions imposed by a claimant's disability reach the point of rendering the claimant unavailable for work. S. 17(1) of the SSA 1975, which refers to the need to be available for work, states that "work" means "work which the person can reasonably be expected to do". Regulation 7B of the Social Security (Unemployment, Sickness etc.) Regulations further define the restrictions claimants can legitimately place on their availability and in paragraph (4)(b) these are defined as "where the restrictions are reasonable in view of the person's physical or mental condition". When should restrictions placed by the claimant because of their disabilities be regarded as reaching the point at which they render the claimant unavailable? Or, to put it another way, how much protection to people with disabilities do the above statements in the Act and regulations offer? The following case illustrates the problem.

> A woman had worked for the same company as a telephonist/switchboard operator. She was made redundant on health grounds as she had to take a lot of time off work. She had polio as a child, leaving her with considerable pain in her back and legs. She signed on in mid 1989 and received UB. She has numeracy and literacy problems, sporadic bouts of illness and requires a job where she can sit down and take occasional walks to ease the stiffness in her legs. Eventually her UB was stopped and she was informed that she "was disallowed for 3 months because she would accept a job only within a limited range of duties" (Slough CAB, 25/4/90).

In the opinion of the advice agency an appeal was likely to have been successful, but because of the long delays in appeals the claimant opted for sickness benefit instead. This illustrates clearly the grey area between placing restrictions on work which are reasonable in view of the person's mental and physical condition and falling foul of the availability requirement.

There are two other points about this case; the first is that the claimant was not redirected towards claiming sickness benefit by the ES, they simply stopped her money and if she had not gone to the advice agency she would have had no money at all. The second is that there is no provision for disallowing benefit on grounds of restricted availability for a specific period of future time, so she should not have been told the disallowance would last for three months; it would last until she was able to make herself available again, whenever that might be.

Incapacity and refusal of employment Regulation 12E of the Social Security (Unemployment, Sickness etc.) Regulations allows for the refusal of an offer of employment where the employment "would be likely to or did cause serious harm to his health or subject him to excessive physical or mental stress". This too gives rise to grey areas where judgements have to be made, as the following case illustrates.

> Client had been in receipt of IS but this ceased after restart interview when he refused a job offered on the grounds of his poor health. He has a bad chest and regularly visits doctor. Job on offer was the same kind that he had given up because of his health problems; not offered any suitable alternative.

> Had no money since 20th April (1989). Submitted sick note but claim would take at least a week to process. Doctor told him he must get food because of poor medical condition. Had not eaten for 4 days. No emergency help available to him from benefit system at all, in spite of long negotiation. No help available from Social Services. Had to refer to Salvation Army for food until benefit arrives (Rotherham CAB, 10/5/89).

This case was dealt with under the old regulations which were more favourable to claimants since jobs could then be refused if they were not "suitable".

Incapacity and actively seeking work If the AO decides that claimants are capable of work, even if only capable of "light work", then they are subject to the full rigours of having to be actively seeking work.

> Long-term unemployed client (four years) has been signing quarterly for some time. Suffers from ill-health, has chronic chest condition of some kind. Aged 53. Doctor considers him "suitable for light work". On attending the bureau, which he frequently does, he has to sit for five minutes or so after climbing the stairs to recover his breath. Wanted help in filling in application for a restart interview following a medical by a DSS doctor.

> Client has previously had to apply for jobs via job centre to prove "actively seeking work". On 15/10/89 he applied for six jobs, helped by UBO and failed to get any, which demoralised him.

The expense in UBO time in encouraging our client regarding job interviews and possible retraining seems to be totally inappropriate for a person with the health limitations of our client (Brighouse CAB, 9/1/90).

There were a number of such cases brought to our attention, including one where a man who had been unemployed for several years and described as "borderline sick", very depressed and on medication was threatened that he would have his benefit stopped if he refused to attend an ET course despite the repeated assurances from the Minister that ET is not compulsory (Pendleton CAB, 3/11/89). More than one advice agency reported a spate of such cases and thought that the DSS was "working down the list" of its IVB cases (Tavistock CAB, 26/9/89).

One case which went to appeal in St Helens highlights both the poor quality of liaison between the ES and the DSS and the bizarre decisions which are sometimes made when claimants move from disability benefits into being considered capable for work. A woman who had been on invalidity benefit for over two years was found fit for work by the DSS on 26th December 1989. She was not notified of this until 19th January 1990. She then made a claim for unemployment benefit for the period from the time her invalidity benefit had been stopped, that is from 26th December. Her claim was disallowed on the grounds that she had not been actively seeking work between 26th December and 19th January, despite the fact that during that time she had no reason to think she was not still on invalidity benefit and therefore exempt from the requirement to be available for work (St Helens SSAT, appeal lodged 6/3/90).

It is clear that the border area between capacity and incapacity for work is one which gives rise to the possibility of widely differing interpretations of the regulations. From the above examples we can see that marginally capable claimants who place restrictions on their availability or job searching activities may

a) if it is pending an appeal, sometimes be required to sign on as available for work and sometimes not;

b) be considered to be unavailable for work and therefore not eligible for UB or IS at all;

c) be considered to be available within the limitations of their physical or mental limitations and so receive full UB and IS;

d) be considered to be unavailable for work and therefore ineligible for UB but allowed by regulation 8(2) of the IS (Gen.) Regs. to be eligible for IS at a reduced rate.

To add to the confusion, there is also provision in Schedule 1(6) of the IS (Gen.) Regs. to exempt from the requirement to be available for work anyone whose mental or physical disability is such as to reduce their likely earning capacity to 75% of that of which a non-disabled person would reasonably be expected to earn, although we did not come across any examples of the use of it. Even the meaning of work itself may be different for disabled claimants; under regulation 7(1)(c) of the IS (Gen.) Regs. the stipulation that for IS purposes work means not less than 24 hours per week is modified in the case of those who are mentally or physically disabled to "such lesser number of hours as, having regard to his disability, he is usually capable of working".

Which of these many possibilities applies in any one case is likely to be a function partly of which interpretation the particular office takes and partly of whether the claimant seeks the help of an advice agency. The consequences for the claimant vary from having benefit in full, benefit subject to the 40% deduction or none at all.

What to do with those on the margins of employability has always been a problem for the ES. Anticipating the introduction of the actively seeking work requirement an area manager of the ES in Yorkshire set out the difficulties of dealing with such people in a letter to his local managers:

> Para 64 of Circular 161/1 suggests that extra care should be taken when dealing with people who have serious mental or physical handicaps which could make compliance with the normal rules difficult. To this group could be added many of those claimants we had to take back on to the register, following the introduction of IS etc. who were considered virtually unemployable and had been on order books. Almost every office has its share of such people including those who are severely mentally disturbed, alcoholics, drug addicts etc. who, if subjected to the full rigours of the new system, would cause our staff no end of problems with not the slightest hope of a positive result. Head Office were asked to advise on what we should do with such people at an early briefing session in July and, as usual, no-one wants to address the problem so nothing is said in the instructions about them (letter from ES Area Office, Wakefield, to local managers, para. 12, 5/9/89).

We sympathise with his sense of the futility of sending many such people on jobsearches which are likely to be unproductive, and with his exasperation at the lack of realistic advice on how to deal with them. The present potential for confusion and different treatment of similar cases in the application of such complex regulations must also be a cause for concern, especially when the benefit outcomes for the claimants can be so varied.

Refusal of employment

> If they turn down a job it is assumed that they already have one, so they pass it to Fraud (worker in Fulham jobcentre).

The regulations: unemployment benefit

Section 20(1) of the SSA 1975 states that claimants may be disqualified from unemployment benefit for up to 26 weeks if "without good cause" they fail to apply for or accept a job offered through the ES, or if they neglect to avail themselves of reasonable offers of employment.

The matters to be taken into account in determining what constitutes good cause are set out in regulation 12E of the Social Security (Unemployment, Sickness etc.) Regulations. These include such matters as where the job would be likely to cause serious harm to his health or subject him to excessive physical or mental stress or in respect of which he had any religious or conscientious objection. Other matters to be considered are travel time to work, expenses where these would constitute an unreasonably high proportion of wages. As importantly, since October 1989 the regulation also specifies matters which cannot be taken into account; notably the level of wages of the job offered relative to the claimant's income on benefit or to his ordinary living expenses, such as for example his mortgage. Travel time to work under an hour cannot be good cause except where the health of the person or the fact that they are responsible for the care of another member of their household would make the time unreasonable.

Section 20A(1) of the SSA 1975 allows claimants to refuse jobs outside their normal occupation and at their normal rates of pay during their "permitted period", the conditions of which are governed by regulation 12F of the Social Security (Unemployment, Sickness etc.) Regulations. This may be any time up to 13 weeks, at the discretion of the ES. Regulation 12E also allows claimants to restrict the jobs they may accept if they have just completed a training course of at least two months; they then have a four week period within which they need only accept jobs for which they had just been trained.

The regulations: income support

The conditions governing claimants for income support are in some respects different. They are set out in regulation 10 of the IS (General) Regulations. This states that a claimant who "without good cause" refuses to apply for or accept a job notified through the ES or DSS, or who neglects to avail himself of a job opportunity, and where in either case the job is still open to him, is not considered to be available for work and is therefore not eligible for income support. There is provision in the IS regulations for a permitted period within which the claimant may restrict his job search to those consistent with his normal occupation for up to 13 weeks. There are no regulations defining what constitutes "good cause", though presumably a claimant could use the UB regulation as guidelines.

The penalties

For UB claimants the penalty under this heading is disqualification of unemployment benefit for up to 26 weeks (SSA 1975 sec. 20 (1)).

For IS claimants it is more complicated. If the job vacancy is still open the claimant is deemed to be not available for work and therefore not eligible for income support (Reg.10(1)(a)). Whether he is eligible for a hardship payment is not clear; the CPAG *National Welfare Benefits Handbook* says that he is (*NWBH, 21st Edition 1991/92*, p.42); Mesher implies that he is not. The only source of possible funds for him would then be a crisis loan from the social fund (*Mesher, note to reg. 10, p. 69 of the 1990 edition of Income Support, The Social Fund and Family Credit: the Legislation*).

Once the vacancy ceases to be open the claimant must no longer be treated as not available for employment (Reg.10(2)(a) of the IS regs). However, he is then subject to reg. 22(4) (c)(iii) and 22(6)(c) of the IS regs. which state that where a claimant for IS would have been disqualified if he had made a claim for UB his amount of IS shall be subject to the 40% deduction.

For claimants of both UB and IS the picture is further complicated by the fact that sometimes the UBO may use refusal of employment as an indication of more general non-availability or of restricted availability and disallow benefit altogether, so a refusal of employment may have different consequences depending on whether it is treated simply as a refusal of a particular job, whether the UBO or DSS know about whether the vacancy is still open, whether they allow hardship payments if it is still open, or whether they treat it as evidence of lack of availability. The outcome for the claimant could be either a reduced rate of IS paid automatically, a hardship payment only, or no benefit at all.

The policies

When the word "suitable" was removed from the regulations in October 1989, which meant that the jobs offered to claimants no longer had to be suitable, and claimants could therefore no longer use the unsuitability of the work offered as a defence against refusing it, the Government argued that penalties only attached to jobs offered through the ES, which ipso facto guaranteed claimants against exploitation since staff in the ES would not offer unsuitable jobs. The Chief Executive of the ES has stated that jobcentres have long standing instructions that they should not handle any vacancy where the wage quoted is below wages council rates, and "in other cases where wages offered are low staff will advise employers about the local prevailing rates for the job" (letter from Chief Executive, ES, to Jimmy Dunnachie M.P., ref.2507/8/90, 16/7/1990). He also claimed that whenever they received reports that wages below legal limits were on offer staff were reminded of these requirements (*ibid.*).

There is now no defence against disqualification for refusal of a job on the grounds of low wages (other than during one's permitted period.). In December 1989 Tim Eggar speaking on behalf of the Secretary of State for Employment made it clear that where the wages left the claimant unable to cover mortgage repayments or child care costs this was still not good cause for refusing a job. To make the point, he went on to add:

> A claimant does not have good cause for refusing any employment if the reasons relate to their income or outgoings, or those of any other member of their family (*Hansard*, 18/12/89, col. 64).

The policy is clear; even where a claimant would be worse off in work than on benefit if he took the job offered that is no defence against disqualification if he refuses it. Asked about this point specifically, the Deputy Chief Executive of the ES said that because the rate of pay must not be taken into account as a factor in good cause, "the question of whether a claimant would or would not be better off in work does not apply" (letter from Deputy Chief Executive, ES, to Clare Short M.P., ref. 2031/90, 12/6/90). He added that the claimant's safeguard was that Claimant Advisers "should give careful consideration to a claimant's circumstances before offering a job vacancy" (*ibid.*).

Illustrative cases The following are some of the cases which have come to the notice of advice agencies which cast some doubt on this assurance.

> A 19 year old who had been in work since age 16 moved to Slough where she signed on for IS, providing the UBO with satisfactory evidence of her active job searching. After 5 months she was given an interview at the UBO and shown a vacancy for a job as a shop assistant paying £80 a week gross. She said she was not interested because of the low wage, out of which she would not be able to pay her rent of £50 plus all her other normal expenses including travel to work. She was asked to put her response in writing without being told of the implications. Two months later her benefit stopped with no written explanation. She had been disqualified for 3 months for refusal of the offer of employment (Slough CAB, 27/4/90).

There are several points about this which are of concern. The wage is very low, but this did not prevent the ES from offering the job. With such a low wage the claimant would probably have qualified for substantial housing benefit, which should have been explained to her and may have made a difference to her calculations. She should certainly have had the implications of a refusal explained, which she claims was not done. Moreover, she should only have been disqualified for as long as the vacancy existed, not for a three month period. As soon as the vacancy ceased to exist she could have requalified for IS. Even during the time she was disqualified she should have been informed of her right to apply for either a hardship payment or a crisis loan from the social fund.

> A young man aged 25 was offered a job with a gangmaster by the claimant adviser. The hours were from 5.45a.m. to 6.00p.m., so he refused, saying that he was however prepared to work from 8.00a.m. to 5.00p.m (Stamford CAB, 13/3/90).

Perhaps not surprisingly, this gangmaster "always had vacancies", which meant that the disqualification imposed by the DSS ran for 13 weeks. As another advice centre pointed out, the existence of these regulations lays the way open for some employers to make unreasonable conditions:

> We are concerned that unscrupulous employers are taking advantage of the 1989 Act and "using" the ES as a free recruitment agency. I was recently approached by a claimant who had been contacted by a Restart Counsellor about a job at Chesterfield Brick Centre for cleaning bricks. I investigated and found that there was no basic wage, that employees would be paid £20 per 1,000 bricks and would be expected to clean 2,000 bricks per day. According to experienced bricklayers this is impossible. However I found out that the jobs had been notified to the Job Centre Counsellors and within half an hour 6 unemployed people had agreed to apply for the jobs. I must stress that claimants were not compelled to apply but it is obvious that, given the current legislation, they feel obliged to follow up notified vacancies (Chesterfield Unemployed Workers' Centre, 19/6/90).

And of course if these claimants then found that the work really was "impossible" and left they would risk having their benefit reduced for 26 weeks for leaving without just cause.

There were several examples of the work offered to claimants being on the face of it quite unsuitable for their personal circumstances.

A married man with a child was offered a live-in job at a stables and disqualified when he refused (Warwick District CAB, 9/2/89).

A "slight, middle-aged" man was sent for a job which involved lifting heavy boxes 4-5 feet on to a platform which he found very difficult to do so was not offered the job by the employer. He was disqualified for failing to accept the job, which he claimed was not offered (Basingstoke CAB, 31/10/89).

A third man was disqualified for refusing a job which was the same kind as he had previously given up on health grounds. He had a bad chest and regularly visited his doctor, and when he was disqualified he submitted a medical certificate. When he attended the advice agency he said that he had not eaten for four days. The agency was unable to get him any emergency help during the week or so it would take to process the claim for sickness benefit (Rotherham CAB, 10/5/89).

The penalty for refusing to take a job also affects the payment of NI contribution credits. A man aged 58 who was pensioned off at 54 from a job where he was working with computers and who claimed to have written over 200 job applications with no success was threatened by the DSS that they would discontinue his credits if he refused the offer of a job stacking shelves at Tesco's (Rickmansworth CAB, 7/12/89).

There are problems with the unpredictable penalties which might flow from a refusal of work, especially for IS claimants. There are also problems for claimants in knowing exactly what constitutes an offer of work and therefore a refusal, as the following case which went to appeal at Oxford in October 1990 illustrates.

A 28 year old man with a degree in zoology who had last worked as a wildlife photographer had been out of work for 18 months. He had applied for a job with the Civil Service, had taken their aptitude test and was waiting for a second round of interviews with them. Meanwhile, he was called in for interview by the Claimant Adviser, who read out some details of jobs to him from her cards, among which was one for a vacancy at W.H. Smith. The claimant stated that "no direct suggestion was made at the time that he should apply for that or the others". He further stated that the Claimant Adviser "did not ask him if he was interested in any of the jobs".

He was subsequently disqualified from benefit for 26 weeks for refusal of employment. In his letter of appeal the claimant said "during the interview I did not know I was being offered any work until I was told that it would be considered that I had refused to accept work".

During the hearing the AO "confirmed that there is no set procedure so far as he is aware in the Department whereby an appellant who is being offered something with the implications that flow from refusal is specifically told in advance that this is the case".

This revealing admission lends weight to the views of the Merseyside Regional SSAT Chairman quoted earlier that claimants may sometimes be the victims of "entrapment".

The appeal failed, but one member dissented from the decision for the following reason:

While it seems very likely that in the interview a number of jobs were discussed or details mentioned to the appellant... it is not reasonable on the basis of natural justice to take his responses as a refusal when they were being given in a situation where the implications had not been explained to him. A fair and proper way of dealing with such interviews would be to tell the claimant at the outset that he is going to be invited to follow up a vacancy and that not to do so may result in a refusal with a consequent disqualification.

There seemed to be no doubt that in this interview the claimant had not had the implications spelt out to him; indeed the AO agreed that there was no set procedure for doing so, which makes it more than likely that other claimants have found themselves in the same disadvantageous position as this appellant. It is difficult not to agree with the conclusion of the dissenting member of the tribunal that:

> On the basis of natural justice, people being put at risk by the answers they may give should be more fairly acquainted with the situation they are in.

The effects on claimants

The effects of the changes in the regulations concerning refusal of employment were not much explored in the course of discussions with either ES staff or advice agencies since both groups claimed that sanctions for refusals of employment were very rare as far as they were concerned. The reasons given were that claimants were seldom offered jobs by the ES, usually only at restart, and if they were the claimants usually pursued them. As a worker in the Brighton jobcentre commented, "People are desperate so they are prepared to work for a relatively low wage".

In Fulham jobcentre the procedure was not to use the refusal of employment regulations because they were too easily overturned on appeal; instead where claimants did refuse job offers they used the "not actively seeking work" sanction or even referred them for investigation by the fraud section.

> If they turn down a job it is assumed that they already have one, so they pass it to Fraud... It is difficult to get someone on refusal of employment. If they are disallowed they usually appeal and get off. They do them on actively seeking work if they don't turn up for a job interview. But Fraud is the easiest; it saves on paperwork and adjudication and it scares them as well.

One advice worker said that the concept of "good cause" legitimately (the ground on which claimants may legitimately refuse offers of employment) was not familiar to claimants and even if it were it is only those who were exceptionally well versed in social security law who would have any hope of understanding it well enough to find their way through the regulations. It may well be the case that once an appeal is lodged claimants have a good chance of winning it, but the strong suspicion must remain that very few would know that they could appeal on grounds of "good cause". If claimants who refuse offers of jobs or job interviews are routinely referred to the Fraud section or suspended on other grounds it would no doubt add to the claimants' sense that the process of claiming and restart interviews are often hazardous and unpleasant.

When claimants were suspended from benefit or disallowed on grounds of refusal of employment once a claim was in progress the DSS computers had no code which allowed the deduction to be made. This, we were told by a worker in the Brixton

UBO, meant that claimants either lost none of their IS or lost it entirely, when they should have been subject to the usual "voluntary unemployment" deduction.

Voluntary unemployment

> They think that they can give up work because they were pressurised into it in the first place, but they can't (worker in Brighton Unemployed Centre).

Despite the recent changes in the 1989 Social Security Act and regulations there was little doubt in the minds of the advice agencies that the biggest problem for the unemployed in respect of losing their benefits was still the voluntary unemployment deduction imposed for leaving a job "without just cause" or for being dismissed for misconduct. The familiar problems were still very much around; unreasonable delays in reaching a decision and the invariable and unwarranted imposition of the maximum twenty-six week penalty.

In Brighton one advice agency had noticed a big increase in the number of claimants being found to have made themselves voluntarily unemployed, which the agency saw as the direct result of the tighter application of the availability regulations.

> The main problem is people being hassled into taking work or just leaving the register... The suspensions we come across are for leaving work voluntarily; this has increased massively recently. They think that they can give up work because they were pressurised into it in the first place, but they can't (Brighton Unemployed Centre).

In London some claimants fell foul of the sanction because they were homeless. The Hammersmith Unemployed Centre had seen three cases of people under 25 who had lost their jobs as a result of their homelessness and who had been subject to the voluntary unemployment deduction. The result was that these youngsters sometimes had very little money to live on; the worker at the Centre gave an example of someone known to him who was living on £1.10p. a week after paying off his accommodation fees and social fund loan, and another who had £4 to live on at another hostel.

Another group of people caught by this sanction were those who had moved off long-term invalidity benefit to try their hand at some light employment, perhaps having been reclassified as capable of work by the DSS medical officer, who had then found the work too much for them, left and been judged to have made themselves voluntarily unemployed. In St Helens two groups were mentioned as particularly likely to be affected. One was young girls who left their jobs because of their pregnancy yet who might still be caught by the benefit sanction, even though pregnancy might afford "just cause" for leaving and so make the sanction inapplicable. The other was married women who, if they were judged to be voluntarily unemployed, usually received no money at all as they would fail to qualify for income support if their partner was in full-time work. Not only would they lose their income but they would also lose entitlement to national insurance credits, thus jeopardising future entitlement to benefit.

Advice workers in Brighton, Newport and London all maintained that when a voluntary unemployment deduction was made it was invariably for the maximum 26 weeks. This is in contradiction both to the internal advice in the AO Guide and to the ruling of the Tribunal of Commissioners which said that a "sensible discretion" had to be exercised in such a manner as the justice of the case requires, taking into account all the circumstances (R(U)8/74T). According to these advice workers, AOs were continuing to disregard these rules and wrongfully penalising claimants.

One consequence of this was that whenever an advice agency appealed against a voluntary unemployment deduction they nearly always succeeded in reducing the length of disqualification if not in removing it altogether. The Brighton CAB claimed to have taken "15 to 20" cases to appeal and got all but three quashed, with the 26 week penalty remaining in force in only one case.

However, while it is relatively easy to win such appeals it was also the view of the advice agency workers that many claimants failed to appeal, either accepting the judgment against them or not realising that appeals were possible. Not only did they fail to appeal, according to a Brighton jobcentre worker and an advice agency, but many of them even fail to sign on if they have left a job voluntarily as they believe they will not be entitled to benefit. In many cases even with a voluntary unemployment deduction the claimant will still be entitled to some benefit if they qualify for income support. Thus, both the failure to appeal and the failure to sign on cause many claimants unnecessary loss of substantial sums of benefit.

Sometimes claimants cannot appeal for several months because it is not uncommon for AOs to take a long time to reach a decision. While the case is under consideration, often awaiting further evidence from the employer, who has no incentive to answer the AOs questions the benefit is suspended but there is nothing against which to appeal. A Brighton advice agency commented:

> They won't make a decision for ages and ages so you can't review it or appeal. That is the problem; sometimes it takes two months or more. I've got one here of four months, and in the end her claim was allowed! (Brighton Advice).

Meanwhile that claimant would have gone without unemployment benefit, or with a reduced rate of income support. Sometimes even the reduced rate of income support was not always paid. Brighton CAB said that sometimes claimants who should have been in receipt of the reduced rate of benefit got nothing at all until they interceded on their behalf.

As we have seen, even when claimants do appeal they may still fall foul of the curious relationship between the ES and the DSS, which means that a claim against a voluntary unemployment deduction on IS may have to have been directed through the ES to have any chance of success.

One welcome change in the 1989 Act which sought to modify the disincentive to return to work brought about by the Draconian penalties for leaving work without just cause was the introduction of a period of employment on trial. Regulation 12G of the Social Security (Unemployment, Sickness etc.) Regulations now provides for a trial period of employment for claimants who have been out of work for 26 weeks. This enables them to take a job and leave it again without penalty provided they stay there for at least six weeks and no longer than twelve. This may become in time a useful means of encouraging otherwise understandably reluctant claimants back to work. Of those claimants we spoke to, very few had yet heard of this provision.

The evidence from the research shows that the voluntary unemployment deduction is still causing major problems for claimants. It affects them in large numbers and it almost certainly results in many thousands of claimants being disqualified for periods far in excess of those required by the Social Security Commissioners and by the ES's own internal guidance. Delays in reaching a decision, claimants' ignorance of the regulations and of the arcane relationship between the ES and the DSS mean that only a small proportion of disqualifications are challenged, and many claimants therefore lose large sums of money unnecessarily.

People with literacy problems and those whose first language is not English

> The ultimate in wild goose chases (Cleveland County Council Welfare Rights Service worker).

People with literacy problems

The policy of the ES is that people with literacy problems should be treated sympathetically when it comes to proving that they have been actively seeking work. The Chief Executive of the ES has stated categorically that "claimants with literacy difficulties would not be expected to keep written job search records and other forms of evidence would be accepted" (letter from Chief Executive ES to David Hinchcliffe, M.P., 14/11/90). Paragraph 39 of Circular 161 (Revised) of the ES acknowledges that people with language or literacy problems will need special help:

> Counsellors will need to explain the requirements to actively seek employment and the need to provide evidence of jobsearch, taking into account any limitations of the claimant. It may be useful to establish local points of contact for people who will need help with supplying written evidence or third person evidence (e.g. CABx, welfare or claimant organisations able to offer translators or interpreters and local authority "Open Door" classes).

> No claimant with literacy difficulties can be criticised for failing to send written applications without access to help.

No doubt these good intentions are often followed, but the fact remains that claimants with literacy or language problems are especially at risk of losing their entitlement to benefit. We had several examples of claimants with literacy problems having trouble proving their active jobsearches.

> Client could not read or write and was turned down for UB; said to not be actively seeking work. After many hassles DHSS [sic] said he could verbally give evidence of seeking work (Rathcoole CAB, 8/2/90).

> Client, single, aged 45, educationally subnormal, inadequate, can hardly read or write. Recently told he will have to sign on by DSS to get his benefit. Falling foul of actively seeking work rules. Does not understand. Has said he's only capable of roadsweeping-type jobs. Not capable of keeping records of attempts to find work. The type of work he is capable of doing does not appear to exist so he would not understand he should apply anyway. Has elderly lodger (80+) and insists he must be home to cook

evening meal for him; is therefore restricting his availability. Disablement Resettlement Officer unable to help on inability to read aspect. Doctor has signed client sick to get benefits. D.R.O. said a lot of their work now involves those falling foul of the UB rules above (Rydale CAB, 28/2/90).

Client illiterate. Client has been looking for work for six months. DSS have threatened to stop IS. Client said he had been applying for jobs but had not kept a record (Portsmouth CAB, 11/9/90).

This last CAB suggested that claimants with literacy difficulties could be given a pro-forma for employers to sign to prove their jobsearch activities.

Immigrants

In respect of those whose first language is not English the official policy is also that they should be treated with special care. In the same letter referred to above the Chief Executive of the ES pointed out that the service provided leaflets about restart, availability and actively seeking work in a number of languages. Perhaps more importantly he set out the ES policy on the use of interpreters.

Although the ES does not employ people specifically as interpreters, we encourage the presence of independent interpreters where language is likely to be a problem. My local offices kept [sic] records of those outside the ES who can provide such services free of charge.

Assuming the "kept" to be a misprint for "keep", this is a laudable policy, though we suspect it will come as a surprise to many claimants.

NACAB carried out its own survey of the difficulties faced by non-English speaking claimants during 1990 and published the results in *Barriers to Benefit, Black Claimants and Social Security*, NACAB, January 1991. In it they say:

Both tests [availability and actively seeking work] cause particular problems for claimants who speak or write little or no English. Claimants are required to fill in the availability for work questionnaire. CABx report that clients are not aware that they have the right to take the form away and to seek advice and help in filling it in. They are not told this by staff at the UBO. The form is in English and the interviewer will almost invariably only speak English. The interviewer writes the claimants' answer for them. This means that the answers are subject to misunderstanding and possible prejudice. CABx have found that claimants have no understanding of the implications the answers can have and, with no advice about the availability of family credit or housing benefit, state a minimum wage required which the UBO consider too high (*Barriers to Benefit*, paras. 7.9 and 7.10).

There are examples from many different parts of the country of such difficulties. Given that many claimants whose first language is English have great difficulty in understanding the complexities of the regulations concerning availability and actively seeking work this comes as no surprise. These complexities soon become totally unfathomable to anyone with language difficulties, and especially so for people newly arrived here who have no idea what they may or may not expect from the benefit agencies.

The most common problem was that of establishing availability for work. The following examples are typical:

> A CAB in the North East reports a client who could not speak English and who was disallowed benefit on the grounds that the type of work and the amount of money he required were not reasonable and he was therefore restricting his availability. The Bureau established that he had not understood the questions which had been asked of him, and when he was helped to fill in the form again by the Bureau his benefit was re-instated (*ibid.*, para. 7.10).

> A CAB in East Sussex reports four cases where the UBO decided the clients were not available for work. On each case the decision was reversed or modified when the clients were helped to explain their situation using an interpreter (*ibid.*, para. 7.10).

These are simple cases where the claimant's lack of understanding of the implications of the questions asked led to the stoppage of benefit. Inevitably this must raise questions about the helpfulness of the interviewing staff, since these same claimants were able to make themselves understood to the CABx. It also raises questions about those claimants in similar circumstances who failed to seek the help of advice agencies and who presumably simply lost their benefit unnecessarily.

A more complicated way, and equally common, in which these claimants lost benefit was when the ES or DSS ruled that their lack of English was ipso facto a reason to disallow benefit on the grounds that it prevented their finding and keeping work.

> A woman aged 20, recently arrived from Bangladesh to join her family claimed benefit. Three months later, having received nothing, she contacted the local CAB. They 'phoned the DSS who advised of their decision that she is not available for work as "she does not speak or understand English". After intervention by the CAB the DSS arranged for her to go on an English language course (*ibid.*, para. 7.11).

> An Asian woman in her mid 40s in receipt of IS was obliged to sign on as available for work. Her weekly benefit was suddenly reduced by 40%. After enquiring at the DSS she receives a letter showing that she has been subject to the deduction because she is unable to speak English and is therefore considered to be voluntarily unemployed. After intervention by the CAB her benefit is restored (Bellshill and District CAB, 2/11/89).

Similarly there are examples of claimants having difficulty proving that they have been actively seeking work.

> A CAB in Devon reports a man who could speak and write little English being disallowed benefit on the grounds that he was not available for work. At the appeal the AO included reference to the lack of documentary evidence supporting the client's claim to have been seeking work. Most of the client's approaches to prospective employers had been in person and there was nothing in writing. The appeal was allowed (*Barriers to Benefit*, para. 7.10).

When poor English is compounded by disability the results can be little short of oppressive for claimants if not dealt with sympathetically.

Client, aged 59, Asian, speaks no English and has numerous health problems. He had been submitting sick notes for some time but for a short period had trouble getting sick notes from his doctor; he therefore had to sign on as available for work. The claimant adviser immediately gave him a list of building sites which he was told he had to visit to seek labouring work in order to show that he was actively seeking work. Given that he could speak no English and could barely walk, let alone labour, this was to say the least the ultimate in wild goose chases. We contacted his doctor and got him to provide backdated sick notes (Cleveland Welfare Rights Service, 24/4/90).

In addition to these general problems there were others to do with the status of the immigrant and whether they were eligible for benefit at all. This is likely to be an immensely complicated area, even by social security standards of Byzantine complexities, given the provisions of our immigration and refugee laws. We do not have enough evidence on these cases to say a great deal, but it is clearly an area which needs a research project of its own. The following is an example of the kind of issue which does arise, and of which there are likely to be many variants.

A CAB in North London reports a black client with a "Right of Abode" who applied for income support. The UBO insisted on seeing his passport and refused to let him register. They said he needed a work permit and so was not available for work. The client returned four times and each time he was refused at the desk. He then contacted the CAB who wrote to the UBO advising that no work permit is required with "Right of Abode". The client was then allowed to fill in a B1 form (*Barriers to Benefit*, para. 7.10).

Another common problem arises for many muslim families when the husband temporarily returns home or goes on a pilgrimage to Mecca. The wife then has to claim, who may often speak little or no English and who often for religious or cultural reasons cannot easily leave home during her husband's absence. As well as the obvious problems of her understanding any communication she may get from the DSS, in one London borough at least the DSS refused to treat such wives as lone parents during the husbands' absence which meant they had to sign on. They were then often refused benefit on the grounds that they were not available for work. The local CAB intervened;

When we challenged this we were advised it was on the basis of guidance from Regional Office on the interpretation of AOG 25072. We succeeded in having this wrongful interpretation withdrawn, but in the meantime several families had borne the consequences (St. Marylebone CAB, September 1989).

Refugees

The status of people from abroad seeking political asylum varies according to how long they have been here and the stage they have reached in their application. During the first six months they are not allowed to work, after which they may be allowed to. Whilst waiting for a decision on their application they are eligible for IS at the reduced rate for urgent cases and they are not required to be available for work. Once a decision has been reached that the applicant has "exceptional leave to remain" the applicant has to be available for and actively seeking work. Once an applicant has achieved full refugee status they also have to be available for and actively seeking work unless they are attending an English language course for more than 15 hours a week, provided that the applicant began the course within 12 months of arrival in this country (IS (Gen.) Regs. Sched. 1 (16)).

The Refugee Council has drawn attention to the general difficulties raised by these rules, in particular that it is inequitable that only those with full refugee status should be allowed exemption from the requirement to be available for work whilst attending an English language course, since those with "exceptional leave to remain" need to acquire language skills just as much.

Given the length of time it takes the Home Office to reach a decision on refugees it is often difficult for refugees to both achieve full refugee status and begin a course as a refugee within 12 months of entry. As for the courses themselves, those providing at least 15 hours of English language are in very short supply, and in any case the teaching of English is often best done when integrated with other subjects. The shortage of courses again makes it difficult for refugees to start one within a year of entry, and it would be better if the range of courses which qualified for the purposes of waiving the requirement to be available for work was widened to include skills courses which included a substantial element of English (Memorandum from Refugee Council to DSS, June 1990).

The same memorandum draws attention to the lack of provision for funding refugees on non-advanced vocational courses for those over 19. Given that these courses improve the refugee's prospects of employment it would make sense to make income support available to those taking such courses, without the requirement to be available for work. The consequences of not allowing refugees to take such courses and to instead require them to be available for and actively seeking work are that they are often forced to leave courses which would have improved their employability in the longer term and instead to take menial jobs.

This can be seen in the application of the actively seeking work regulations to refugees. Stating that "there is growing evidence of refugees who are in fact suffering unfair treatment of these new regulations" the Refugee Council gives the following examples:

> Miss D. (Ethiopian.) Obliged to take a job in McDonalds and thus to drop an English/ study skills course with a view to entry into higher education at a later stage. She was intending to study for a BTEC Business studies course.

> Miss C. (Eritrean.) Obliged to leave an English course to take up a low-paid cleaning job. Benefit reinstated after Social Services intervention, and considerable social distress.

> Mr B. (Cambodian.) Arrived in U.K. with refugee status, speaking no English. Honestly (but inadvertently?) filled in the box when signing on saying he was not available for work and added the words 'learning English'. Had arrived during college vacation – no classes nor advice available. Benefit disallowed until study over 15 hours was possible. It took 2 SSATs to authorise his repayment of lost benefit.

> Mr E. (Ethiopean.) Studying on a 2 year B/TEC national course in photography (under 21 hours.) Obliged to leave course after 1½ years to attend a Job Club after benefit

was stopped for not "voluntarily" attending this activity. Had stressed willingness to attend Job Club at end of course (*ibid.*).

The Refugee Council recommended that refugees seeking employment ultimately should be "deemed" to be actively seeking work, provision for which already exists in the regulations for other categories of claimants. One could also argue that taking an English course, or any skills based course, comes within regulation 12B, the criteria for the steps to be taken by those actively seeking employment in that it may offer the "best prospects of receiving offers of employment." This is all the more the case if the ES staff continue to deem claimants unavailable for work simply on the grounds that they cannot speak English.

In the light of the above examples we would agree with the conclusion of the NACAB report that inability to speak or write English should be explicitly excluded as a reason for disallowing benefit under the availability or actively seeking work rules. This would be a much firmer way of ensuring that such claimants were not disallowed benefit just because of misunderstandings than optimistic exhortations in ES circulars.

We would also agree with the conclusion of the Marylebone CAB that treatment of those with language difficulties can only improve if sufficient money is provided to local offices to provide a pool of interpreters who can be called on when necessary, and information is provided in leaflets in languages other than English (St. Marylebone CAB, September 1989).

Hardship

The AO's submission frequently failed to address the question of hardship (*Chief Adjudication Officer, Annual Report*, 1989/90, para. 5.4).

Under regulation 8(3) of the IS (Gen.) Regulations claimants who fail the availability test can be awarded a payment of IS if the AO believes that either they or any member of their family will suffer "hardship". Under reg. 10A(2) similar provisions apply to those who fail the actively seeking work test. If a hardship award is made the amount of IS is reduced by 40% of the claimant's personal applicable amount, or in certain prescribed exceptional circumstances, by 20%; the allowance for dependants is paid in full. Hardship is not defined and is at the discretion of the AO, and could be challenged on appeal.

As we noted in the chapter on the statistics relating to hardship payments, according to ministerial statements and guidance in the Adjudication Officers' Guide, every time a claim is disallowed the AO should automatically consider whether a hardship payment is payable and if so, should make the payment (*Hansard*, 212/2/91 and AOG Vol.3, para. 25300 and 25481). As we also saw in that chapter the practice is considerably at variance with this policy. Of 66,819 claims for UB and IS disallowed on grounds of doubtful availability in 1990 only 3,311 were considered for a hardship payment and of 5,227 claims disallowed because the claimant was judged not to be actively seeking work only 926 were considered.

In London, according to a Fulham DSS appeals officer, the procedure is that decisions about disallowance for availability or failure actively to seek work were taken by unemployment benefit AOs and "are not the subject of further adjudication in the DSS". The AO in the DSS stops payment and considers whether a hardship payment is appropriate, though "in most cases a hardship payment is not forthcoming". Even before the AO in the UBO reached a decision, the AO in the DSS would usually have stopped benefit once the UBO had suspended benefit pending a final decision, (under IS (Gen.) Regulation 22(4)(c)). Since there could be a six month delay between the initial suspension and the final decision the claimant could spend months with no money if they failed the hardship test, which, as we have seen, most do, and with no decision against which to appeal. (They could appeal against the decision of the DSS to stop payment, but would find it very hard to win given the wording of reg. 22 which requires the DSS to act once "a question has arisen" over availability, whether or not the question is reasonable.)

In St Helens hardship payments were very rare; the staff member in the UBO could remember none. In the DSS the staff member said that many new claims were delayed because claimants had to wait for their new claims interview at the UBO. They issued emergency B1s "only if the claimant insisted", though he conceded that many were unaware that they could ask for one. The guidelines on "hardship" were "not very specific" and payments were "very few and far between".

In two areas we were told that even when a payment is authorised it is not always made. In St Helens the UBO might issue a claimant with an emergency B1 if they were to "plead poverty" or were "an obvious hardship case".

> Then we give them an emergency B1, but even then the DSS won't always pay; it depends what side of the bed they got out of.

In Brighton it was the UBO who were blamed for the failure to pay even when the DSS had issued instructions. In cases where the claim was delayed because of the delay in offering a new claims interview the DSS were making hardship payments, but sometimes these were not reaching the claimant:

> At the end of the first two weeks we send down instructions to the UBO to pay (having received the first B1) and if they haven't had a fresh claims interview they'll send the order book back saying they haven't claimed. They are not treating the B1 as the actual claim until they've had a claim interview.

A Brighton DSS supervisor also stated that they would only consider hardship payments if the claimant asked for one; it was not done automatically.

Claimants should not have to apply for a hardship payment. In those areas where the local policy is nevertheless to wait for claimants to apply before considering a payment it is imperative that claimants are told that such awards are possible. The following cases from Cleveland show that claimants are not always told about this possibility.

> Mr A. aged 23 and single, unemployed since leaving school is suspended for one week and referred to AO for decision as to whether benefit should be disallowed for this period on the grounds that the claimant did not satisfy the ASW conditions. Claimant's

benefit was stopped without any written explanation being offered. Claimant was not advised that he might qualify for IS on hardship grounds.

Mr B aged 20 and single, unemployed since leaving school, in receipt of IS which was suspended for two weeks on the grounds that the claimant was not ASW. Claimant had not completed record of job search. This was due to problems with literacy, a fact which when communicated to the UBO resulted in benefit being restored. However this was only after a four week period in which Mr B. had ceased to register for benefit because he thought he was no longer eligible. Again the decision to suspend was not communicated in writing nor was he advised that he might be eligible for IS on grounds of hardship (Cleveland County Council Welfare Rights service, 24/4/90).

Not only were these claimants not informed of the possibility of hardship payments but it looks as if they were not even considered for them in the absence of applications from them. The worker in the Cleveland Welfare Rights office stated:

Whilst trying to sort out the suspension with the UBO I contacted the DSS to ask why no payment had been made on hardship grounds under Reg. 8(3) of the IS (Gen.) Regs. I was informed that claimants had to make a separate application for IS under this regulation. I told them this was nonsense and they subsequently backdated reduced IS under Reg. 8(3). A colleague telephoned another DSS office with a similar query and was also informed that a separate application needed to be made under Reg. 8(3). The consequences of this misinformation are obvious – some clients whose benefit is suspended are left with no money at all unless they are aware of the complexities of Reg. 8(3) (ibid).

If the practice of these DSS offices is widespread it explains why so few hardship payments are made.

Even when claimants were considered for a payment, whether they got one or not could depend on the whims of the local office policies. In Merseyside the rule of thumb was that people with partners or families would not be considered for hardship payments, while in Brighton the policy seemed to be to give hardship payments to families but not to single youngsters. In Newport the DSS only make hardship payments to 16 and 17 year olds and refugees; other claimants are referred for a social fund crisis loan. A worker in the Newport DSS office explained that "the normal course of action if someone came in on hardship was to direct them to the social fund first". This is in direct contravention of the guidelines. In Brighton too it is recognised that claimants can apply for a crisis loan during the delay between the claim and the first interview. Crisis loans are subject to all the well-known vagaries of the social fund so there is no guarantee at all that an application will be successful, and even if it is it is a repayable loan, unlike the hardship payment which is a sum of money to which the claimant has legal entitlement if he or she satisfies the conditions and it is not repayable.

Finally, further confirmation that AOs do not consider hardship payments as automatically as they should is provided by the Chief Adjudication Officer. In his annual report for 1989/90 he states:

In appeals against disallowance where a claimant has failed to attend for interview with an ES claimant adviser under the restart scheme, the AO's submission frequently failed to address the question of hardship. If hardship is likely to result from disallowance, the AO should consider the payment of income support at a reduced rate (*Annual Report of the CAO*, 1989/90, para 5.4).

They should do, but from the evidence we have they often do not. It is abundantly clear that the statement made by Michael Jack, a Social Security Minister, that "a payment to avoid hardship will be automatically considered by the adjudication officer where someone fails to fulfil this condition [to be available for and actively seeking work]" (*Hansard*, 21/2/91, col. 260) is more a reflection of what should happen than what does happen. The reality is, as the figures show and the cases and interviews confirm, the hardship provision is failing to protect vulnerable claimants.

Part 3
THE EFFECTS ON THE
LABOUR MARKET

8 The search for work

One of the questions which this research set out to answer was whether or not the requirement to actively seek work has improved claimants' prospects of obtaining employment. But what is meant by actively seeking work? Does it mean looking for work, rather than not looking at all; or improving one's methods and search techniques; or altering the type and location of the work one is searching for? This section looks in detail at how claimants search; the changes which claimants have made to their search; the extent to which they are attributable to Employment Service advice or insistence; and perceptions of the outcomes.

Types of work sought by claimants

Although the types of work that claimants seek will be covered in more detail under 'Attitudes To Taking Work' in Chapter 10, it is necessary to consider what claimants would like from work in order to understand how they go about searching.

It is often assumed that claimants have very set ideas about the type of work that they desire, particularly the type of occupation that they wish to work in – and that this, in itself, presents an obstacle to their searching for other work that might be on offer.

In fact many claimants did not specify particular occupations which they were searching for. Instead they stipulated certain aspirations that they had – in terms of money, learning a skill, doing something enjoyable, 'something I am confident in doing', or 'something in which I feel I can be of use'. The search for work brought the claimant into contact with specific vacancies, which were then considered against those criteria.

Claimants who did specify a particular occupation or area of work (such as 'hotel work' or 'factory work') were those with a skill or qualification which suited them to that work; those who had spent a considerable period in an area of work, and wished to return to it; and those who, although they had not worked in the area they mentioned, were keen to get into it – including graduates with little or no work experience, and women returners looking for a 'new direction'.

Those in current employment (all of whom had experienced unemployment since the introduction of the Act) fell into three categories: those dissatisfied with their current job who wanted a change but did not cite particular occupations; those who had taken their current job as a 'stop gap' , for instance to pay off accumulated debts, but were keen to move into a particular occupation; and those who were not searching.

That people considered their search as a search to fulfil personal aspirations, rather than as a search for this or that occupation, reflected the work histories of the job seekers. Most did not regard themselves as having a 'usual occupation' because they had undertaken a variety of jobs in their working lives. Their 'work identity' was not that of a well-defined 'occupational identity', nor necessarily that of a 'jobchanger' who could not settle to a job, but as one who responded to changed circumstances, both personal and in work, by taking work that was offered. It was often a case of Hobson's Choice.

Searching, with the realisation that vacancies were scarce, had involved being 'open' to different occupations – being receptive to whatever might 'come up', rather than pinpointing one or two occupations which one might never have the chance to pursue. That claimants did not always look for particular occupations also reflected dissatisfaction with previous work experiences and uncertainty as to what work they would really like to do. Such claimants were often looking for training or basic skills to help increase the opportunities available to them.

Advice on occupational search and change over time

There is evidence that the most effective method of job search is an initial period of occupationally focused search. If unsuccessful, the search should be extended over a wider occupational band (W.W. Daniel, *The Unemployed Flow*, 1990; Helen West, *Labour Market Flexibility: The Attitudes and Behaviour of Unemployed People. A Review of the Literature*, Research and Evaluation Branch ES Report No.7, 1988).

This is the theory behind advisers giving claimants a permitted period at the start of their claim in which to stipulate occupational areas on which they will concentrate their search. The Back To Work Plan entails completion of initial claim forms, which ask what jobs you are 'now looking for' and an interview reviewing the claimant's search once the permitted period expires or after 13 weeks. The Employment Service is now committed to reviewing all claimants in this way, although this was not the case when the research began.

There was evidence that claimants spontaneously widen their job search to areas of work not considered initially – often when met by a lack of success through intensive, occupationally-focused search. For example, graduates' expectations as to the work they can command on leaving college were adjusted over a six month period following the 'discovery' that their college city offered fewer opportunities than they had previously thought, and that the competition for those jobs was often great from job seekers of similar age with work experience rather than a degree qualification. Likewise claimants with professional qualifications began to contemplate applying for jobs beyond the realm of their experience following a poor or non-existent employer response to written applications.

In these cases it was the searchers' knowledge, acquired in the first few months of unemployment, about local demand for labour and the competition for jobs which brought about a broader occupational search. Rarely, if ever, did the broadening of one's occupational search result from Employment Service advice. This was because this advice was generally lacking. The major reason for this was the failure to follow up after the initial claim interview.

Whilst claimants were often questioned about the search they had undertaken since their previous signing day, Signing Clerks rarely gave advice as to changes claimants could make in their search for work. Only with the introduction of Active Signing in the first half of 1991 have Signing Clerks been given a pivotal role in the review process, now that they have a responsibility for funnelling claimants who they believe would benefit from advice to Claimant Advisers. Nevertheless, their role still does not incorporate a counselling function.

The first opportunity for review of the claimant's search tended to come at restart interviews, that is, after six months. However, even here, suggestions that a claimant ought to consider broadening his or her occupational search were infrequent.

Claimants with previous experience of unemployment noticed that they had to be more specific in answering the question 'what job, or jobs, are you now looking for?' than they had been in the past. Some recalled having to put down three separate specific jobs. While the first one or two tended to correspond to what the claimant wanted, specifying jobs on a form was not associated with the process of searching but with the process of claiming benefit. Consequently it did not have a major impact on actual searching.

'Back To Work Plan' was a phrase which few claimants had heard and none could describe its intention. Virtually no claimant had heard of the 'permitted period'. This is not very surprising given that, in interviews with Employment Service staff, it was apparent that the phrase was not used, although advisers did set periods in accordance with the legislation, using their discretion and official guidance in setting their length. It was clear from interviews with Employment Service staff and claimant advice agency workers that permitted periods ranged from the full 13 weeks for some claimants, including the skilled and the qualified, down to no permitted period at all for those with no work experience or no recent work experience, such as college leavers and women returners.

In the absence of explicit references to the 'permitted period' one would nevertheless have expected New Client Advisers to make apparent to claimants that they might be expected to broaden their occupational search over time. However, whilst many claimants were aware that their search, and their ability to show evidence of that search, could be checked and reviewed at any time, they were not usually aware that they were being given an initial period to look for work which they wanted and that, after that, they might need to look for other types of work. For those aware that their search could be reviewed, the prospect was associated with 'checking up' on whether they had been looking, rather than assessing what they had looked for, and advising on what they could do in the future. Others were not aware that their job search could be reviewed at all. This is part of the more general absence of Employment Service job search counselling (see below).

Search channels used, and why

In deciding on search methods claimants relied on the methods that they thought were best for the work that they wanted, which in turn were determined by their personal experiences of past searching, hearsay and the advice of others – both informally through friends, colleagues and relations, and formally through careers advisers.

Claimants and non-claimants alike are able to use the self-service Employment Service facilities which normally result in a counsellor contacting the employer to arrange an interview. A counsellor may also suggest vacancies to a claimant during an interview, and contact the employer there and then: this is most common during restart interviews. It is almost exclusively claimants who are able to make use of facilities such as those offered through jobclubs, leading to telephone calls and written applications to employers, speculatively or in response to jobcentre-registered vacancies. (Indeed there is growing pressure on the Employment Service to target all their facilities towards the needs of the claimant unemployed.) It is, of course open to claimants to simultaneously apply for jobs through speculative visits and calls in their own time without Employment Service assistance, in the same way as non-claimants would do. The other major way in which claimants come into contact with employers is through work-related government training programmes, such as Employment Training and Employment Service courses like restart courses and the Job Interview Guarantee Scheme. Advisers may also suggest third parties, like employment agencies and careers offices, as a way of pursuing job search.

All but a few of those interviewed were searching for work. In the main they were looking for full-time permanent work, although there were some who were using agencies to find temporary work at the same time, to help 'tide them over'. Those who were not searching included those currently on Employment Training and those who were seeking accommodation, either as homeless or living in hostel accommodation. These claimants had informed Employment Service counsellors who had accepted their need to find permanent accommodation before searching for work. The regulations allow for claimants' steps in obtaining living accommodation to be taken into account when assessing what it is reasonable for a claimant to do in seeking work in any one week of a claim.

The interviewees included those in work, some of whom were searching for other work either because they had taken their current job as a stop gap or because they were not happy with their work for other reasons. They included some people working part-time and claiming benefit, despite the financial disincentives to do so: they were seeking full-time permanent employment, finding it very difficult to manage with fluctuations in their net income resulting from different amounts of work they obtained each week and the impact on benefit levels. For part-timers and full-timers alike serious job search beyond their existing work establishment proved a very difficult and stressful activity.

The actual 'mix' of job search channels used by those searchers interviewed depended primarily on the work being sought, how the claimant came to be unemployed, and whether or not the claimant had had any recent experience of unemployment.

One of the most surprising findings when interviewing claimants was the number of people who had moved into unemployment following the completion of fixed-term contracts, or as the result of 'lay offs' and redundancies. For those used to working in the building trade, for example, this was a very regular occurrence. Consequently there were a number of claimants who were faced with extended periods of unemployment when the demand for their labour was no longer required, to be taken on again at some point in the future for similar work. With the downturn in labour demand over the last year claimants reported longer than usual bouts of unemployment.

These claimants, whose movement in and out of work consigns them in many peoples' minds to the fringes of the labour market, actually appear to be a far more extensive part of the workforce. Recent research supports this (Daniel, 1990). They were people who were capable of 'seeking out work', and had been successful on a number of occasions in doing so, although the work that was available to them was often only temporary or fixed-term.

Many of the claimants were well-acquainted with the search for work. They tended to rely more on informal methods of job search, through former colleagues, ex-employers and friends, than searchers as a whole.

Amongst those reliant upon more structured search channels and job search assistance through the Employment Service were those who found themselves unemployed after a long history of stable employment: these included those made redundant from permanent skilled and semi-skilled work, such as factory operatives and those in staple industries like steel (important in Newport) and coal mining (important in Newport and St Helens). Likewise, those who had entered unemployment following personal trauma – a breakdown, marital problems, or a job just 'folding' under them – were often leaving full-time permanent work behind, and looked to the Employment Service and other agencies to assist them in reestablishing themselves. The other group who looked for structured assistance in finding work were those returning to the labour market after an extended absence – mainly women whose care responsibilities had been shed, some were claimants and some were non-claimants.

There were very few who stuck to only one method of search. These included those looking for very specific forms of work, such as a qualified chartered accountant seeking business consultancy work through national newspapers, and a qualified Heavy Goods Vehicle driver who, through experience, had always found 'word of mouth' to be adequate on its own. The less specific the searcher was about the type of work s/he was looking for, the more diverse the number of search methods used. This was typified by long-term unemployed men who, driven by the need to secure a 'family wage', used all means at their disposal to obtain it.

The vast majority of seekers used Employment Service jobcentres and unemployment benefit offices. Those who did not tended to be those with specific types of work in mind, such as those with specialist skills, and college or professional qualifications. In these instances the New Client Adviser had invariably informed the claimant that s/he was unlikely to find the type of job s/he wanted through the Employment Service, and suggested looking elsewhere.

A number of claimants, having experienced jobcentre assistance, expressed negative views about it (see below). It was less usual for a person to refuse to use a jobcentre without previous experience of one. It did occur with some claimants who had spent most of their lives in work, were fiercely independent and determined to re-enter work through their own efforts; and in exceptional circumstances, where the claimant was highly qualified and believed that jobcentres were merely interested in 'processing claimants as quickly as possible'.

In the main claimants were receptive to suggestions about using various search channels. It was rare to encounter antagonism to any type of search channel before it had been tried. However, counsellors did not tend to suggest search channels, other than when commenting on the need to prove job search. The exception was at restart when counsellors often suggested jobclub or referred claimants to outside advisers such as adult guidance counsellors and careers officers.

There was a high degree of consensus that, whilst the newspapers tended to be the best source of information as to the jobs available, 'word of mouth' was the best way of securing work. A number of people said that it wasn't 'what you know, but whom you know' that counts in getting work. Alongside this there was a recognition that perhaps the most important thing was luck – being in the right place at the right time. This view was held across the board by claimants and non-claimants alike, almost irrespective of employment experience or qualifications.

Attitudes to the effectiveness of other search methods were more mixed. A lot of searchers felt that the rates of pay offered by agencies, for example those operating in the transport industry, were 'exploitative' in terms of the pay and conditions they offered. Some refused to use them point blank whilst others said that they only used them if it was 'absolutely necessary'. Others did not use them because they resented the commission taken by the agency. One claimant said he would not use an agency for driving work again because co-drivers resented the fact that he was used by a company at a lower rate of pay than the regular workers – there was a feeling that he was 'undercutting' their rates of pay, even though the company might have been paying more for him when the commission to the agency was taken into account. Agencies were viewed more positively by women who used them to search for secretarial and clerical work, both temporary and permanent. However, it was necessary to pressurise the agency by telephoning them and, in the case of temporary work, the agency would only give you a steady supply once you were well known to them.

Use of Employment Service as search channel and usefulness of job leads

Despite nearly all the searchers interviewed expressing negative feelings about the usefulness of the Employment Service as a search channel, and the type of vacancies it had available, it was widely used, even by those who said that they had never seen a job there that they had wanted. This 'brand loyalty' to jobcentres in particular (as opposed to unemployment benefit offices which in some cases were beginning to take on a job placement function) had resulted in some offices being renamed 'Jobcentre' following a change of corporate identity to 'Employment Service'.

Some had not used jobcentres having been told at new claims interviews that the type of work they were seeking could not be obtained through the jobcentre. Some said that the work they wanted was offered by employers who did not register their vacancies with the jobcentre whilst others had stopped using them because they had never found a job vacancy that had interested them. There were conflicting views as to whether or not the Act's requirements had dissuaded the unemployed from claiming and, if they did claim, from using jobcentres. Certainly some interviewees had delayed their claims citing the 'hassle' they had to go through, and some said that they only used the jobcentre when called to do so because they expected pressure from advisers to consider government training programmes.

Employment Service staff reported considerable demand for their self-service facilities; it had increased recently, something that was to be expected with growing unemployment. The non-claimant unemployed and job changers were also frequent users.

One Employment Service Regional Director described part-time jobcentre vacancies as 'indispensable to the likes of women returners'. The women returners interviewed did use it regularly. One lone parent looking for part-time work in 'hours that suit' regarded it as a particularly fruitful source of job leads. 43 per cent of the vacancies notified to St Helens jobcentre and 33 per cent notified to Newport jobcentre were part-time. This in itself is a problem for claimants who have to seek and be available for full-time employment: it means that claimants must look beyond the public job placement service if they are to satisfy the conditions for claiming benefit.

The majority of those seeking part-time employment tend to be non-claimants. Despite the importance of jobcentres as a channel for seeking such work, local Employment Service staff in all four labour markets said that advice on reception and self-service was increasingly geared towards claimants rather than non-claimants. (This may reflect the requirement in the Service's Agency Agreement with the Department of Employment to give priority to the placement of claimants into work or other 'positive options'.) Consequently, since April 1990, it had been the practice in some offices to ask all enquirers at reception desks whether they are claiming benefit. Non-claimant seekers said that Employment Service staff 'didn't want to know' when asked for advice or assistance, although some claimants expressed the same view.

This shift in emphasis is also reflected in the discontinuation of services used mainly by non-claimants – including holding vacancies in higher occupations, for example those contained in local authority, health authority and college 'job opportunity' listings. There was also more concern to avoid competing with private employment agencies, so that Temp Desks dealing with temporary jobs were discontinued, and employers occasionally encouraged to place vacancies with private agencies instead of the jobcentre.

Local Employment Service staff regarded the transfer of jobcentres away from prime high street sites as intended to deter the casual passer-by.

Some said that their use of jobcentre self-service facilities was not purely voluntary; they used them only when a counsellor 'insisted' that they did so. Others said that using jobcentres for searching was 'stressful' whilst others 'disliked' using them. These views were associated with claimants' experiences in signing on for benefit, a process which some regarded as 'intimidating' or 'embarrassing' and where they were subject to criticism by counsellors or Signing Clerks.

Many felt that the chances of obtaining work that one wanted from a jobcentre were not high. It reflected the narrow range of occupations, often at the 'lower end' of the job market, which they dealt with. Employment Service Regional Directors accepted that the Service operated at that 'lower end' of the market, but stressed that in doing so they performed a vital placement function which was not attractive to commercial agencies. This fact was nevertheless a cause of frustration amongst Employment Service local staff.

While technical and supervisory job vacancies were also registered with jobcentres claimants felt that their chances of getting them were small. In the first place 'decent jobs' required qualifications or experience which the seekers did not possess. There were particular problems for older claimants were often precluded from applying by age restrictions, with 'maximum ages of 30 or 35 at tops'. Secondly, one had to be very 'quick off the mark' – some felt that it was a waste of time pursuing vacancies when you knew that 'there are always 200 applicants'. One claimant had darted off for an interview only to discover that he was the sixteenth person to arrive; he didn't bother waiting. Another interviewee explained that he had been very lucky in using the self-service facility because the printing job he managed to get had 'only been on the board for 25 minutes'.

The rapid takeup of vacancies contrasts with the assumption that there is a large pool of inactive claimants shunning jobcentre vacancies.

In fact, the turnover of vacancies is so high that it occasions one of the most common complaints about the Employment Service – that is, that many of the jobs applied for 'don't exist any more', as one claimant put it. They are what the Employment Service terms 'dead orders' – vacancies that have already been filled. Claimants found it disheartening to check the self-service boards, choose a handful of vacancies, chase them up with the help of the staff, only to discover that they have already been filled – often some weeks ago. Employment Service staff found this to be a very regular occurrence. Searchers put this 'inefficiency' down to under-resourcing. It was also due to the fact that some offices, particularly unemployment benefit offices to whom job placement was relatively new, were not equipped with the Supervacs system which gives advisers up to date information of the vacancies registered with them. Some unemployment benefit offices were still relying on jobcentres for print outs from Supervacs which, by the time they arrived, were out of date.

That said, one or two seekers had noticed that unemployment benefit offices had become 'more like jobcentres' and felt that they were more capable of matching them to suitable vacancies than in the past. There was one instance, however, in which 35 lorry drivers had been made redundant and were in receipt of registered vacancies, which had included a 'kissogram' vacancy. The claimant wondered 'how stupid can you get'.

134

Personal experiences of how helpful staff had been when enquiring about self-service board vacancies varied considerably. Some felt that it was 'too much trouble' for staff to bother and that they 'remained behind their desks' at all costs. One dyslexic claimant had informed staff that he had trouble reading the cards but his request for help was flatly refused: this had severely restricted his ability to make use of the self-service facility. Another claimant who had transferred from sickness benefit to unemployment benefit said that she had been 'helped round' the boards by a member of staff.

Other than assistance in pursuing the vacancies taken from the boards, Employment Service staff offered little assistance to those using the self-service boards. Seekers did not believe that they could receive assistance with travel to interview expenses: none had received such help. Some said that, if they had known that it existed, it would have encouraged them to pursue vacancies further afield.

Some of those who had used jobclub found that the assistance that they received there was markedly different. Jobclub users had been impressed with the availability of free facilities such as stamps, telephone calls, and specialist newspapers. They felt this saved money, as did assistance with the costs of travel to and from jobclub. They valued previews of jobs registered with jobcentres before they appeared on the boards, as well as the assistance they received in applying for non-jobcentre vacancies. Others who had used jobclub or turned it down criticised the types of jobs participants were encouraged to apply for, with some saying that whilst the facilities were useful, well-presented applications could only 'get you so far'.

One Employment Service Regional Director said that, whilst pay rates were often low for registered vacancies, unless the vacancy was covered by a Wages Council order requiring the payment of the legal minimum, the rates of pay could only reflect what was offered in the local labour market. 'Decent pay' or 'good money' were amongst the key aspirations which searchers mentioned when interviewed. Yet jobcentre vacancies were regarded as poorly paying, even when taking account of the types of jobs they were; one claimant for example, said that if he could get a joiner's job on site, it would pay twice the rate advertised in the jobcentre. Despite this, claimants continued to use the Employment Service in their jobsearch. This reflects the fact that, although Employment Service registered vacancies appear to be low paying when compared to other available work, claimants' expectations are such that they are not deterred from searching through jobcentres and unemployment benefit offices.

Jobsearch advice and Employment Service counselling

The public job placement service entered a new phase with the introduction of the Act: the corollary of the claimant's requirement to seek work was the provision of more structured job search assistance and counselling. A Department of Employment Report (*Claimant Advisers: Their Advice to Unemployed People on Job Choice and Job Search*, Psychological Services Report no 322/S) published two months before the introduction of the Act found that Claimant Advisers only gave job search help to claimants who had no idea or were very vague about the type of work they wanted;

that the advice on searching for work 'usually concentrated on notified vacancies' and that knowledge of local labour markets and job requirements was variable.

The introduction of the Back To Work Plan, Active Signing and the New Framework (see Chapter 2) were intended to provide the structure against which claimants could expect to receive consistent job search advice on making an initial claim, at review interviews and at restart interviews.

By the spring of 1991 these structures were not in place in the four local labour markets studied. Almost without exception claimants had received little or no job search advice or counselling, other than through jobclub participation. The suggestions and assistance proffered were of a rudimentary nature which many claimants regarded as 'obvious' or 'common sense'. Furthermore, claimants felt that references to job search – such as 'look everyday' – were normally made in the imperative, rather than as part of constructive counselling: the large majority of claimants considered these comments to be part of a 'checking up' exercise instead of genuine assistance, even if they were only 'soft pedalled'.

The initial signing on with a New Client Adviser was regarded by claimants as a 'formality', something that the adviser and claimant had to go through in order for a benefit claim to be made. Few had heard of the 'Back To Work Plan' and those who had were unsure what to do with it. One unemployment benefit office receptionist said:

> claimants don't know what to do with their Back To Work Plan – you see them plotted in their wallets when they are signing off. It's seen as just a part of what you've got to go through when you claim.

Others felt that the rudimentary advice given was 'common sense' or 'obvious'. Some felt that any advice was irrelevant because the most important thing was to be presentable, and sell yourself as best you could. In this sense, the way in which one searched was regarded as something personal, which could not be passed on by a counsellor.

New Client Advisers made their own assessment of the claimant's 'job readiness'. It was the most 'unready' who obtained the greatest assistance, particularly women returners. Often they only had vague ideas about the type of work they wanted and were initially more interested in building their self-confidence rather than moving into a job straight away. They tended to be the most receptive to advice on training and methods by which to obtain the qualifications necessary to move into skilled but poorly paying work such as sewing or typing. They had the most positive attitude to the advice received: it was often followed up at restart where Employment Training was suggested as the best way to obtain experience and a City and Guilds qualification.

Not all women returners had had the same experience. In particular lone parents, some searching for part-time work, felt that 'they don't seem to bother if you're not signing'; and one non-claimant said that they had shown no interest in her at all. In these instances the women had been very keen to work but felt that their efforts had been frustrated by Employment Service indifference; the progress they had made had been 'off their own backs'.

There were firm ideas as to why different claimants appeared to be treated differently by Employment Service staff. The quality of advice was seen to depend heavily on the counsellor you got: it was suggested that counsellors reacted more positively to those who seemed to genuinely want work, although some counsellors appeared keen to assist each claimant they dealt with, irrespective of the claimant's attitude. Some felt that the advice received was based on more arbitrary factors, such as whether or not 'your face fits'. Nobody referred to their status as a claimant in the advice they received, other than quarterly attenders and lone parents, who felt that counsellors' lack of interest in them was due to their not having to sign on every fortnight.

A majority of claimants felt that Employment Service staff were primarily interested in 'processing' them as quickly as possible. Some referred to being treated as 'a statistic', with one saying that signing on was 'more like joining the Army'. Claimants were offended by the impersonality of the process, saying that advisers were more interested in their National Insurance numbers than their names. This processing began at the initial claim, followed by fortnightly signing on (with the exception of Quarterly Signers, claimants who did not have to sign on but claimed by book, and those who, with no safe address, had to sign on everyday).

Attitudes to their treatment at signing on determined many claimants' attitudes to the job search advice that they received. It was generally felt, as one claimant put it, that:

> they are only interested in processing you as quickly as possible and if you don't fit into the category they want they'll squeeze and push until you actually fit it.

As a consequence some claimants had paid no attention to what the Client Adviser said to them at interview and others had discarded job search advice sheets on leaving the interview. For some the experience was clearly negative. The 'processing' was regarded as 'degrading', an experience in which the claimant was accorded little or no respect, and in which the fault for being unemployed was being laid firmly on his or her shoulders.

These claimants were aware that advisers were determined to get them back into work, but regarded this as more of a threat than helpful, largely because it felt as if the adviser was less concerned than the claimant as to what sort of work it would be. Some felt the importance of having a firm idea about what they wanted to counter pressure to move into something that they did not want.

When asked why advisers should wish to behave in such a counterproductive way claimants said that they were 'making work for themselves' to keep them in work, 'making themselves important', or just 'going through the motions of what they are supposed to do'.

There were claimants who felt that Employment Service counsellors had been 'obstructive' and even 'hostile' to them. By inferring that the claimant did not want to work, some were intimidated so that the option of using Employment Service counsellors for positive help was effectively foreclosed.

Throughout counsellors' job search advice, there was a marked reluctance to 'network' with organisations ready to assist claimants. There was little or no advice, for example, on local voluntary agencies with job search resources, such as unemployed centres. Careers offices and adult guidance counsellors were suggested in certain cases, for example with graduates and those recently made redundant, but most submissions tended to be to organisations responsible for 'positive options' such as Employment Training, EAS and private jobclubs – perhaps because, as far as the Employment Service is concerned, it is these which count as 'positive outcomes'.

Adult guidance counsellors and careers officers made the distinction between their work, which tended to be 'seeker-oriented', and the role of the Employment Service counsellors, which also had to take into account the needs of employers and benefit entitlement. It meant that the advice given to the seeker wasn't necessarily always in the best interests of the seeker. For example, it was often better for somebody who had been out of the labour market for some time to undergo basic skills training and confidence building before being expected to seek work – yet this would not necessarily fulfil benefit entitlement requirements. Counsellors were often obliged to inform claimants of their need to seek work, even if they were considered far from 'job ready'.

One adult guidance counsellor went further, saying that Restart Counsellors 'are not really counsellors. They don't have the knowledge or skills to counsel, they only run through lists'. She went on to say:

> Client Advisers don't have an overall view of employment prospects in each field. It is unrealistic advice if you don't know the avenues into things.

Similar views were expressed by others about the Employment Service's knowledge of local college courses.

The value of the advice proffered by Employment Service counsellors is brought into question by their responsibility to enforce benefit regulations and their lack of local knowledge, which is partly a function of their failure to 'network' with outside organisations – as well as outside organisations' concerns about communicating with the Employment Service. This point is graphically illustrated by the dilemma faced by one adult guidance counsellor when she was advising a claimant who was finding it increasingly difficult to search for work, and was considering signing on as incapable of work. The adult guidance counsellor had decided against contacting the unemployment benefit office for advice as to what level of search would be required in his case because there was the danger that the claimant could be called in for interview as a result.

Virtually none of the seekers interviewed had been for a review interview between their initial claim and their restart interview at six months so that reviewing job search patterns after the permitted period was not possible. What's more, for most claimants the restart interview was regarded as 'more of the same' – that is, merely as an extension of the signing on process. Restart Counsellors checked what the claimant had done to seek work but the main focus of their advice concerned the menu options which the claimant could chose from, rather than job search assistance. The main reason for this is that one of those options, jobclub, is specifically geared towards offering structured jobsearch advice to claimants who, normally, have been six months' unemployed.

A number of searchers had used jobclub, all but two after six months of signing on for benefit. Some had refused the jobclub option at restart, believing that, whilst the free search facilities might be of some use, it would only intensify demands to look for work.

Jobclub provided the only structured job search advice for claimants. This is surprising given that recent changes have been explicitly linked with the need to prevent movement into longer-term unemployment by targeting those deemed most susceptible to it at an early stage in their unemployment (Paul Mooney, *Factors Influencing the Duration of Unemployment: A Review of the Literature*, ES Research and Evaluation Branch Report No.31, para.7.2, 1989).

Free telephone and post facilities were valued, as were the job leads. Most claimants felt that the help they had received in compiling curricula vitae, making job applications, and telephone and interview techniques were of use, although only one claimant had actually obtained work following jobclub applications (he had done this twice). The advice itself was often contrasted with that received at interviews and when signing on.

Only one claimant expressed uniformly negative feelings about her experience with jobclub. She described it as a 'waste of time', a place where advisers 'pull you down' and 'tell you what to do': she had left after a few visits. Others expressed mixed feelings about their experience with jobclub. One woman returner had managed to join a jobclub following a restart course although she was not a claimant. She found that 'most of them went because they would get their benefit stopped if they didn't'. She felt that this had created the 'wrong atmosphere'. She strongly believed that:

> for it to work, you have got to want to go... If it was up to me, it would just be people who really wanted to look for work.

Jobclub participation had helped some claimants by remotivating them after an initial intensive but unsuccessful period of search. This was the case for one man who had lost motivation at an early stage in his search because of personal problems and a belief that the local market for jobs had suddenly collapsed. He had been accepted for jobclub before six months' registered unemployment and had welcomed the feeling of mutual support and help engendered by looking with others.

'Discouraged' job searchers were not confined to the long-term unemployed: some would clearly benefit from access to structured job search assistance at an earlier stage in their unemployment. Careers officers and adult guidance counsellors felt that 'the damage was done' once six months' unemployment had elapsed, and that access to structured assistance ought to be considered on an individual basis as part of reviewing one's job search.

None of the claimants interviewed had experienced a restart course although a number had been unemployed for some time. Indeed, some of those who had been unemployed for over two years had not been interviewed in the last six months or, if they had, it had been a perfunctory restart interview. The Employment Service in the four local labour markets studied were concentrating their advice resources elsewhere.

Awareness of actively seeking work

At their initial claim, claimants were usually asked whether they were searching for work, the steps they were taking, where they were searching, and the work they were looking for – although, for the purposes of the regulations, claimants are excused from seeking work for the first week of their claim.

This 'check' was often made when claimants signed on subsequently. Some said that Signing Clerks were sometimes prompted to ask: it was obvious because, on certain days, they asked the same repetitive questions to everyone – as one claimant put it, it's 'like the patter at McDonald's, asking everybody the same questions exactly'.

It was firmly impressed on most claimants that they were expected to seek work and, if requested, show evidence of that search. To that end, it was normally explained how they could show proof of their search. Whilst this advice varied depending upon the type of work the claimant said s/he was searching for, it normally included keeping newspaper cuttings, recording on forms provided the telephone calls and visits made to employers; photocopying written applications to employers and replies from employers.

Claimants knew that their search could be reviewed at anytime, either when they were signing on, or if called in to interview by a counsellor.

Sometimes claimants were told that seeking work and furnishing proof were conditions of benefit entitlement; but even if this was not made explicit, it was apparent to most claimants that there was a strong link between satisfying advisers that they were looking for work and the receipt of benefit. However, when asked what precisely did they think could happen to their benefit if they did not look for work, although some imagined that their benefit would be stopped, they did not know how much of it would be stopped or for how long. Few had received a warning letter and none were aware that their benefit was only suspended for the period in which the counsellor felt that job search was in doubt – that is, normally the one or two week period since their last signing day. Some felt that the money that was stopped could not be recouped, whilst others said that they would appeal, if they had a right to do so.

Nor were claimants aware of what might be expected of them if their benefit was suspended for failing to actively seek employment. Some hazarded a guess that they would be expected to try harder, but for most it was no more than a guess. Others felt that they would be required to make a fresh claim for benefit.

Only sometimes was advice about the need to search couched in terms of 'actively seeking work' or 'actively seeking employment'. The extent to which claimants had heard the phrase was very variable. Some said that they had seen the phrase on their claim forms. But irrespective of whether they had heard the phrase, most were aware of the need to search for work and provide evidence if requested.

Even so, there were some claimants who had never heard of 'actively seeking work' and could remember no reference to the need to seek work. These tended to be claimants whose claim began before the introduction of the Act, and who had been registered for some time. Some hazarded guesses as to why they had not come into contact with the requirement to search for work: a claimant wondered if it was due to his jobclub participation; some thought that they had not been claiming long enough to be told; a quarterly attender felt that he was treated differently but wasn't sure why. (In fact, quarterly attenders are also subject to the requirement to seek work but there has been some doubt about advisers' ability to ensure that they do so, so the Employment Service has recently taken action to seek to rectify this.) A lone parent said that she felt she was not expected to search, assuming that the Employment Service was 'happy to let women stay at home and look after the kids' – she even seemed desirous of the 'hassle' that other claimants said that they were getting because it would, at least, be a recognition of her existence. A graduate said that he had been claiming before the changes were introduced – in fact he was mistaken, they had been introduced, but he was not aware of them.

While many understood the need to search for work and keep proof, only a few were aware that searching for the type of work that they wanted was time-limited. This was normally only apparent to the claimant if the New Client Adviser said that the claimant could expect to be called in for a review interview whereupon s/he could be expected to broaden her or his search to other types of work. Very few claimants had been advised that this might happen – they included those who had recently graduated.

Claimants' attitudes and response to actively seeking work

Flowchart 1 explained how a benefit sanction, or the threat of a benefit sanction such as suspension for not seeking work adequately, is intended to affect the behavioural patterns of claimants.

This model did not apply in the four local labour markets studied because claimants either were not aware of the possible benefit consequences or, in most cases, were aware of them but did not believe that their benefit would be threatened. Claimants did not believe that Employment Service staff were deploying the sanction – or, if they were, they were doing it in only very exceptional circumstances which did not apply in their case. Some were aware of claimants who were receiving full benefit despite little effort to seek work. Indeed, most claimants fervently believed that they were doing all that they could to find work. Suggestions to the contrary were regarded as insulting, as was the idea that an Employment Service counsellor could judge the effectiveness of their search better than the claimant.

The most significant impact that the requirement had on searchers' behaviour was their preparedness to keep proof of their search. Some had continued to do this for some time, 'just in case' – that is, to cover themselves, through fear of benefit loss. This was a small minority, however, with most claimants' efforts tailing off after a few weeks when they realised that counsellors and Signing Clerks were not requesting it.

141

Some said that it was very difficult for them to procure evidence due to the nature of the work they were looking for. One man, who had been searching extensively and intensively for labouring work, said that the site foreman 'would probably punch me' if he asked for evidence of his search – in fact, the only conclusive evidence he could show would be if somebody 'took a photograph of me on site'. Like many other claimants he resented the implication that it was necessary to check up on whether he had 'really' been searching: he said that if they really wanted to see how much searching he did, they ought to come with him in his car.

Others, such as the dyslexic claimant, said that they had had difficulties in gathering evidence of their job search. Requests for staff assistance in filling search forms were sometimes turned down. Many claimants said that, despite large volumes of applications, employers rarely responded, leaving them with no evidence of their search.

Those more confident of themselves said that, even though they were not collecting evidence, their current search was sufficient and they would not find it difficult to collect proof at short notice if necessary. The legislation had effected a preoccupation on the part of some claimants in 'manufacturing' the proof necessary to receive their benefit. For some, this meant 'rustling it up' quickly, regardless of the quality of the applications or whether the claimant wanted the job. This hardly seems to be a desirable outcome if the objective of the legislation is to assist claimants in making effective job search.

For those seeking semi or unskilled manual work, one of the most common methods of seeking work was to make speculative visits to sites and factories. Some said that this could prove a fruitful way of obtaining work but that, if the first objective was to ensure that one had the right proof to establish one's rightful claim to benefit, it often meant going to employers who you knew did not have work to offer, but who would be prepared to sign a card or form stipulating that you had sought work. This practice had proved detrimental to some claimants' job search because it had interfered with serious attempts to obtain work and, in some cases, accentuated the demoralisation which came with extended, unsuccessful job search. Technically this type of search does not satisfy the regulations since the claimant must take the steps which, in his or her case, offer the 'best prospects' of obtaining employment. In practice, the need to obtain proof, particularly in areas where few jobs were available, meant pursuing employers who claimants knew were very unlikely to offer them work.

When Employment Service advisers had asked for proof of job search, claimants were usually able to satisfy them. There was evidence that some advisers were just 'going through the motions, doing what they have to do' and that this made them less fastidious than they otherwise would have been.

That proof of job search could be expected at any time was treated by claimants as a clear indication that the actively seeking work requirements were more concerned with the process of claiming – and eligibility for payment – than with effective job search. Claimants saw themselves as having to fulfil the expectations of a 'doubting' and sometimes 'hostile' bureaucracy before 'their money' could be handed over. It was difficult to see how fulfilling the requirements could improve their prospects of obtaining work. As one claimant put it:

(the chances of getting work won't improve) not if the jobs aren't there, you won't find 'em will you? We'd all be working if that was the case. Nobody wants to be unemployed.

The insistence on being able to show proof of searching caused perplexity when claimants were also told by the counsellor that there were very few jobs available in the locality.

For one claimant it was

> all about messing you about, making you go out, get all your 'no's', send 'em in... They're not giving you anything, not offering you nothing.

For others it served to keep Employment Service staff in work.

Stipulating time limits for searching for the work that one wanted was deemed to be very difficult. Careers officers said that even 13 weeks was not sufficient for searchers such as graduates when making applications for posts in the civil service, or in artistic pursuits where they had to engage in some initial, perhaps unpaid work, in order to build up a portfolio. A full-time Regional Chair of Social Security Appeals Tribunals felt that strict time limits were wholly inappropriate for jobs such as teaching where there was a 'closed season': he felt that if the 13 weeks had been used as a guide, alongside common sense, then the guidance offered by counsellors would be more satisfactory.

What would claimants do if the regulations were fully enforced?

There was no instance in which a claimant's search patterns had been substantially altered by the threat or actual use of an actively seeking work benefit penalty. But interviewees were asked what would their reaction have been if they were subject to a penalty for failing to satisfy a counsellor that s/he had sought work adequately.

Most felt that they were already doing enough to find work, and could hardly do any more: all they could do was make sure that they had better proof of their search. However, they said that, faced with the prospect of benefit loss, they felt that they would have to try to do more. 'I suppose I'd have to' was the most common response. It was a question of doing more of the same, rather than changing tactics; most felt that they were already using the most effective means available.

There was strong resistance to searching for lower paid work, even if faced with benefit loss. This was due in large part to claimants' feeling that they were already looking for work which did not pay well. One or two, fearful of any reduction in their income, would have searched for and taken anything to satisfy the counsellor that they were doing all they could.

Those intent on obtaining work with a particular occupational status were loath to search for anything else, whatever benefit threats they faced. But their antipathy to the idea was motivated by the belief that they were either too highly qualified or educated to be considered by employers for other types of work.

It was those who fervently defended their current efforts to seek work – often men, including those searching for a 'family wage' – who were likely to be the most defiant if faced with a benefit suspension for not seeking. There was a feeling that the penalties could hit the family more than the claimant, even if it was only their personal allowance that was affected. Some said that they would 'present the wife and kids, say 'you feed them'.' It was also felt that the policy was self-defeating in creating financial constraints on claimants' ability to search, especially if deductions were already being made from benefit, such as crisis loan repayments (which some of the claimants were making or had made in the past).

It was often younger claimants, living alone or with parents, who felt that benefit withdrawal for not seeking work could be easily rectified – either by readily obtaining proof of search, even if one did not want the job applied for, or by moving into a stop gap job, so that the suspension would not affect them. Those able to move in and out of work generally tended to be less concerned with benefit withdrawal than other claimants. For them, benefit loss for a short period was of little consequence.

9 The search for workers

Claimants' attitudes towards search channels, including the public job placement service located largely in jobcentres, depends crucially on the use made of them by employers. This in turn depends upon the nature of the local employers and, of course, what they regard to be the best way of advertising their vacancies.

Although claimants are not required to register with jobcentres, they must attend Client Adviser interviews and, in most cases, sign on regularly. To that extent the Employment Service can count on dealing with the claimant. For employers, on the other hand, the association is voluntary. As a result, only about one third of all vacancies are placed with jobcentres.

This chapter considers what use employers make of the public job placement service, and why; as well as assessing their awareness of the actively seeking work requirements, and the impact they have had on the recruitment process.

The extent to which jobcentres are used depends a great deal on the ability of employers to use the unemployed, either immediately, or after initial training; on the type of work that is on offer; the size of the establishment – particularly the resources that can be devoted to recruitment; and attitudes to the unemployed and jobcentres themselves.

How suitable are jobcentre applicants?

That an employer is using a jobcentre would suggest that it is providing suitable candidates for the vacancies notified. This is not necessarily so. Some employers interviewed were using jobcentres as a matter of company policy, even if the local manager was not happy with the quality of labour supplied; or as part of a wider commitment to the unemployed. For many it was a major source of recruits, despite the fact that a large proportion using it were not suitable.

Few found that all their recruitment needs could be met by jobcentres alone. Even when jobcentre applicants were heavily relied upon they were supplemented by those who had applied speculatively, those who had been kept on file, and those who had heard through 'word of mouth'

Most found jobcentre applicants to be 'variable' in quality, ranging from 'very good to absolutely appalling'. But there were a range of responses from employers showing different levels of tolerance.

Some had stopped using jobcentres. They were in a position to fill their vacancies through other means, either because their demand for new workers was small and could be filled by informal means, such as personal contacts and advertisements in the window, or because the employer was prepared to devote greater resources to recruitment.

Some tended to be very exacting in the standards that they wished to achieve – this normally resulted in their resorting to agencies to undertake meticulous screening of candidates before they were submitted to interview – a process which, while costly, they regarded as worthwhile in ensuring the right calibre of candidate. Jobcentres were liable to send 'everyone and anyone', in contrast to commercial agencies who could screen candidates before they were submitted to interview. One firm explained:

> if you want black and white cups you go to a shop selling black and white cups – you don't go to somewhere selling everything.

Although some firms shared this view, they were prepared to continue using jobcentres, either because they had a personnel department capable of 'fielding' candidates, and so were not unduly concerned about the occasional unsuitable candidate, or because they were more reliant on jobcentres. For example, some needed large numbers of workers, supplied quickly and cheaply – jobcentres were capable of doing this, although there were some applicants who were totally unsuitable. This was regarded by some to be 'par for the course' and did not occasion any action.

Amongst those most satisfied were employers whose only specification was physical health: for them 'suitablility' was measured in terms of the quantity rather than quality of the labour supplied.

In other instances employers had been moved to complain to the Employment Service about the unsuitable candidates sent to them. A large hotel related how it had been faced with jobcentre applicants with

> no references, vagrants, some mad, absolutely filthy; one wore a glittering clown's hat and had dirty long finger nails. Others have come with tattoos.

This was described as 'fairly typical' and was 'not ideal'! At the same time, the jobcentre remained a valuable asset in providing candidates who were basically suitable, often very quickly, with the minimum call on resources.

In those cases where employers had complained to the Employment Service about the candidates sent the local office had responded positively, often undertaking rudimentary screening on the basis of newly drafted, more detailed job specifications. Jobcentre staff did not believe that it was their responsibility to screen in instances where the job specifications were broad and ill defined.

In other cases companies had altered their own recruitment processes to 'weed out' unsuitable jobcentre applicants. Some had introduced the requirement for all applicants to fill in an application form, and a few were introducing their own screening interviews prior to a full interview.

'Suitability' was normally characterised as suitability for the type of vacancy that was on offer. That was why employers, in the main, did not treat jobcentre applicants as uniformly unsuitable or suitable – rather, they had firm ideas about the types of work which jobcentre applicants would be suitable for. This regularly meant notifying jobcentres of part-time, temporary, casual and seasonal posts – even if the permanent version of the same job was placed elsewhere. Those permanent jobs that were notified to jobcentres tended to be for unskilled or lower grade posts, or for jobs where the employer was looking for aptitude and was capable of training the person taken on. While some technical and supervisory posts were notified, most employers mentioned a job level beyond which they would not place vacancies with the jobcentre, normally because they did not expect to find suitably qualified or experienced candidates using it as a search channel.

Some had interviewed jobcentre applicants who had not wanted the vacancy, something that was apparent where applicants were non-commital, unpunctual or poorly prepared. Such applicants had 'obviously been forced into it' by the Employment Service. It was as a direct result of this that some had introduced their own screening mechanisms. Smaller firms were more fatalistic, accepting that this was the price to be paid for depending on jobcentres: they were unable to commit further resources to recruitment.

Awareness that attendance at interview may not be purely voluntary was associated with the belief that jobcentre users had to look for work, although in most instances this did not entail awareness or understanding of the requirement for claimants to actively seeking work.

Distinguishing features about jobcentre applicants

Particularly in cases where jobcentres were being used alongside other recruitment methods it was not always easy for employers to distinguish those who had applied through or at the behest of the Employment Service. Much depended on the type of contact. Where the seeker was put in touch with the employer by a counsellor, or had used an application form with a jobcentre or Employment Service stamp, then the employer was in no doubt. But if the seeker had used the company's standard application form or had walked in off the street, it was not as easy to know whether the applicant had used the jobcentre. In these cases it was only when the applicant had to fill in a form which asked where s/he had seen the vacancy that the employer would know.

It was still more difficult for the employer to determine whether or not the applicant was claiming benefit. Most employers did not make it their business to know, only doing so in exceptional circumstances such as when the employer was offering temporary contracts and wanted to avoid answering the Employment Service's queries concerning leaving employment voluntarily. Consequently, even when an employer was aware that the searcher had come from the jobcentre, s/he was not normally aware of his or her claimant status.

When asked, employers were capable of making informed judgements as to the employment status of jobcentre seekers. Most of the firms interviewed required all applicants to fill in an application form, which invariably contained information as to the applicant's recent work history and time out of work. Some were even able to estimate which jobcentre searchers were liable to be claimants because they assumed that the majority would be men and would be seeking full-time permanent work, perhaps offering a 'family wage'. It was with this rationale that some employers said that the types of jobs that they offered did not attract benefit claimants.

By and large, then, it was of little interest to employers whether an applicant was a claimant. However, they were often able to determine who had applied through the Employment Service.

There were a number of employers who said that the applications made through jobcentres were of a higher standard than speculative applications and other applications, and that jobcentre applicants had clearly benefited from the advice given in jobclubs and by advisers generally in the Employment Service.

There were those who expressed the contrary opinion: that speculative applicants, because they had applied 'off their own backs' were more strongly motivated, something that showed through in the efforts they made on their application forms. These employers were critical of the guidance given by Employment Service advisers because it had failed to prevent jobcentre applicants from making elementary mistakes, such as failing to address the correct recruitment officer or company, or incorrectly completing the application.

Jobclub applications were heavily criticised by some employers as being akin to 'painting by numbers': these employers showed signs of irritation with jobclub applicants 'manufacturing' applications without due regard for details, using identical formats, completing them without really knowing what they were applying for. Some, receiving such applications, expressed sympathy for those clearly keen to work who were 'trying their best'.

Unfortunately, even when jobcentre applicants had 'tried their best' in producing presentable curricula vitae and application letters, it was not good enough because they did not have the supporting experience or qualifications to obtain an interview. So, while their applications were sometimes presentationally superior to other applicants, they were inferior substantively, particularly where the employer was looking for more than basic skills, needed the applicant to start straight away, or preferred a ready-trained applicant to one who had aptitude but needed training.

If jobcentre applicants obtained an interview, employers tended to feel that there was little to distinguish a jobcentre applicant from other applicants, with the exception of the small minority who attended to satisfy the Employment Service rather than obtain employment.

Where employers often drew a distinction between jobcentre applicants and others was in their propensity to turn up for interviews arranged. Some employers strongly associated failure to turn up with jobcentre applicants. The owner of a small nursing home in Brighton said:

(they are) not unemployed... they are unemployable... You get 10 applicants of which 5 turn up; 2 are unemployable; you choose one of the remaining three, who then doesn't turn up. It's a big joke.

In his case it had led to his taking people who he regarded as 'clearly unsatisfactory', but he felt that he had been left with little choice due to the high drop out rate between arranging interviews and somebody finally starting work.

Some felt that the Employment Service ought to take action against those who failed to turn up because it wasted so much of employers' time and prevented them from arranging interviews with those who might have attended. (See later for jobcentre enforcement of actively seeking work requirements.)

Reasons given for jobcentre applicants' failure to attend interviews included the fact that they may have obtained other work already, a point supported by the fact that non-attendance was most acute when there was a delay between making the appointment and the interview date; the possibility that the applicant had 'got cold feet' or reconsidered; or that the applicant had done enough to satisfy the Employment Service that s/he was seeking work, so that there was no necessity to attend.

Some employers' experience was that it was other applicants who were the most prone to non-attendance, particularly job changers, who were viewed by many to be unreliable. Others felt, on the other hand, that jobcentre applicants had all the relevant information about the post through the counsellor or the self-service boards, and so were unlikely to reconsider having made initial enquiries.

There were other employers who felt that, whilst non-attendance was a problem, it affected jobcentre and other applicants alike, and related to the turbulance of the labour market rather than factors specific to either of the two groups.

A minority of employers had altered their recruitment procedures, successfully reducing non-attendance. The most successful method involved personal telephone contact with the seeker, sometimes on more than one occasion, so that any fears that the applicant may have had about the job could be cleared up. Some emphasised the importance of not misleading the applicant or raising expectations unduly by witholding information. For some jobs, such as security guard, the employer undertook elaborate screening procedures before inviting an applicant to interview. Knowing this in advance, any applicant in doubt normally dropped out before an interview was arranged.

Employers' perceptions of jobcentre users and the effect on vacancy notification

Even those employers who made little or no use of jobcentres had strong opinions about them: often it is was a result of these views that they decided not to use them. Their perceptions of the seekers using jobcentres were a crucial factor.

Companies such as banks and large manufacturers offering apprenticeships geared their recruitment almost exclusively to school and college leavers: often they were looking for academic credentials. They rarely considered using jobcentres because they had made the assumption that the type of worker they were looking for would not be using the jobcentre. Likewise, those needing qualified professionals did not expect to find them through a jobcentre, assuming that their jobsearch would revolve around private agencies and newspapers. Others assumed that the jobcentre was a place of last resort for jobsearchers and that a number of searchers were likely to be using other means first, such as the local newspaper.

Employers were 'second guessing' where the people they wanted were searching. Sometimes this was based on intuition about the local labour market, while on other occasions it was the direct result of having failed to obtain the people wanted through jobcentres. One employer who had tried the jobcentre for registered nurses found that 'they just don't use them'.

Jobcentres were strongly associated in employers' minds with the unemployed, particularly the long-term unemployed. While unemployment was rarely a criterion for 'screening out' candidates, the fact that such applicants were less likely to have recent relevant work experience meant that they were not regarded as the most suitable candidates. For some, particularly the more 'risk-averse', this meant that jobcentres were not considered. Others, either more confident in their own screening ability, or offering jobs which only required basic social skills, or with the facilities to train the unemployed, were using jobcentres for at least some of their vacancies.

A majority expressed concern about long-term unemployment, which was normally regarded as unemployment for six months or more, Whether or not the employer had had experience of interviewing the longer-term unemployed, there were doubts about their genuine willingness to work, unless there was 'good reason' for their time out of work such as illness or childcare responsibilities.

Employers sometimes expressed the more general belief that they would not get 'the right calibre' of candidate through jobcentres. Some referred to this as an 'image problem': it led to employers such as a small burger chain in Brighton saying that jobcentre applicants' calibre was 'not good... many are itinerant... applicants are often just going through the motions'. This resulted in the employer not using the jobcentre at all or else confining the vacancies notified to it to occupations requiring only basic skills, and to temporary work. One employer bluntly pointed out that her local jobcentre

has got a name for itself that it has got to get rid of... Until it changes they'll only (get) subordinates.

To an extent, the notification of lower grade jobs to jobcentres in the belief that the supply from the jobcentre would not be adequate to fill other vacancies was self-fulfilling, in so far as searchers associated jobcentres with this work, and so those seeking other vacancies used other search channels.

But jobcentres were not associated merely with the claimant unemployed. They were also regarded as the best source for women – those returning to the labour market having shed their childcare responsibilities searching for full-time employment, and those who still had childcare responsibilities looking either for part-time employment or for short-term full-time work. They were also known to be popular with students looking for evening and weekend work, as well as seasonal work.

The desire to recruit maturer part-time workers was linked to a perceived decline in the quality of school leavers, many of whom were being 'encouraged' to 'stay on', as well as to the need to more closely match the supply of labour to peak demand, as was the case in some restaurants and retailers who wanted more 'lunch time fillers'. The strategies to attract such workers invariably involved placing the vacancies with jobcentres, even where there was little or no use of the jobcentre otherwise. One firm was using it to target women returners for telephonists whereas most of their vacancies required clerical insurance experience and so were not notified to the jobcentre: the personnel manager felt that women would 'shop around' in a jobcentre, 'like a supermarket, whereas going to an agency is like committing yourself'.

Employers' attitudes towards Employment Service offices

Employers' decisions about using methods to recruit staff depended on how they thought different means would meet their labour demands. As far as jobcentre use was concerned, this depended upon the suitability of the candidates supplied (discussed above) and their attitudes towards using jobcentres.

For employers jobcentres have an advantage over many other recruitment methods in that they are free to use. When asked why they used jobcentres most employers mentioned that they were 'cheap'. Companies with a centralised personnel function often required local managers to explore relatively cheap recruitment methods, such as jobcentres and schools careers fares, only resorting to more costly methods such as newspaper advertisements and commercial agencies if the number or quality of applicants was inadequate. Even when other methods were regarded as more desirable, they were often supplemented by jobcentre notification because it involved no extra cost. This involved the notification of particular vacancies, or sending an internal vacancies list to the jobcentre at regular intervals.

Despite its cheapness some employers had never thought of using the Employment Service. They were usually content with their existing recruitment methods, which had served them well for some time, or else their labour turnover was so small that they were capable of filling vacancies without resorting to formal advertising. Companies with established reputations for good employment practices received sufficient speculative applications to fill their vacancies with suitable people. So did smaller firms in areas of high unemployment. When the employer was contacted by seekers directly, this could prove to be still more cost effective and less time consuming than dealing with jobcentres.

In such instances the employer felt no need for jobcentres. However, this did not mean that they would not be prepared to use them. Some were prepared to notify their vacancies to the jobcentre, but 'have never been asked'. They were even prepared to consider lists of jobcentre applicants sent periodically, provided that they did not have to justify their recruitment decisions.

These employers were very open minded about using jobcentres, but it had never occurred to them to do so. They were generally ignorant of the Employment Service, and rarely knew where their local jobcentre was. However employers refused to accept any blame for their ignorance of Employment Service practices. On the contrary they felt that the Employment Service had a responsibility to employers to inform them of the service it offered. It was regarded as naive on the part of jobcentres to assume that employers would automatically contact them with their vacancies. One employer suggested that:

> employers need to know what the objective of the organisation is... So jobcentres need to befriend employers.

The onus was placed on the Employment Service to 'sell themselves' to employers, who were often capable of surviving without them. That they had not been contacted by their local jobcentre was considered to be evidence that the Employment Service needed to do more to raise its awareness of the local labour market and the employers with vacancies to offer.

It was unlikely that the situation would change unless the Employment Service could attract employers with what they had to offer. However, if the effort was made, there appeared to be a fund of good will towards the public job placement service, which emanated from a desire to assist the unemployed.

At the same time, employers said that they did not want their time wasted. Some stressed that they were not prepared to see applicants 'merely because they have been unemployed for six months and need a job interview'.

More caution was expressed by those who might be termed 'risk averse' – those who wanted to 'play safe', minimising the chances they took in recruitment. They were often attracted by commercial recruitment agencies because it was their business to shoulder the administrative burdens and responsibilities of initial selection which would otherwise fall on the employer. A large majority of the employers interviewed welcomed the discounts they received in agency fees for taking on the long-term unemployed, seeing it as an incentive to take a perceived risk.

More important still, a majority of employers interviewed relied on taking new recruits for probationary periods before guaranteeing a permanent post. For some this meant offering temporary contracts in the first instance, usually running for between three and six months. (There were instances in which temporary contracts were used for peak period and seasonal employment, rather than as 'trial periods', where an offer of a permanent post was the exception rather than the rule.) Some had established ties with recruitment agencies, all of whom offered such a facility: for example, the nationwide Office Angels agency had a Hire After Lease Out scheme whereby there was no initial commitment by either party to a permanent contract – the introduction on a temporary basis, made at a reduced fee, was very popular because it reduced the risk that employers perceived in taking new recruits.

Employers were aware that claimants who left employment after a short period were investigated for leaving voluntarily. Some complained that responding to Employment Service requests for information was time-consuming and irritating. It added to the risks in recruiting claimants when compared to other applicants. However, none of the employers interviewed were aware of Employment on Trial whereby a claimant who had been registered for six months or more was able to leave a job after six weeks but before the end of the thirteenth week in employment without benefit being jeopardised for leaving voluntarily. When informed of the concept

152

employers found it appealing, and most felt that it would meet some of their concerns when wishing to 'try out' a jobcentre applicant without the prospect of being drawn into benefit-related matters.

Employment on Trail was regarded as a refreshing exception to some employers' views of the Employment Service – users and non-users alike – as overly bureaucratic. Jobcentres were associated in some minds with rules and regulations, and procedural niceties. Checks on claimants for leaving voluntarily often cut across jobcentres' user-friendliness to employers.

Employers' risk-averseness also led them to place great stress on the advantages of screening candidates before they attended interviews. That commercial agencies were geared to matching applicants to detailed job specifications was the reason why some employers relied so heavily on them. But for jobcentre users as well screening was regarded as highly desirable. Very few expressed satisfaction with jobcentres' efforts to screen out unsuitable candidates, some devising their own strategies, others requesting action on the part of counsellors to ensure basic screening.

Although Employment Service staff sought to respond to employers' requests for better screening, interviews with staff indicated that simple screening did occur, and that, rather than allowing 'everyone and anyone' to approach employers, staff were keen to match searchers to jobs as much as possible. Claimants confirmed that there were occasions when they had been dissuaded from applying for a vacancy by a counsellor who had advised them that they did not meet the employer's specification. The unpalatable truth for some employers was that the jobcentre applicants they were seeing were those who had been sent after basic screening. One jobcentre receptionist explained:

> somebody ought to talk to employers to tell them that this is all we've got, and ask them isn't there something that they can do for them. The trouble is they don't train anymore.

The discrepancies between employers' demands for labour and what the unemployed had to offer may have been as much a function of more stringent employer demands (with an ever-increasing number of vacancies requiring ready-trained, well-skilled and experienced workers) as it was a reflection of poor Employment Service screening.

Some employers did not blame the Employment Service for the service that they provided, sympathising with the enormity of the task that they had and their limited resources. Others were less forgiving. There was considerable frustration amongst those who had sought to build up contacts with their local jobcentre. Employment Service staff turnover militated against continuity and against jobcentre staff's knowledge of employers' needs. Some had noted sporadic efforts on the part of the Employment Service to meet local employers and acquaint themselves with recruiters personally: these efforts tended to fade quickly and, in most instances, employers had not been visited recently. Employment Service staff explained that, whilst establishing local employer knowledge through regular contact was seen as important, the Service was forced to respond to continually changing priorities with limited resources in such a way that it was often neglected.

That is why some employers maintained that, no matter how good one's local jobcentre was, it was necessary to continually work at the relationship in order to maximise the benefits from it. Some employers remained dispirited at the jobcentre service they received, despite their best efforts to acquaint Employment Service staff with their needs. One employer regularly invited them around for tea but 'even this doesn't seem to work'.

At a more practical level, employers felt that there was much room for improvement. Jobcentres' failure to appreciate employers' needs created a lot of work for employers. For example, large employers were regularly contacted by jobcentre staff who were very unclear as to whom they had to talk to about the vacancy in question; some observed that the Employment Service computer for storing jobcentre vacancies ('Supervacs') was not able to take detailed job specifications which would facilitate applicant screening, thus avoiding time spent considering unsuitable applicants.

The most widespread concern was that Employment Service staff offered candidates for posts that had already been filled. This was a very frequent occurrence, resulting from poor communication amongst jobcentre staff and inefficiency in taking down 'dead orders'. In many cases employers were forced to contact the jobcentre on more than one occasion to prevent further applicants being directed to them – even when jobcentre staff had already rung to check whether the vacancy had been filled.

In suggesting changes some employers advocated the adoption of commercial agency methods. Those who used public and private placement agencies remarked on the financial incentives private agencies had to find the right person for the vacancy as quickly as possible. It meant that a client-relationship was established as a matter of commercial necessity, the financial incentives underpinning agencies' interest in ensuring that they knew what their client wanted.

Some employers felt that the public job placement service would benefit from a more commercial orientation, which would guarantee a better service for them. Others recognised the special role that the public job placement service performed for employers and jobsearchers alike; they were very satisfied with the service that they received which was often courteous as well as efficient; and they were not convinced that the Employment Service could be successfully 'commercialised', primarily because of the types of vacancies it dealt with, many of which would be unlikely to command placement fees, and because the essence of the system was seen to be its effectiveness in placing large numbers of seekers quickly and cheaply.

The impact of labour market conditions on jobcentre use

Employers are often seen to be 'for' or 'against' using Employment Service facilities. The interviews with employers showed that this was not the case: we have already seen how employers discriminate in determining which of their vacancies they notify to jobcentres. It is rare for an employer to notify vacancies at all levels in his or her company or organisation. Other important factors affecting jobcentre usage were the state of the labour market and large fluctuations in an employer's demand for labour.

The biggest deterrent to employers using jobcentres was the fear that they would be 'inundated' with applicants; this was particularly prevalent amongst smaller employers who did not have the facilities to 'field' a flood of applicants. Some employers, particularly in St Helens, explicitly stated that they would not consider notifying vacancies to the jobcentre because they would be unable to cope with the response. Others had had to contact jobcentres asking them to stop mentioning them to those wishing to make speculative applications because they had received so many. This phenomenon was most prevalent in areas of high unemployment.

For others the major reason for using jobcentres was in order to get as many applicants as possible, for example when local authorities were seeking seasonal workers or companies needed to respond to sudden increases in demand, for instance, hotels hosting large conferences or banquets. They were regarded as a very reliable source of temporary, seasonal and casual staff.

There were those who, feeling that the quality of jobcentre applicants was variable, only used the Employment Service when they had to, or as a last resort. This often occurred when a local labour market was particularly tight and the response from other channels was not great enough. Paradoxically, jobcentre usage also grew during periods of rising or high unemployment because the quality of the labour that the Employment Service dealt with was greater, and because those currently in work were less inclined to change jobs.

Awareness of actively seeking work among employers

There was a very limited awareness of the requirement for claimants to seek work among employers interviewed. The majority had never heard of the requirement, some explaining that 'income support doesn't affect us' or that 'we don't deal with that type of worker'. Some had 'no wish to be involved in regulations', assuming that the requirement was another manifestation of bureaucratic government procedures.

Some looked absolutely blank once the requirement was described to them, a number finding it hard to comprehend its objective. However, some said that, although they were not familiar with the phrase 'actively seeking work' or 'actively seeking employment', they had a 'vague awareness' that, as one employer put it, 'you can't claim ad infinitum without making the effort to find work'. In some cases the employer had been convinced that claimants had been expected to do that for some time – well before the legislation came into force in October 1989.

Those employers who were aware of actively seeking work either had a managerial responsibility for recruitment or legal matters in a sizeable company (even if situated on a small local site) or large personnel department, or else they had heard of the requirement through friends, relatives or acquaintances who had claimed benefit – not in connection with their work reponsibilities. Their awareness rarely entailed anything more than a vague understanding of what could be expected from claimants.

Employers with a good understanding of the actively seeking work provisions were in a small minority. They included employers who had had to advise staff about redundancy matters, and those who had noticed a considerable impact on the number and type of speculative applications they had received since the latter part of 1989. The latter, for example, were aware that claimants needed proof of their search for work. One employer, when asked whether he had heard of 'actively seeking work', said:

we get them. We sign a book for them. The number of casual callers has risen in the last 18 months, asking for a job. If we haven't got one, they still ask us to sign. It has tailed off in the last few months, the pressures on the claimant seem to have reduced... Before that we had people coming along who normally never would... with pinched wizened little faces.

While in this case and others the fall in the number of speculative enquiries after the initial rush was associated with less stringent enforcement, in others it was apparent when employers ceased to provide written evidence for searchers. One employer explained:

when it first came in we had a whole series of calls asking if we had vacancies; when we said 'no' they asked for a letter. We did some then we stopped. Then the calls dried up quickly.

Others who were not aware of the actively seeking work provisions had nevertheless detected some changes in the quality and quantity of applications they had received in the latter part of 1989. One reported seeing:

all sorts of odd characters – I don't know if pressure was being exerted on them. I rather think it might have been. It seems to have died away now.

But on the whole employers had not detected any major fluctuation in the number or quality of speculative applications they had received since the autumn of 1989. Where there had been an increase in the number of applicants it was often associated with increasing unemployment locally or sectorally. It was only possible to extract the 'local labour market' effect from the 'actively seeking work' effect in the small number of instances in which employers had noticed a marked increase coinciding with the implementation of the Act.

The bulk of interviewees had noticed no marked increase in speculative applications from jobcentre candidates since October 1989, nor a decline in the standard of applications which would have been consistent with claimants' efforts to please Employment Service counsellors, rather than making serious efforts to obtain employment. Conflicting views were expressed as to whether the number of candidates 'compelled' to attend interviews had risen, or whether there had always been a residual group who were not really interested in obtaining work.

The only significant change in the type of applications reported by employers was that there had been:

an increase in the number of manufactured curriculum vitae in the last few years, especially from jobclubs.

This may have been associated with the need to seek work, or merely with increased jobclub activity and coverage.

There were suggestions that the Employment Service was not enforcing the requirement to seek work, or that if they had initially, they were no longer doing so. Certainly it was very rare indeed for Employment Service staff to check up on whether claimants had attended the interviews they said they would attend. Such enquiries had been more regular shortly after the Act's introduction. It was common, however, for Employment Service staff to ask employers whether vacancies had been filled and, if so, by whom. This information is necessary to up-date jobcentres' vacancy lists, as well as to record 'positive outcomes' when a jobcentre applicant has been successful. These appeared to be higher priorities than checking whether claimants were fulfilling their responsibility to seek work.

Employers' attitudes towards actively seeking work

There was little sign that the actively seeking work regulations furthered the prospects of claimants obtaining work. Employers needed to be sure that the people they considered were genuinely interested in the work offered rather than merely satisfying the conditions for receipt of benefit. One employer said he often wondered:

> are they coming for a job or because they've got to present themselves for a job?

Claimants' desire to work – particularly the long-term unemployed – was often viewed with scepticism by the employers interviewed. A number felt that the regulations would make little difference to the 'hard core' who would be able to satisfy the benefit authorities through 'superficial gestures', not least because the Employment Service rarely checked on interview attendance.

Those who genuinely wanted work were already thought to be seeking it. Employers felt that claimants should be expected to look for work, that it was a reasonable requirement. They looked favourably on those who made efforts to seek work. However, many pointed out that regulations premised on the assumption that claimants needed the threat of benefit loss to make them seek work sent perverse signals to employers. It merely confirmed the image of claimants as 'dependent' – a group who needed to be forced to do things. The view was most succinctly expressed by an employer who said:

> if you are told people won't look, that they are dross, you can't blame employers for thinking that way... Employers are risk-averse. It's all contradictory sending people you are expected to perceive as a risk.

This view was shared by many employers who already knew of the benefit penalties attached to not seeking, and those who were informed during the interview.

Employers echoed claimants' views that the need to seek work had not improved the chances of getting work because not only were the vast majority already looking for work, with competition for vacancies very intense, but in some instances, there were no vacancies to find.

Some employers sympathised with claimants being required to seek work while employers were not required to notify jobcentres of their vacancies. They were seen to be in something of a 'Catch 22' situation. They suggested that employers should be expected to notify their vacancies to the Employment Service, although voluntary registration was deemed preferable to compulsion. Employers would respond more positively to efforts to sell the advantages of vacancy notification, whereas compulsion seems liable to cause resentment.

Although many said actively seeking work would make them more wary of claimants and their motivations, only a few said that knowledge of it would cause them to reconsider their use of jobcentres. Others were confident that they were able to screen out unwilling candidates.

It is sometimes regarded as self-evident that claimants' requirement to seek out vacancies benefits employers in filling vacancies. This view was not supported by employers. Only a handful of employers said that they would diligently file speculative applications and call them up when vacancies arose. Regardless of how well presented they were, applications from those with little or no relevant work experience were often discarded immediately. There was some irritation expressed at the number of jobcentre applications received from unsuitable candidates, one or two saying that they felt like they were running their own jobcentre.

Although the regulations stipulate that claimants should take the steps which offer them the best prospects of obtaining employment, this was not always employers' experience. Some had received full curricula vitae and application letters which they regarded as inappropriate for the types of vacancies they were offering, for example in waitressing. Claimants were not furthering their prospects of employment by making such applications.

It was not easy for claimants to obtain written evidence of job search from employers. Employment Service staff said that they had been concerned that claimants' requests for evidence would act as a disincentive for employers to notify jobcentres of their vacancies. There was no evidence that this was the case, although some were loath to 'waste their time' to satisfy rules and regulations which they felt had nothing to do with them. Many had initially sought to respond to each enquiry but had found that the number of applicants made this impractical. Those with less formal recruitment procedures only dealt verbally with applicants; not all were happy to sign a form or book at the searcher's request.

The evidence suggests that no matter how hard claimants are prepared to search, they are not able to alter how suitable they are to the employer – a matter which will often turn on the searcher's qualifications or experience. Nor is there much of an advantage accruing to the individual seeker when, as employers reported, vacancies were already heavily over-subscribed. Employers did not need more applicants per se, although they were always keen to receive more applications from suitable people. With unemployment rising in all four of the labour markets studied, an increasing number of seekers were competing for a diminishing number of vacancies, with the opportunity for employers to pick better quality candidates than would otherwise have been the case. Under these conditions it was increasingly difficult for claimants to obtain employment, no matter how hard they searched or how well they presented their applications.

10 Attitudes to taking work

It is the Government's view (*Employment in the 1990s*, HMSO, 1988) that there are local labour markets in which the number of vacancies outstrips the number of claimants, and that the failure of some to take those vacancies is due in part to their harbouring unduly high wage expectations and exhibiting occupational inflexibility.

The Social Security Act 1989 sought to provide the legislative framework in which the Employment Service could engineer changes in claimants' expectations such that they would be more likely to take up available vacancies, or, if eligible as six months' registered unemployed or one of a 'special' group, the positive options (primarily Employment Training, Enterprise Allowance Scheme, Jobclub, and Job Interview Guarantee Scheme) offered through restart.

Legislation exposing claimants to loss of benefit for refusing offers of employment, neglecting to avail themselves of employment opportunities, failing to attend Employment Service interviews or to carry out written recommendations, and restricting one's availability for employment, was well-established prior to the Act. The changes, through the introduction of a limited period in which claimants can legitimately restrict their pursuit of vacancies to those in occupations and at rates of pay they would like, and by removing the onus on the Employment Service to show that the job offered by the counsellor was 'suitable' for the claimant, reinforced the expectation that claimants should seriously pursue vacancies, attend interviews, make efforts at presentability, and accept jobs offered, unless they had a good reason not to.

This chapter considers claimants' awareness of the legislative changes; the impact they have had on claimants' propensity to take work and their attitudes to 'positive options'; and, more broadly, what factors lie behind claimants' attitudes to jobs on offer.

What do claimants want from work?

The research revealed that claimants saw work as a means to an end, rather than an end in itself. They wanted work because it enabled them to fulfil a number of their aspirations. These revolved around

- improving one's quality of life, either materially, or through access to wider social circles at work and, with a greater disposable income, beyond;

- attaining status, for instance, as a 'breadwinner', or merely as a worker – this was bound up with the desire for an identifiable role and perhaps being of use to others;

- fulfilling responsibilities towards others, primarily to dependants, often expressing itself through the need for a family wage or income;

- personal satisfaction, often following a long period out of work when the desire to be in earning employment had come second to other responsibilities;

- security, not purely financial, but as the basis for 'sorting out' personal difficulties;

- money, sometimes purely for one's own ends, but often linked to other responsibilities such as debt repayment or family;

- finally, there were those factors which relate more directly to jobs themselves, such as terms and conditions, occupational preferences and career development.

Consequently when asked what types of work they were prepared to take, and what they had taken in the past, the issues of pay and occupational expectations were merely two of a number, and, whether or not they were significant in determining a claimant's actions, they were invariably linked to other goals and desires. Claimants considered taking work or training in the context of what it could do for them, rather than entering the labour market with the attitude, 'this is the sort of job specification that I want'.

Their attitude contrasted starkly with employers' (see Chapter 11) who tended to seek an 'ideal' candidate to fill the requirements of a specific job. The difference lies in the fact that, when a claimant searches for work, s/he is looking for something that will help satisfy a range of aspirations, whereas the employer has a more precise objective in mind – finding the right person for the job.

However, in the case of employers and claimants, it was rare to find a perfect fit and so compromises had to be made. But whereas employers were capable of altering job specifications and labour requirements more generally – for example, by altering shift patterns or mechanising – and thus overcoming difficulties in mismatch between the demand and supply of labour, it was not so easy for claimants to change who they were. None of the interviewees felt that they had ever had any real control over their job content or specification, nor had they been in a position to negotiate on such matters during the recruitment process. Instead, they were faced with a range of 'set'

160

options, whether they were available government training programmes, or specific vacancies. Claimants were required to make decisions between concrete options.

Below we look at what affected claimants' labour market decisions, and the role played by the Employment Service. Different aspects of claimants' flexibility are examined in turn.

Occupations claimants are prepared to consider

As mentioned in Chapter 8 few claimants had set ideas about the type of occupation that they wanted to work in. Those who did tended to be people with a specific skill or qualification which suited them to that work; those who had spent a considerable period in an area of work and wished to return to it; and those who had not worked in the area mentioned, but were keen to get into it, for example graduates with little or no work experience.

Most did not have a 'usual occupation' because they had undertaken a variety of jobs in their working lives. They had responded to changed circumstances in their personal and working lives by taking the opportunities which had been offered to them.

Some younger claimants had yet to take their first job. They regarded their lack of work experience as a bar to obtaining work; this was compounded in some instances by what they perceived to be the stigma of long-term unemployment. This group had been unable to show how occupationally flexible they could be because they had not been offered employment. Consequently they had taken Employment Service training options such as Employment Training: in a number of cases they had been 'recycled' through government schemes. Employment Service staff found it hard to place some who had already exhausted the menu of 'positive options' by their middle 20s, but were yet to experience their first 'real job'.

Claimants and those in work who had had a 'usual occupation' were often dissatisfied with it and were keen to take other employment. Some, for example those who had taken their current job as a 'stop gap' to meet short-term objectives, such as debt repayment, had other occupations in mind. However, for most the priority was finding any other type of work, provided it took them away from the facets of their work which they had disliked. For example, some had left split shift work for 'day jobs', others wanted to leave office work for work 'outside'. Other than this, little thought had been given to alternatives.

The desire merely to leave current employment or not to return to work undertaken in the past was in itself a product of claimants' occupational flexibility, whereby jobs that were less than ideal had been taken in the absence of other offers, so that in many instances workers had found themselves working in an area of employment for some time even though they had no particular attachment to it.

It was common for claimants to have performed a number of different occupations, even over short periods of time. Many were currently unemployed because they had completed fixed term contracts, or other forms of temporary work, such as casual employment: only those who had worked in the building trade expected to work in a similar occupation next. For others, short-term employment was associated with

161

the need to be occupationally flexible – that is, to be receptive to whatever might 'come up'.

Claimants' loss of permanent employment through dismissal, redundancy or in circumstances in which they had felt obliged to leave regularly led to occupational flexibility.

Concerns about the lack of occupational flexibility among the unemployed have often focused on those made redundant from heavy manufacturing industry, invariably male manual workers in skilled or semi-skilled occupations. In fact, although older workers often feared occupational change, those used to work, especially if they had dependants and needed to secure a 'family wage', were keen to move into alternative work quickly. Unless they were fortunate – as was the case with some ex-colliers who had found work in the steel industry – this normally entailed movement into work offering lower wages, less security and relatively unskilled. This was largely due to the fact that they were narrowly skilled and were not sufficiently acquainted with the practices necessary to take work in other companies, even in related disciplines; consequently they were considering either unskilled manual labour or other work in the services sector.

Employers reported that ex-colliers and those who had left the Services were sought after for security guard jobs and other work where reliable, stable workers were prized.

For many, the priority given to financial support for the family meant that they were prepared to take work that was beyond their traditional area of expertise. However, this preparedness was not sufficient for some who had found it necessary to build on, or discard their specific skills through re-training in order to obtain work. Evidence for this occupational flexibility came from employers, claimants and those in work, and trades union representatives interviewed: it is well-documented elsewhere (e.g. S. Moylan, J. Millar and R. Davies, *For Richer, For Poorer: the DHSS Cohort Study of Unemployed Men*, DHSS, 1984).

Those made redundant or suddenly faced with unemployment and no prospect of returning to the work they had habitually undertaken often considered vocational retraining. For most, this involved self-financing vocational courses, with one or two successfully exploiting the opportunity offered through the Enterprise Allowance Scheme.

Those who had used Enterprise Allowance successfully had had more capital than was required to enter the Scheme and stressed that sufficient capital was an absolute prerequisite, without which failure was guaranteed. Others had considered it, either to work in their 'usual occupation', as was the case with those in the construction industry, or to retrain, but had decided against it, often having attended the 'Aware Day' run by the providers, either because they felt that they did not have enough capital, or because they felt that there was not the prospect of sufficient reward for the time, effort and stress that self-employment entailed. A number had tried self-employment in the past, in occupations such as taxi and lorry driving, but had left them for similar work as employees. They had found profit margins to be low and the stress and hours involved considerable. Even when they had found themselves unemployed again, none were contemplating a return to self-employment.

Some factors in determining what alternative work claimants would consider and what they were offered were gender-related. Men who had undertaken various occupations in the past, or whose working life was dominated by one occupation, were contemplating a number of alternatives now that they were unemployed. However, there were some jobs that they had never considered because they were 'womens' jobs', either because of the job content, for example light industrial work or caring occupations, or because they did not offer a 'family wage' but a wage only sufficient for a 'secondary earner'. Perceptions of being the 'breadwinner' meant that such occupations would not be considered under any circumstances. They were reinforced by the belief that they would not be seriously considered by employers even if they did apply for such work. The employer interviews confirmed that this was the case, with some explicitly stating that they would not take men for work – sometimes because they would have had a disruptive effect, because they were not as good as women at jobs requiring dexterity, or because the employer shared the searchers' views that they were indeed offering 'womens' work'.

There were instances in which women had retrained for occupations which were treated as the traditional preserve of men: even where they had obtained the suitable vocational qualification through retraining, as was the case with one claimant who had financed herself through a weight training vocational qualification, they had been unable to secure a job.

Employers' attitudes were also treated as a major bar to occupational flexibility for older claimants. They had found that employers' desire for workers with relevant experience, or young workers who they were willing to invest in, effectively precluded them from obtaining employment outside their area of expertise. Some felt discriminated against on the grounds of age per se, so that they were not confident of finding work again, even if they had an established skill or occupation. These concerns were confirmed by employers in their comments on recruitment policies, and often reflected in job specifications for jobcentres and newspapers.

Consequently some older job seekers believed that, although they were willing to be occupationally flexible, they were not given the opportunity by employers who overlooked them in their recruitment processes. However, it was sometimes searchers' self-perceptions as being 'too old for employers to consider' that prevented them from applying for jobs in the first place. This 'self-deselection' was recognised as a problem by careers and adult guidance counsellors but, although there were formal schemes for older claimants, such as Jobstart for the Over-50s, run through the Employment Service, none of the claimants interviewed had received any advice or counselling on the matter through the Employment Service.

Employers' perceptions of job seekers had proved to be an impediment to claimants' occupational flexibility in other respects as well. Some with personal attributes, such as educational qualifications or being well-spoken, had been denied unskilled manual employment by employers who had not been convinced by protestations that they needed the work, sometimes to overcome desperate financial difficulties. Employers, they felt, perceived them as a risk, and as unlikely to settle to mundane work. Others, who had established professional qualifications, argued that it was not worthwhile applying for lower grade jobs, even within their own profession or occupation, because employers would have treated such an application with suspicion, wondering what was wrong with the applicant. Some explained their lack of success in applying to targeting jobs that they were over-qualified for.

Claimants' experiences suggest that preparedness to be occupationally flexible was only of limited assistance in obtaining employment.

The motivation for occupational flexibility

Interviewees' work histories and the jobs they were considering revealed considerable occupational flexibility. However, it normally entailed movement from one job to another that was at least comparable, in terms of the wage on offer, skill level, or the 'status' that the interviewee attributed to it. This is to be expected when workers have left voluntarily for more desirable employment and in sectors dominated by short-term and casual employment. But it was also the case when workers had been forced to leave employment, either through redundancy, dismissal, or as a result of a change in personal circumstances. It was most common among those who had worked in semi- or unskilled employment and, on the termination of one employment contract, were willing to 'turn their hand' to whatever came up. This was a regular feature for those who had worked in hotel and catering, retailing and associated work such as butchery, and cleaning.

That, as benefit claimants, they were expected to show a willingness to be occupationally flexible after an initial permitted period in which to find work that they preferred, would have had little or no impact on those used to shifting lower grade occupations in response to turbulent labour markets and short-term contracts. The concept of 'downward occupational flexibility' meant little to them because they were hovering around the lower end of the occupational ladder anyway, and because they normally worked, not for the love of the occupation they were pursuing, but as a means to achieving other ends. In other words, the flexibility which the 1989 Act sought to engender already existed as part of the 'natural' workings of labour markets.

Those who had shown 'downward occupational flexibility' had normally done so following redundancy or dismissal from permanent, full-time work which was no longer available in the locality, either because adverse economic conditions had severely reduced the demand for such labour or because the specific sector or employer was shrinking or closing down. In such circumstances, that is where the claimant cannot show 'reasonable prospects' of obtaining offers of work in his or her chosen sphere, it is a condition of eligibility for benefit not to restrict one's availability to that work, and to take offers of employment in other occupations. Where this had been necessary to obtain work, those interviewed had shown such flexibility. The only cases in which there had been some reluctance to do so had been in instances where the claimant had had considerable experience in a skilled occupation, or was well-qualified for specific work which s/he enjoyed, or which commanded a higher wage than alternative employment.

Even when the claimant was reluctant to be 'downwardly flexible', s/he was resigned to it after unsuccessful job search. Some, such as graduates with little or no work experience, had 'lowered their sights' once, through the knowledge they had picked up in searching, they had accepted that there were very few suitable vacancies.

Others recognised that, despite their considerable expertise, their lack of recent work experience made it unlikely that they could command a similar job immediately: this was the case with narrowly skilled craftsmen unfamiliar with multiskilling; and with those in professions such as accountancy where proficiency depended on familiarity with knowledge acquired through recent practice.

An Employment Service Regional Director suggested that industrial restructuring in the last decade had fostered an acceptance of occupational flexibility. The claimant interviews suggested that it existed not only in local labour markets which had experienced major industrial change, but in service sectors – where full-time permanent employment was not always the norm. Occupational flexibility was something that featured in most claimants' work experiences as they had responded to employers' demands for more flexible working patterns and more flexible attitudes towards the tasks that they undertook in particular jobs.

The role of Employment Service counselling in promoting occupational flexibility

Employment Service counsellors saw their role as ascertaining what job-related preferences claimants had (as opposed to what they expected to achieve more generally through work) and, if they were deemed unreasonable in the light of vacancies on offer in the locality, to guide claimants in being more realistic about their job prospects.

Counsellors were also able to use the benefit sanctions contained in the 1989 Act where persuasion had failed and claimants were refusing to be occupationally flexible after the expiry of their permitted period (a period of up to 13 weeks in which claimants are able to restrict their availability and acceptance of job offers to those in their preferred occupation).

The setting of permitted periods had had limited impact on occupational flexibility, firstly because it was common among claimants anyway, but also because, although the interviews with Employment Service staff confirmed that permitted periods were being set, they were of no practical significance because review interviews were not being undertaken, and claimants were not aware that they had a limited period in which to take work in their preferred occupation.

That they were expected to specify three occupations on their benefit claim forms was associated with the process of claiming, rather than being linked to the reassessment of job expectations over time. What appeared on the form were either ideal preferences, or options entered merely to fill the form, rather than seriously considered occupational preferences. It meant that many could not remember what they had put on their forms.

Although there was no awareness of the permitted period, and claimants did not make the connection between their benefit claim and reevaluating work preferences over time, a majority remarked on the pressures they had felt from counsellors to lower their initial expectations. This pressure usually occurred at the new claim or restart interview, with some feeling that they were being expected to 'take anything'. The best way to counter this pressure had been to convey a firm idea as to what one wished to do.

Counsellors' comments about the types of work that claimants' might wish to consider were rarely treated as helpful, but as a means of lowering claimants' expectations from the outset. Exceptionally claimants welcomed the advice, including those who were searching for work after a long period outside the labour market, or working with one firm. Others, better acquainted with the local labour market and with firmer ideas as to the aspirations they wished to fulfil through work, regarded counsellors' suggestions as inappropriate to themselves, the advice being proffered indiscriminately – that is, it was not perceived to be individually-oriented. Claimants referred to being 'herded', treated as 'statistics' or 'numbers'. There was resentment that claimants' own efforts to obtain work were discounted or ignored, and that counsellors felt themselves to be in a better position than claimants themselves to determine what was 'good for them'.

Negative attitudes towards counsellors' advice centred on suspicion as to their motivations. Many said that counsellors were most interested in removing them from the unemployment register and, to that end, were not concerned about whether the job that a claimant obtained was necessarily in the claimant's best interests. Others said that the process of claiming and advice served no other purpose than to ensure the continued functioning of the Employment Service. Contrasts were made with the advice proffered by careers and adult guidance counsellors.

However, just because claimants responded negatively to counsellors' references to occupational flexibility did not mean that, when faced with real job offers, claimants rejected them. Their work histories showed this not to be the case. Many had taken work in occupations which they might not otherwise have considered – including casual and permanent posts with the Employment Service!

There appeared to be a distinction between accepting work which was immediately available, (and, though far from ideal, held some advantages), and agreeing to gear one's efforts towards working in an occupation that one didn't like, at some unspecified time in the future. This might explain why, according to Employment Service staff and benefit advice agencies, claimants rarely turn down job offers.

However, only two of the claimants interviewed could recall being offered job interviews through counsellors – vacancies were normally pursued through the self-service facility or jobclub. That job interviews were hardly ever arranged through counselling interviews is one of the most surprising findings of the research. It reflects the emphasis that counsellors placed on other aspects of their work – namely benefit checking, job search advice and the promotion of 'positive options'. In some cases it also reflected the small number of vacancies available. It meant that no claimant had experienced a situation in which their benefit had been threatened for refusal of employment or neglect to avail oneself of an employment opportunity.

Attitudes to other options

Suspicions as to the motives of Employment Service counsellors' were most pronounced at restart interviews, where the acceptability of specific occupations and restart 'menu options' were discussed in greatest depth. For most restart was the first

166

opportunity for counsellors to raise alternative occupational preferences. However, no claimant could recall specific job interviews being offered to them at restart, or indeed anything other than cursory discussions about job prospects. Instead the bulk of restart interviews concerned the take up of other 'positive options' – namely Employment Training, jobclub, the Enterprise Allowance Scheme and Job Interview Guarantees.

One advice worker said:

> it is the whole atmosphere and how people perceive restart.. which makes it so difficult and daunting, rather than the legislative changes (which many don't know about).

The restart process was perceived as an effort to remove claimants from the unemployment register. There was widespread awareness that participation in Employment Training and the Enterprise Allowance Scheme removed claimants from the register.

Many were convinced that taking one of the restart menu options was obligatory, and that to refuse all the options led to benefit penalties. A number said that they had been explicitly informed that if they refused all offers of help, their benefit could be stopped. Others were less sure of the position but had felt that they had not been give the option to refuse – that, as one claimant put it when describing her decision to take Employment Training:

> I feel I was forced into it; I wasn't give the option to refuse – it was more or less suggested, you know, to keep them happy... I wasn't sure if I was allowed to stay on unemployment benefit.

Legally the receipt of unemployment benefit and income support is not dependent upon taking any one of the 'positive options'. In practice the situation was not so clear cut. One of the Employment Service staff interviewed said:

> there's no way that you can't take up anything unless you sign off.

Benefit Fraud Officers were regularly called in to investigate situations in which all options had been turned down; in other instances claimants were treated as having made themselves unavailable. There was intensive follow up in cases where claimants had originally agreed to take an option which they had subsequently refused.Concerns about loss of benefit were strongly associated with the take-up of Employment Training. Some preferred 'an extra tenner' to no benefit at all. ET and EAS were treated as ways to avoid the pressures of claiming; for some take-up avoided benefit deductions which would have applied for leaving work voluntarily.

Those who refused Employment Training generally felt that they had nothing to gain from it. There was doubt about it being a stepping stone back into employment – because the training and on the job experience were regarded as unsuitable or of poor quality. They were looking for a more 'concrete' means of moving back into work. This applied to previous participants who, although they had been willing to try ET, had found it to be of limited value. None had moved into work as a direct result of participation on ET, although some had been offered employment at the end of it.

Employment Service staff were concerned that younger claimants in particular had been willing to take training schemes but, having been through a couple, further 'recycling' was pointless. There was, it seemed, little or nothing that the Employment Service could do for such claimants in the absence of suitable vacancies.

But the experience of being offered 'options' was by no means wholly negative. Previous sections referred to jobclub and EAS positive experiences. The best response to Employment Training came from those who had access to it as 'special groups' – those with basic skills needs, lone parents, and women returners. Although, because these claimants did not fall into the categories guaranteed ET offers, and so were faced with a limited number of places, they did not need to be registered unemployed for six months in order to qualify. In fact they were offered ET at their new claim and usually began shortly afterwards.

ET proved valuable to lone parents who were able to take advantage of assistance with childcare costs; women returners using it as an opportunity to build their confidence and obtain a qualification before considering applying for work; and those requiring assistance with basic skills, including literacy and numeracy. Take-up was not associated with counsellor pressure in these instances, perhaps because they were not associated with restart.

Because there were limited ET places for non-guaranteed claimants many were frustrated at being unable to take a place, or having to wait six months before doing so. There was evidence that some found this demotivating, while others were concerned that they would be 'labelled' as long-term unemployed by employers purely because they had had to wait for Employment Service assistance. Employment Service staff said that this frustration would grow: in the course of 12-18 months the situation had changed from one in which counsellors had filled ET places with 'special' category claimants to one in which, with rising unemployment and tighter resources, there was increasing competition for the remaining places.

Financial considerations in moving into work

After the 1989 Act refusing employment or restricting one's availability on the grounds of pay could attract benefit penalties after the expiry of the permitted period, unless the claimant could show good cause, or show that s/he had reasonable prospects of obtaining employment regardless.

The legislative changes were motivated by a concern that claimants appeared to have insufficient financial incentives for taking employment. In particular there were worries that claimants' 'reservation wages' – the wage levels at which job seekers were prepared to work, were unduly influenced by what the claimant had received in previous employment and currently through benefits.

By tightening up the conditions in which claimants could lose entitlement to unemployment benefit and incur income support benefit reductions, it was hoped that the incentive to take work would increase, without having to tamper with market-set wage levels. This would occur because the gap between what the claimant could command on benefit and what s/he could obtain through work would widen.

Technically speaking, this involved reducing the 'replacement ratio', that is, the extent to which unemployment benefits can replace what one could receive through earnings. Reductions in the 'replacement ratios' were also achieved through the replacement of family income supplement by the more generous family credit in 1988 – an in-work benefit available to those with children working 24 hours or more each week, and who fall below specific net earnings thresholds.[1]

Wage levels were the most important consideration for most claimants in deciding whether or not they were prepared to take employment. Even when this had not been the case initially, for instance with those merely wishing to reestablish themselves in the labour market after prolonged absence, financial pressures meant wage levels soon reasserted themselves as of prime importance. Mounting pressures from bank managers to repay debts were instrumental in making some claimants reduce their wage expectations over time.

It is difficult to disentangle the factors which influenced the setting of reservation wages. They appeared to revolve around commanding a better life style than the subsistence possible on benefit – this, in turn, was sometimes associated with meeting financial commitments originally incurred while in previous employment, or that had resulted from unemployment.

The wage flexibility expected during claimants' permitted period was relative to what the claimant could reasonably expect to receive in his or her usual occupation. After that s/he could be expected to be fully flexible in taking the wage offered by any job which s/he had no good reason for refusing – irrespective of benefit levels, financial commitments, previous wages commanded and the wage received by others doing the same job. The research suggests that while most claimants were very flexible relative to their previous earnings and the pay offered by local vacancies, there was resistance by the majority to the flexibility envisaged in the legislation. This was particularly so when expected to disregard existing financial commitments and existing benefit entitlement.

Only occasionally did claimants refer explicitly to previous earnings levels when stating what they would hope to receive in the future. But, for the most part, claimants were prepared to accept well below that level after an initial period of unemployment and, in some cases, had done so. The exception to this was when previous employment had been low waged or failed to meet financial commitments. In such cases claimants didn't see further downward wage flexibility as either feasible or desirable, given that their expectations were already in line with wage levels on offer.

In obtaining work the crucial factor was whether claimants were prepared to take the wages that were on offer locally. To that extent it was not relevant how flexible they were relative to previous earnings, since a claimant who had worked on lower wages than those currently available could actually specify higher wages and still obtain employment at rates employers were willing to offer.

It was very rare for claimants to consider work offering wages below their benefit levels. Most said that they had struggled to subsist on benefit and that, if they were to make the effort to work, they would expect to command a living standard above that feasible on benefit.

In the few instances in which claimants said they would consider or had taken wages below benefit level, they had done so in the belief that 'in-work benefits' (mainly housing benefit and family credit) would raise their income to at least that which they had been on subsequently. They had offset financial rewards against other advantages such as training opportunities, or merely acquiring work experience.

In reality, those eligible for income support who wished to earn would receive their benefit plus the appropriate earnings disregard (usually £5 for single claimants, £15 for couples and £25 for single parents) provided they worked less than 24 hours; eligibility to family credit, which usually took claimants well above their unemployment benefit entitlements, is confined to those working over 24 hours with children. Those in receipt of unemployment benefit could earn no more than £2 per day, and below the national insurance contributions threshold (£46 during the period of the research) before losing entitlement to it for that week.

At the very least most claimants expected the wage offered to compensate them for their loss of benefit. The costs of moving into work were much more broadly defined than the loss of housing benefit (rent, mortgage and community charge assistance) and 'passported benefits' such as free childrens' school meals and milk – although these were very important. They included the cost of work clothes, eating out in the daytime and the cost of travel to and from work. There was widespread concern that, given the jobs on offer, claimants would be little better off if they moved into work.

If costs 'necessarily and exclusively incurred' through work represent an 'unreasonably high proportion of remuneration' claimants can refuse work offered; however, this does not include child care costs, which were particularly important for lone parents, or mortgage interest payments. It is worth noting that work-related expenses have been treated differently in the benefits system since 1988, in so far as they can no longer be disregarded for the purposes of benefit entitlement; and, in contrast to supplementary benefit single payments, the social fund does not offer assistance in meeting work expenses or travel to work costs. Some claimants were aware of this and it featured in their concerns that they did not seem to be able to obtain assistance from the DSS or Employment Service in meeting such expenses.

In fact, claimants may not have lost entitlement to housing benefits and, if they were in receipt of family credit would have remained entitled to some passported benefits such as free prescriptions. Nevertheless, their perception that they would be little better off in net income terms does accurately reflect the rapid withdrawal of means-tested benefits once claimants earn above income support levels.

Claimants were often making judgements as to how much better off they would be on the basis of partial knowledge. The level of knowledge about family credit was far lower than that for Employment Training, for instance. But even those who had received family credit regarded it as of little assistance, not least because it was offset against housing benefits.

Many judged that, given the benefits they were receiving and the jobs on offer, they would only be marginally better off in work. But that a claimant felt that s/he might be marginally better off in work rarely featured in deciding whether to take work: when the income level was of most significance to the claimant, it was normally necessary for him or her to feel that s/he would be substantially better off in work than unemployed.

Of course claimants' views as to what 'marginally' and 'substantially' better off meant varied greatly. But claimants usually had to feel that they would be able to command a significantly better standard of living for themselves, and their families, if in work. They referred to the demands that would be made of them at work, and felt that they should receive a 'fair reward' for the efforts they made in travelling to work and working.

There were those who felt it imperative that they earned well in excess of their benefit levels, including those with financial difficulties, and those seeking a 'family wage'. They were not contemplating remaining on benefit either, because this would not help them meet their financial responsibilities. It did mean, however, that they were not prepared to take work whatever the wage.

This 'holding back for something better' was also a feature with younger, single claimants who received family support, or else preserved high expectations as to what they could command, as was the case with new graduates.

Nevertheless, there was much evidence that, when faced with real job offers, claimants were prepared to take work at rates of pay below what they had originally stipulated – that is below their 'reservation wage'. The most flexible were those with no financial or family responsibilities who were prepared to 'trade' wage flexibility for other desirable ends – such as work in a specific occupation or moving from night to day shifts.

Decisions about moving into work could not be understood in terms of trade offs between the marginal benefits accruing through time in work and leisure time. In the first place most claimants were driven to find work through fear of unemployment – the isolation it entailed, the boredom that went with it, and the sense of uselessness felt by some. Some had taken work that they disliked and at rates of pay that they would not have considered originally because they had been unable to contemplate further time out of work. Because paid employment had been hard to come by this had led some to take voluntary work.

Secondly, and perhaps more importantly, claimants were concerned above all to ensure that they maintained a steady, reliable flow of income. Although all found unemployment benefits to be inadequate in meeting their material and social needs, claimants were secure in the knowledge that, unless their personal circumstances altered, it was likely that they would be able to rely on receiving at least that level of income in the future. Movement into work was associated with risk – in particular the risk of disrupting existing income levels.

Payment of wages in arrears had created debt problems which, if one had accepted low paying employment, were hard to resolve. If there were doubts about the continuity of the employment – either because it was temporary or fixed-term, or because the claimant was not wholly sure whether s/he would like the work, or the employer like him or her – claimants feared having to go through the process of claiming afresh. Even if the claim was processed swiftly, it still meant benefit payment in arrears. But many had experienced great difficulties in establishing benefit claims – for example, following enquiries about leaving voluntarily, or administrative delays, or while awaiting a new claims appointment – so that many regarded the risks of taking work available as substantial.

The risks were viewed as particularly acute by those with family responsibilities because many claimants were sanguine about managing for themselves, but feared their children suffering through their actions. In this respect family credit was of little or no use. Indeed it was considered to be part of the problem. There were a number of examples in which claimants had pursued vacancies but had decided not to take them when it had been unclear to them what they would receive through benefit top-ups. Those on family credit had not been persuaded to take work because of it. Indeed most had not found it very helpful. One recipient explained:

> it is not worth it for the trouble you go to to get it. I had to work five basic weeks, then wait 3-4 weeks for them to tell me I was entitled to £21... But then you lose your housing benefit.

Others, who had received less in cash terms, felt it had made little difference to their ability to make ends meet.

Uncertainty about the levels of net income claimants could get in work and worries about the impermanence or suitability of available work meant claimants regarded movement off benefit as 'risky'. Although it was a risk that many were required to take through financial necessity, few were happy at doing so unless they were sure of commanding a wage in permanent full-time employment which paid well above benefit levels.

Only two of those interviewed were working while claiming unemployment benefits. Both were engaged in part-time work and were aware of the financial disincentives they faced through the loss of benefit as their net earnings rose. They also faced regular problems with the processing and calculation of their benefits. Both were single and motivated by the simple desire to be in work: in the absence of full-time permanent work, they had to 'make do' with what they could get. For the vast majority of claimants, however, the need for a secure, reliable level of income meant that combining earnings and benefits was not practical or feasible.

Employment Service counselling on wages and flexibility expected

From the research it is apparent that most claimants were strongly opposed to taking wages below benefit levels, or which were insufficient in meeting existing financial commitments. And yet, as Chapter 3 makes clear, the Adjudication Officers Guidance states that such flexibility can be expected after the permitted period.

The issue of wage levels was most significant in decisions to supply labour for:

- those seeking a 'family wage', unconvinced by in-work benefits, and faced with low wages locally;

- young workers, living at home or on recently leaving college with debts;

- older workers looking to the longer term, with no desire to take 'stop gaps';

- and women who, because their husbands had become unemployed and because their own wages barely compensated for the loss in benefit, left work.

Our sample was heavily weighted towards those who had 'signed on' for unemployment benefits, and so did not include women who had withdrawn their labour following their partners' move into unemployment, it being the man who was claiming in these instances – there were only a few references to their withdrawal from the labour market by men who felt that it had been the rational thing to do. (Although some benefit advisers mentioned the importance of 'tactical' decisions taken by partners claiming benefit to maximise income, the study dealt primarily with the decisions of individual claimants.)

Those most likely to come into conflict with Employment Service counsellors were those who were generally inflexible over time, or were initially adamant about the wages they were prepared to accept when making a new claim. Older workers and those seeking a 'family wage', because they tended to be more flexible on non-wage matters such as occupational preferences, were often capable of finding work within the first six months of their unemployment. If they did not, counsellors recognised that they were willing to show flexibility where they could and did not pursue them vigorously.

In contrast, there was some evidence that counsellors had targeted younger workers, students and those who had recently left college, as well as those who refused to alter what were considered to be unreasonable wage expectations at their initial claim.

Nevertheless no claimant had suffered a benefit reduction as a result of restricting his or her availability or refusing employment on the grounds of pay. This was largely due to the fact that claimants were prepared to lower the wages they had specified on their new claim or restart forms, and because it was not counsellors' practice to offer jobs at very low rates of pay.

One of the reasons why claimants were so ready to revise the wage they had entered on their new claim or restart forms was that, rather than specifying 'the lowest weekly wage' they were prepared to work for, they had specified the wage that they would have liked to receive. It was misleading as a guide to what work claimants were available for.

As with the specification of occupations on claim forms, citing a wage was treated by most as part of the claiming process, rather than a figure relating to their real aspirations and search for work. The counsellor practice of crossing out 'unreasonable wages' was treated as helpful in recording a successful claim, rather than as part of counselling geared towards reducing claimants' real wage expectations.

Even for those aware of family credit, it rarely featured as a positive encouragement to move into work. But most had not heard of it. Surprisingly, given the clear commitment of the Employment Service to in-work benefits assistance, it was rarely 'sold' at counsellor interviews. Those who had received it felt that they had had to 'fight for it'.

Where there was awareness of family credit it was often vague, stemming from television advertisements and 'the grapevine'. In those cases, there was much antipathy towards it, mixed with disbelief that it could make families substantially better off. One man said:

I've seen an ad with people in a bus smiling, saying 'I get £100 and I also get something else'. It's a con.

Such attitudes were often grounded, not so much in a knowledge of family credit, but in the experience of claiming benefits from the DSS and Employment Service.

Travelling to work

The distances claimants were prepared to travel to work were contingent on what they thought they could get out of particular jobs. Those who placed a general limit on their willingness to travel tended to name places, rather than the time they were prepared to spend travelling. Nevertheless, when told that they could be expected to travel for an hour either way each day, many thought this to be excessive. Only one claimant had been told that her benefit could be threatened by travel restrictions.

Most were prepared to travel anywhere 'if the money is right'. However, many vacancies were deemed to offer wages that were insufficient to compensate for the cost and effort of travelling. As one claimant put it:

some don't pay enough to feed you let alone give you transport.

Few had their own transport, but those that did placed few or no restrictions on the locations they were considering.

Some had worked away from home in the past, returning at weekends, and would do so again if the work paid well enough. The exceptions were normally those with families. Being single or married emerged as the key factor limiting claimants' daily travel expectations. Yet even those with families were happy to leave their locality permanently 'for the right job'. This was not so for those with strong attachments to the local community such as older claimants.

Some claimants had been impatient with counsellors' questions concerning travel to work. Their purpose was not apparent to claimants. They resented answering a lot of what appeared to be totally irrelevant questions, when they had been hoping for assistance in returning to work.

Hours of work

Many had experienced long hours in previous employment and were unconcerned about working long or unsociable hours again, provided they were paid overtime rates for doing so. There were objections to working very long normal hours. For example, some had turned down offers as security guards when they had discovered that the normal working week was 60 hours. One man said that he'd been told that overtime was available but:

how much overtime is there left after 60 hours?

The problem facing many claimants was that available vacancies offered too few hours, rather than too many. Partly because they were required to be available for 24 hours work per week, and partly because they wanted full-time permanent

174

employment, all but lone parents (who are not subject to the availability rules) were not considering the part-time work which abounded in jobcentres.

Awareness of the refusal of employment and availability changes and their impact on movement into work

There was very little awareness that refusing employment could result in benefit penalties, never mind the fact that the legislation had changed in 1989. There was more awareness that claimants could lose benefit for restricting their availability and failing to attend Employment Service interviews. But again, there was no awareness of the 1989 Act.

Some said that they understood that a claimant could refuse two jobs before being penalised. This seems to have been the practice of counsellors in the past. But when the October 1989 benefit changes were mentioned, most interviewees referred to the end of supplementary benefits single payments and the introduction of the social fund, both of which occurred in 1988 and are more closely associated with the Department of Social Security.

When discussing benefit penalties more widely, some were aware that they had been penalised for leaving work voluntarily; others thought that they had been subject to benefit reductions but were unsure why and unaware of the precise impact they had had on their benefit income.

Given that most claimants were totally unaware of the benefit penalties for refusing employment and restricting their availability on the grounds of pay or occupation, and that even those who had suffered reductions were regularly unaware of the connection between their loss and their actions, it is not surprising that the changes have had so little impact on claimants' behaviour.

Claimants felt that their benefit was more likely to be threatened if they refused 'positive options' at restart interviews. This did make them more likely to take one of the 'options' offered to them.

Interviews with claimants and Employment Service staff revealed that, in the main, pay and occupational expectations were not severely out of line with the vacancies available. Where they had been, they had normally lowered their expectations after some time out of work – in response to their lack of success in applying, and partly to pressures they felt from others, including Employment Service counsellors.

It was this 'indirect' effect of the legislative changes, in the context of new priorities set for the Employment Service by its Agency Agreement, which some Regional Directors believed had contributed to increased placement ratios.

An Employment Service Regional Director, seeking to explain why it was that there was so little awareness of the permitted period, or that failure to lower occupational and pay expectations after a specific time period had elapsed could result in benefit penalties said:

> discretion and direction lie ill together.

And yet, 'discretion and direction' appear to be at the heart of the Employment Service's dual function in checking benefit eligibility and placing claimants into jobs. In fact, counsellors had leaned towards 'discretion' rather than 'direction'. For example, the legislation appeared to have no effect on the vacancies that counsellors offered to claimants. Although there was no longer a statutory duty on them to offer jobs which were 'suitable', they felt that their role as brokers between searchers and employers meant that there was nothing to be gained by suggesting work at wages below claimants' existing benefit levels or significantly below those hoped for by the claimant.

It is not surprising, then, that the legislative changes had little or no impact on claimants' decisions to take work, or the type of work offered to them. But what, if any, would the implications be if the legislation was fully enforced, and claimants were aware of the benefit consequences?

Although some were strongly resistant to the idea of taking work paying below benefit levels, for example, most said that, if faced by the choice between unsuitable work offering low wages, and receiving less benefit than they were currently receiving, they would – albeit reluctantly – take the work offered.

Some said that they would take the work offered as a 'stop gap' in the hope that something better would turn up quickly. There was evidence that such a situation already existed in the case of Employment Training offers. One DSS Adjudication Officer said,

> we get a lot of D2s [orders to lapse benefit claims] saying 'Such and such started work'... A month later they're back on the register... Often they're just signing off for ET.

It is easier for claimants to sign off for ET only to make a new claim shortly afterwards, thus circumventing the pressures of restart, than it is for them to take unsuitable work, leave it and register again, because there are no penalties attached to leaving Employment Training voluntarily. Claimants were well aware of the benefit penalties attached to leaving employment voluntarily. This awareness featured significantly in decisions to stay in work until another job had been found and, if unemployed, wariness in taking work which might prove unsuitable.

So, the leaving voluntarily benefit deductions acted as a disincentive to changing jobs and taking work if unemployed. The interviews suggest that, if claimants felt greater pressure to take work they did not really want, then labour turnover would rise as they left 'stop gap' jobs, either voluntarily or on dismissal by dissatisfied employers. Such a policy was regarded as short-sighted and did not serve claimants or employers.

Only one or two of those interviewed were aware of the Employment on Trial provisions whereby those registered unemployed for six months or more could try a job and, if they left after the sixth week but before the end of the thirteenth week, they would not face a voluntary unemployment deduction. Interviewees responded very positively to the idea because it went a long way to allaying the fears associated with trying jobs which might not work out. However, virtually no-one had heard of the provision and nobody had had the opportunity to use it.

176

What claimants thought militated against their obtaining work

The Act relies on the concept that there are 'barriers to employment' which stem from claimants' high wage expectations and lack of occupational flexibility. The research indicates that these are not, in most cases, significant factors barring claimants' movement into work. A range of other factors emerged from interviews with claimants, including:

- the stigma attached to being unemployed, particularly long-term unemployed; claimants said that employers often felt that they would be 'taking on a person with a problem, rather than merely somebody who had been unable to find work';

- lack of employment experience, creating a spiral in which claimants are unable to obtain experience because employers will not take them on. This applied even to low paid employment such as waitressing;

- the absolute dearth of full-time, permanent vacancies, or at least those that could be regarded as even remotely suitable;

- the lack of vacancies paying substantially more than unemployment benefits – a problem which was particularly acute for particular groups such as lone parents and others with family responsibilities;

- the financial risks associated with moving off benefit and into employment;

- the difficulties of matching benefits with earnings;

- age discrimination, so that older claimants are not given the opportunity to work in areas beyond their work experience;

- the labelling of specific types of work as gender-specific, regularly excluding women from consideration in a number of occupations;

- 'self-deselection' by those lacking confidence, for example. It is an issue on which the Employment Service do very little counselling;

- the lack of basic skills such as numeracy and poor literacy;

- physical impediments to doing some, but not all jobs;

- the 'vicious circle' of homelessness and joblessness – some of the interviewees were homeless, some were living in hostels; they had found it very difficult to get work without a permanent address;

- material deprivation, making it difficult for claimants to afford interview and work clothes, and travel to work costs;

- personal attributes, including educational qualifications and work history which preclude employers from accepting claimants for lower grade occupations.

This list does not cover all the problems referred to in this chapter. But it does serve to put in perspective the dangers of concentrating on the 'barriers' which some feel claimants place in the way of obtaining employment. As indicated at the start of this chapter, claimants wanted jobs in order to fulfil a range of social, financial and personal aspirations they had. Whether or not they were able to find work which helped meet those objectives was, for many claimants, as much a matter of luck as anything else. Certainly the problems faced require a broad set of employment, training and counselling policies which do not reflect the emphasis of current government policies.

Note

1. Table C on p.110 of the *Tax/Benefit Model Tables*, November 1990, shows the replacement ratios as they stood in April 1990 and affected the claimants interviewed – other than lone parents, for whom the earnings disregard increased in October 1990.

11 Employing the unemployed

We have seen in the last chapter that claimants show quite a degree of flexibility in the work that they are prepared to take. From the claimant interviews it appeared that flexibility was only of limited value in actually obtaining work. But how valuable is flexibility to employers? Are they more likely to offer work to somebody who is prepared to travel further, earn less or switch occupations?

This chapter considers whether the flexibility required by the 1989 Act has, or could, make any difference to the propensity of employers to take claimants. It also assesses employers' awareness of and attitudes to the provisions.

How suitable can claimants be?

For the most part, 'suitability' depended upon the extent to which an applicant matched the requirements of a specific job on offer. These requirements were either explicit in the job specification, or else lodged with the employer in his or her head – the product of experience as to who would suffice.

It was regularly the case that, no matter how willing claimants might have been to take work available, they were unable to meet the prerequisites. Unemployment was not a hinderance if the claimant met the job specification; but in practice, many jobs required recent relevant work experience and/or qualifications. In these cases, it was not possible for claimants to 'make themselves suitable' over a short period of time, without retraining or educational courses.

A lack of recent, preferably relevant, employment experience, was often a criterion for 'screening out' candidates. Those without experience were only considered for lower grade work; in the NHS this meant that only auxiliary work was available for those without health service experience. Only very occasionally did employers positively discriminate in favour of those without recent experience. This was the case with some who welcomed the fact that a new recruit could be 'moulded' and would not be 'set it their ways', and with those who were eager to recruit women returners (regarded as reliable, mature, stable workers) despite the fact that they might take some time to readjust.

The search for experience frequently meant employers taking those already in work. One employer said:

> I won't pretend I'm going for claimants without experience when there are people in work with experience applying.

Whether claimants were considered depended to a large extent on the availability of other, more experienced labour. As one employer put it:

> it's a question of supply and demand... a person generally unemployed for a long time will not get the job, but it depends who comes in over the next 3-4 days.

Employers proved still less compromising where educational or professional qualifications were called for. In smaller firms particularly there were few training resources so that employers were hoping to recruit skilled, trained workers, normally by 'poaching' from other employers. There was evidence that this practice was on the increase, with larger firms either temporarily or permanently stripping back the resources devoted to training staff.

Even well-qualified claimants were at a disadvantage in competing for such jobs because employers were wary of taking applicants who were not acquainted with the latest developments in the field. Employers were making demands on applicants which those who were unemployed after some years in stable employment were unable to meet. For instance, employers sought multiskilled fitters with training which had broken the traditional demarcation patterns.

In firms where the demand was primarily for skilled workers and training facilities were minimal the only opportunities for the majority of the unemployed were in unskilled permanent, and temporary or casual employment. However, there was evidence that the demand for wholly unskilled work was in decline. This was due to automation – as was the case in one company whose:

> only unskilled work (was) store cleaning and warehousing, but even here there is now an aptitude test for MRP.

It was due to firms moving 'up market', as was the case with some burger restaurants seeking to provide a better quality service, dependent upon smart, intelligent staff capable of using hand-held computer pads. And it was due to a fall in the absolute number of semi- and unskilled jobs in the public sector resulting from cash cuts and in response to compulsory competitive tendering.

Together these trends meant that employers were making greater demands on applicants, demands which some claimants found difficult to meet.

Employers were most likely to be taking claimants where the job requirements were very straightforward – where applicants' suitability was judged by their appearance, their physical attributes, or by their possession of basic social skills. Even here, however, some employers held negative perceptions of claimants which dissuaded them from placing their vacancies with jobcentres, or led them to 'screen out' unemployed candidates. In these instances, the unemployed were associated with instability, unreliability and uncleanliness. This negative image was sometimes based on experiences of having employed claimants who had subsequently proved unpunctual, poorly motivated or had left after a short period. More frequently, it was a view held by employers who had had little or no experience of recruiting the unemployed, but had considered applications from them.

Claimants were also in demand in those firms which looked for aptitude and were capable of training staff on the job, that is, where experience and qualifications were of least relevance. Such firms included hotels (the larger ones with training managers and departments), restaurants (mainly through informal on the job training), large retailers, private manufacturers (both those offering relatively unskilled process work where dexterity and reliability were most important, and in skilled work such as sewing), and ex-public sector services with apprenticeship schemes. There was firm evidence through personnel monitoring and personal recollections that jobcentre applicants (though not necessarily claimants) had been as successful as other applicants in passing aptitude tests and obtaining employment.

Many employers used initial probationary contracts, usually of 12-13 weeks duration, in which to assess the suitability of applicants before considering them for permanent posts. These 'trial periods' were viewed as indispensable by those who used them, in allowing the employer to judge the suitability of those taken on in the work environment.

'Trial period' use was associated with recruiting from the unemployed, because those currently in work were unlikely to leave permanent employment for temporary employment. But some were concerned about the implications for claimants' benefits on the completion of the trial. None were aware of the Employment on Trial provisions allowing claimants who had signed for at least six months to try out work and leave without benefit loss. When advised about it, most felt it to be a very welcome development.

The long-term unemployed

Despite some employers' 'blanket' negative image of the unemployed, the majority of employers said unemployment was incidental to an individual's employment prospects if s/he could show his or her suitability for the job on offer. But most employers shared negative images of the long-term unemployed – which, for most employers, meant unemployment of six months or more. Some specified 'cut offs' – six months, a year, or two years unemployment – whereupon applicants were 'screened out'.

Even if they were not screened out, there appeared to be a greater burden on the long-term unemployed to show their suitability for work than was the case for other applicants. This was because they had to overcome a number of doubts about their attitudes towards work. Although one or two were prepared to discriminate positively in favour of the long-term unemployed, most were not. One employer said:

> I am not prepared to see people just because they are six months' unemployed and need an interview.

Every employer asked long-term unemployed applicants why they had been unable to find work. They were confident in being able to 'weed out' those who did not have a genuine desire to work, because they did not provide satisfactory reasons for their time out of work. Being unable to find work was not considered to be a legitimate reason by those who maintained that there were 'jobs about'.

Others said that they were 'less likely to get involved' with those who had been out of work for some time because the long-term unemployed were characterised as 'people with problems', only one of which was the lack of employment. Above all, employers were concerned not to risk taking on somebody who might be 'a problem'.

Doubts about the motivation of some who had been out of work for some time were confirmed in some employers' minds by their experiences in interviewing applicants who clearly did not want to take the job on offer, a matter that was regarded as self-evident by attitudes shown during interview, and occasionally references to being 'forced' to attend by the benefit authorities.

Attitudes towards the long-term unemployed were not wholly negative, however. One employer felt that:

> being unemployed means nothing. They just need a chance. Sometimes they are the best (employees) because they want to keep the job when they get it.

Smaller employers and those with 'flat' career structures sometimes welcomed taking those who had been out of work for months in the belief that they were likely to stay for some time, and would not be career-oriented, or impatient to move on, as was the case with other 'better' candidates.

There was also a group of employers, the health service among them, who admitted to the fact that the long-term unemployed were recruited in the knowledge that they were 'desperate for work' and so would be prepared to work under great pressure for relatively little money.

Of course attitudes to the long-term unemployed were conditioned by previous experiences. Often this meant experiences with Employment Training trainees. The experience had convinced some that the long-term unemployed could be trained and become a valuable source of labour. Some were currently employing Employment Training trainees. Others had used them in the past but had not found it a rewarding experience, or else, as had occurred with some schemes where the Training Agents or Managers had changed, had found that the quality of trainees they received had deteriorated, whereupon they had discontinued their association.

On the whole the employers interviewed had taken on very few long-term unemployed. One organisation who had, through the Job Interview Guarantee, had been disillusioned by the post-placement problems they had had with recruits. Although claimants had been presentable and acceptable at interview, problems had developed once Employment Service counselling had ceased. The employer had experienced punctuality and absence problems, as well as a deterioration in the quality of work, which had resulted in disciplinary measures. This experience is particularly worrying since the employer was keen to discriminate positively in favour of long-term unemployed claimants, and had found their job interview presentation to be more than satisfactory, only to face considerable difficulties post-placement.

'Jobchanging'

Concern about 'jobchangers' – those who had undertaken several jobs in their working lives – was widespread among employers, being the most common 'screening out' factor. It was most marked where a reliable job record was all important, such as in the security industry, and where heavy training costs were incurred.

The impact of labour market conditions on suitability

Applicants' suitability for vacancies was measured against the labour market competition so that a claimant who may have been suitable for a vacancy at one moment in time could find himself 'less suitable' when the employer had a wider pool of labour to choose from.

Claimants were finding it increasingly difficult to obtain work as unemployment rose in the four labour markets studied. This was partly due to reductions in labour demand resulting from redundancies and redeployment in large firms, less mobility among those in work and lower labour demand generally, induced by lower consumer demand. But it was also due to the fact that competition had intensified as better quality, recently employed labour came onto the market. A number of employers said that it would be increasingly difficult for claimants without recent employment experience, or without educational or professional qualifications to be short-listed for vacancies, let alone obtain work. Not surprisingly, employers welcomed the opportunity to recruit better quality applicants.

It was suggested by the Employment Service and some local authority Economic Development Units that 'backfilling' was occurring, whereby vacancies appeared in firms which were taken by internal applicants, leaving room for claimants to enter firms at the bottom. There was little evidence that this was occurring to any great degree due to the lax demand for labour, and the volume of redundancies leading to substantial redeployment of existing staff in major manufacturing firms, as well as ex-public sector service industries and local authorities. In a number of instances recruitment freezes had been instituted.

Impact of recruitment methods on claimants' chances

Falls in labour demand accentuated the problem that claimants faced in having access to vacancies in the first place. This was an important factor helping to determine how successful claimants were in getting work. Larger firms, particularly those undergoing redundancies and seeking to redeploy existing staff, had to look no further than their own firm and did not notify vacancies externally, effectively precluding applications from claimants.

More generally, employers regularly concentrated their recruitment efforts on sectors of the workforce which are not heavily represented among the claimant population. This was the case where recruitment was geared towards school leavers – for instance, with gas and telecommunications apprenticeships and bank clerks. In other instances employers concentrated on internal applicants for posts which they thought needed intimate knowledge of the industry, as was the case with driver-operators in the waste disposal industry.

No matter how 'flexible' claimants were prepared to be in the terms and conditions they would accept, the segregation of the vacancies market, by denying them access to vacancies, precluded them from consideration in the first place.

Downward wage flexibility: desirability and practicality

Employers had rarely thought of reducing the wages they offered. The only instances in which employees had suffered wage reductions had been following competitive tendering where new terms had been set by private contractors.

Pay rates were employer-set, either at establishment level, or 'externally' – through Review Bodies, national collective bargaining, company policy or Wages Councils. The majority of jobs attracted a rate of pay, or a pay band, which was not negotiable with applicants. The rate or band was either formally set through a pay structure, or else approximated to what the employer regarded as appropriate given the job's content and responsibilities.

Consequently, employers did not seek out applicants' wage expectations. Rather, they advertised vacancies that attracted pay rates which the employer thought appropriate, or else was obliged to pay due to company policy, negotiation or statute.

Claimants interviewed had complained that when they had pursued jobcentre vacancies where wages were 'negotiable', they were not. One claimant recalled going for a 'wages negotiable' job to find:

> they weren't negotiable. £60, that's your lot. Take it or leave it.

Some employers using jobcentres said that they did not specify 'wages negotiable' because they were not. None of the employers interviewed admitted to using this device to assess a claimant's desire for a job, and set the rate accordingly – a process which could allow for reductions in the wage which the employer might have been prepared to pay initially.

The only instances in which there was real negotiation between applicants and employers were for managerial and professional posts. Those with scarce skills or valuable experience sought to maximise the wages offered by employers. Ironically, it was only in such cases – that is, those which conform to the classical economic model of employer and applicant freely negotiating on an individual basis – that employers regularly met with resistance to the wages offered. As one employer explained:

> although pay rates are good, there is a problem with pay expectations, but more at managerial level than below because it is more of a negotiation situation.

However, whenever wages were negotiable, employers did not take applicants on purely because they could get them at a 'discount'. Applicants had to be basically suitable; there were no advantages in paying less for somebody if s/he was the wrong person. Some preferred not to fill a vacancy at all than have the wrong person in post. 'Discounts' were only appealing if the quality of the applicant could be guaranteed, as was the case with candidates provided through reputable employment agencies.

In the light of employers' attitudes to pay levels, it is by no means certain that those with a high degree of pay flexibility spend less time unemployed than those with lower expectations. Instead, obtaining work depends upon the individual's suitability for the vacancy, and then on his or her preparedness to accept the wage offered – a wage which could be lower or higher than his or her previous earnings.

The attitude of most of the employers to pay setting was characterised by the employer who said:

> at the end of the day you've got to make a profit, but you've also got to get and hold people.

The recruitment of staff of the right quality and their retention depended crucially on pay levels. Employers who had not considered wage adjustments regularly had no difficulties in recruiting and retaining staff at rates of pay they were prepared to offer. Where wage adjustments had occurred, they were almost invariably upwards, in response to 'tight' labour market conditions.

Frequently employers were paying close to the minimum they thought they had to pay to recruit staff, and often below what was needed to reach acceptable levels of labour turnover. This was the case in a number of hotels and restaurants, as well as small retailers and manufacturers. It meant that reducing wages further was inconceivable without raising turnover to unsustainable levels or expecting a substantial deterioration in the quality of applicants. This was of less concern to those recruiting casual or temporary staff, or where training costs were minimal; but it was almost invariably of great concern when it affected permanent full-time and part-time staff.

It is interesting to note that although some firms were already suffering high labour turnover rates, due in part to offering wages which proved uncompetitive, they rarely raised pay rates in recognition of the hidden costs incurred, but only if the situation suddenly deteriorated through pay rises elsewhere.

Most firms were acutely aware of the pay rates being offered in the locality and the travel to work area (that is, the area from which employers expected to be able to recruit staff, rather than the official TTWA). Some, particularly larger firms in sectors like the security industry, retailing, banking and insurance ensured that they kept a competitive edge by maintaining rates slightly above what they considered to be the 'going rate'. National firms were assisted in doing this through supplementary allowances available where recruitment and retention problems were acute.

Intra-sectoral wage competition was very apparent in the hotel and catering sector, and inter-sectorally, for example, between hotel and catering and retailing, where the latter tended to pay higher rates. When competing for the same or similar labour, pay comparability between and within sectors was as significant a determinant of pay levels as comparability between firms offering the same goods or services.

This 'cross-checking' among firms able to set rates locally, meant pay was highly susceptible to general local market fluctuations affecting the demand and supply of labour.

185

Even within the same firm, pay rates varied considerably in response to the amount of work available to those the firm wished to attract. For instance a cleaning firm in Sussex offered between £3.00 and £4.40 per hour for part-timers, depending upon the demand for private cleaning work in different towns. Such sensitivity suggests that employers were prepared to pay what they had to pay to acquire staff, but no more than was necessary.

Some of those who were free to raise their wages locally had done so in the last eighteen months in response to local labour market pressures. However, none were considering reducing them again as unemployment rose because they did not think employers competing for the same labour would do so, and there was concern about 'poaching' by those offering better rates. Instead they hoped that they would be able to obtain better workers because upward wage adjustments meant they were better placed relative to employers in other sectors competing for the same labour.

The marked reluctance to reduce wages related to concerns about recruitment and retention. It was not pay expectations which dissuaded employers from reducing wages; in the main, these were in line with the wages on offer. Indeed expectations were perceived to be well below market wages in many instances. One employer even felt that:

> if we reduced wages to £2 per hour (from £2.50) we would still have no problems recruiting – desperation leads the way.

The difficulty for employers was that the quality of labour was intimately linked to pay levels, so that:

> if I paid £1 an hour I daresay I'd get waitresses but what would I get?

These concerns were mixed with objections in principle to paying 'exploitative wage rates'. What were regarded as 'exploitative rates' varied, but levels below Wages Council rates were regularly considered 'very low'. Out of 'fairness' some had continued to up-rate under-21s' pay rates by the Wages Council percentage increases, despite their removal from Wages Councils' remit in 1986.

A clothing manufacturer paying £2.50 per hour remarked:

> our philosophy is that no-one should work for less than £1.50-2.00 net per hour, so we don't exploit them.

Some regarded national pay rates to be too low and argued that reductions in those rates would be 'criminal' and 'immoral'.

The practicalities of reducing wage costs

By no means all employers shared the view that wage reductions were undesirable, although nearly all agreed that the 'laws of supply and demand' meant that direct wage cuts were usually impractical.

There were other methods by which employers successfully reduced direct wage costs, including the subcontracting of ancillary functions; increasing the number of part-timers earning below the national insurance contributions threshold; organising 'twilight' shifts to avoid the payment of overtime to full-time staff and increase line production; taking advantage of government financial incentives for jobsharing; and using Youth Training trainees (although some had ceased their involvement with YT following deteriorations in the quality of trainees).

Direct wage reductions were impractical for a number of reasons. In the first place, wage rates were often set 'externally', that is, not at local level, but through national collective agreements, Review Bodies, Wages Councils, the Whitley Councils in the case of the health service, and company or local authority pay scales. Sometimes there was room for the local employer to set differential rates above the minimum, taking account of qualifications, experience, and local labour market conditions, but wage floors were set by 'external' factors over which the local employer had little or no influence.

Even if wage rates were set at establishment level, where this process involved a recognised trade union, employers envisaged strong opposition to pay reductions, or the employment of new staff on lower rates. One or two employers had sought to institute such a change in the past, but to no avail.

Even where there were no unions, employers felt that such moves would be met with 'uproar' by existing staff. One employer felt that:

> you are heading for trouble if you say you like him better than him so I'll pay him more.

Dealing unfairly with staff was regarded as dangerous by employers desirous of keeping unions out of their workplace.

Finally, pay arrangements which involved differential payments for groups doing similar work was regarded as potentially too complex to administer – as being 'more trouble than it's worth'.

Attitudes to and awareness of pay flexibility envisaged in the Act

There was very little awareness about provisions sanctioning claimants for refusing employment or for restricting their availability. However, many said that they had dealt with applicants who they felt had not applied through their own volition, and some knew that 'something might happen' to claimants if the benefit authorities found out that they had refused work, or had 'made themselves unsuitable' at interview.

The levels of awareness about these provisions, which have been part of the benefits system for some time, was much lower than awareness of the relatively new actively seeking employment provisions. In contrast most were aware that claimants could suffer benefit losses for leaving work voluntarily; those used to recruiting claimants had regularly dealt with benefit enquiries pursuant to an employee's departure. However, those who knew of these provisions were not normally aware that the period of disqualification could extend to six months, most citing six weeks (the designated period until 1988).

Only those who had friends or relatives claiming were aware that there had been changes in the circumstances in which claimants could legitimately refuse employment or restrict their availability on the ground of pay or occupation.

There was no evidence at all that the changes had in any way affected employers' recruitment practices or the terms and conditions they were offering. Some trade union officials and local authority personnel suggested that the provisions could have a major impact in areas where compulsory competitive tendering laid a premium on reducing direct labour costs. There was no firm evidence that this had occurred – those who had lost employment had turned down 'the same' jobs on lower rates with private contractors because they had been redeployed or obtained other work.

For employers to utilise the extra pay flexibility expected on the part of claimants, they had to know which applicants were claimants. They sometimes knew who had applied through a jobcentre, because they were contacted by a counsellor; because the applicant carried an identification card; or the application form was stamped. Employers were often aware that an applicant was unemployed through the application form, instinct or direct questioning. But even then there was no guarantee that the applicant was a claimant.

It was only apparent that an applicant was a claimant if the employer made it his or her business to know (for example, to avoid dealing with 'leaving voluntarily' enquiries if seeking temporary workers); where it was evident through applicants' references to benefit levels; through jobclub applications; or once the applicant had been recruited, as was the case with employees investigated by Benefit Fraud Officers.

Normally employers were unaware of applicants' benefit status because it was of no interest to them. So it was not possible for them to treat claimants differently in terms of the pay and conditions they are offered, for instance.

So far as they were aware, employers felt that claimants' wage expectations were usually in line with the wages that they were offering. Some firms had monitored the reasons given by applicants for refusing employment. The major reason for refusal was wage levels, but those who refused work on that basis were normally jobchangers, not the unemployed.

Some claimants had cited what they received on benefit during interviews. Some employers felt that this was indicative of a poor attitude and had rejected applicants on that basis. Others had asked applicants whether they felt they would be better off unemployed, judging by the answer whether it was worth taking a risk with an applicant who could be poorly motivated.

Other employers felt:

> it's commonsense to work out your best bet.

Employers were sometimes aware of the calculations applicants had done. In one case claimants had worked out that:

> they are working for 50p an hour because the dole is £37 and their take home from £100 is £60.

Although some employers agreed that 'some bright people will wonder if it's worth it' claimants regularly took the work if it was offered to them. One employer pointed out:

> they are not much better off than on benefit, what with £36 rent, so it takes you to £70 or £80, so it's £20 at most better [than benefit].

Few were prepared to blame claimants for refusing employment which made them little better off than on benefit because:

it's not benefit that's too high but wages that are too low.

There were very strong objections to the expectation that claimants should take employment irrespective of their existing financial commitments after a permitted period, or at rates below existing benefit levels. Indeed, the vast majority felt that family and financial commitments should be central in determining what could be expected of claimants.

The amount of pay flexibility which should be expected from a claimant depended upon his or her personal circumstances, as far as most employers were concerned. While they did not want people to receive 'something for nothing' there was a strong belief that, if claimants with family responsibilities or high financial commitments were expected to move into work, then it was incumbent on the State to pay the 'mark up' between the market wage and the claimants' assessed needs.

That claimants should legitimately take such matters into account was regarded as a matter of

self-preservation; it's got to go through their minds. If they tried to make me [take pay which did not cover her family needs] I'd tell them where to go.

Another employer said:

if I was unemployed and on unemployment benefit, say I got £25 from work, but then there was travel and childcare costs, I'd say 'to hell with it'.

This sympathy for claimants faced with wage levels which employers themselves thought to be low, extended to preparedness on the part of some to pay part of the wage in cash to allow for family credit and to payment of cash-in-hand to allow claimants to avoid benefit withdrawal as net earnings rise.

Most objected to employers paying 'off the books' or 'in hand' because it enabled those employers to recruit staff at lower rates of pay than those operating 'above board'.

None of the employers interviewed said that they would take advantage of the provisions which could require claimants whose permitted period had expired to take rates of pay below those offered to others working in the same establishment. Many employers concurred with the employer who said:

I wouldn't treat them any different just because they were a claimant... It's not fair. I wouldn't like it if I was the only odd one out...

Not only did most believe that it was unfair to pay two people doing the same job different rates of pay, but some wondered:

how do you expect people to get an incentive to work if you are paying them less than others on the job?

In addition some felt that the wage they offered reflected the value of the job they were offering and that to go below it was to 'cheat' the applicant by paying him or her less than s/he was worth. There were instances, for example during a probationary period, or when one worker had much more experience but was doing the same job as another, when some differential was regarded as acceptable. But on the whole employers were not happy with the idea that one worker should be paid more than another for the same work.

Even when claimants were prepared to take work at pay rates below those offered to others, this did not mean that employers would take them on. There were particular concerns associated with taking claimants who had previously worked in well-paid employment in 'good firms'. Some employers had a policy of not recruiting them for fear that they would not be sufficiently motivated.

But this concern was small compared to the fear that claimants were not taking work through their own volition, but to avoid benefit deductions or stoppages. The worries were summed up by one employer who stressed:

> If we took someone on like that, how long do you think they would stay with us? One thing we are trying to do is reduce our staff turnover... The willingness has to be there, even if they are free. To do a job you have to want to do it... We can't afford to have people who don't. Having someone pressurise them can be of no use to us.

The wish to do the job was regarded by all as the most fundamental prerequisite for taking an applicant. Without willingness no applicant was suitable. While the benefit provisions might have been able to assist employers in recruiting workers, it would worsen their retention difficulties and jeopardise the level of service they were able to offer to customers. Some said that they would rather pay an unwilling claimant to stay away than to take the vacancy.

The employment outcomes

None of the employers interviewed had adjusted the pay levels offered to claimants as a result of the changes, not only because they had been unaware of them, but also because of the undesirability and impracticability of doing so. Claimants that were being required to consider vacancies on pain of benefit loss were considered unsuitable because their motivations were considered suspect, and so would not have been offered employment. Employers sought to weed out those who displayed the 'wrong attitude'.

It appeared unlikely that any claimant would have gained a 'competitive advantage' by displaying considerable pay flexibility because suitability for vacancies did not depend upon claimants being able to undercut the rate offered.

It also appeared unlikely that the provisions would widen the pool of vacancies offered to claimants, since even if jobs were offered to claimants rather than other candidates, it was likely that they would have been offered to them in the first place. Secondly, as one employer put it:

> even if you could cut wages by half and retain (staff) you wouldn't necessarily increase your staff.

This was because staffing levels depended on meeting the demand for the good or service, as well as on the price of labour.

It appeared that employers did not need the social security provisions because they used market indicators to set pay rates. If labour markets were 'tight' they had to increase wages as a response to recruitment and retention problems – the provision of a cheaper pool of potential unsuitable labour was therefore not relevant. Then, if labour markets were not 'tight', labour was plentiful at the wages that employers were prepared to pay.

Responses to labour shortage

There were three employer responses to shortfalls in labour supply. They either intensified their efforts to find suitable candidates, widening their search over time; took 'less suitable' applicants; or did not appoint anybody, waiting for a suitable candidate to apply. The idea that employers could use occupationally flexible candidates relies heavily on the assumption that they are prepared to take candidates 'less suitable' than those who are more qualified or experienced.

The centrality of relevant work experience and/or qualifications to candidates' suitability often meant that occupational flexibility was regarded as a major risk. For occupations such as cookery and nursing appropriate qualifications were indispensable. Even flexibility within occupations was often wholly inadequate. One interviewee pointed out that, under no circumstances could a pastry chef ever suffice as a grill chef.

For some posts basic qualifications were used largely as a mechanism for 'screening out' applicants, although they were not absolutely necessary to undertake the job. This was the case with banking clerks who needed two 'O' level passes.

Sometimes, although particular qualifications were not called for, employers did not fill vacancies if candidates did not possess the attributes which the employer thought vital for the job. This was so in occupations often regarded as 'low skilled', such as supermarket cashiers who required dexterity, patience and problem-solving abilities. Those failing aptitude tests for such posts were not taken on.

Employers with less formal recruitment techniques were able to describe in some detail the attributes they looked for in 'suitable' candidates. They tended to be personal attributes, not directly related to the candidate's employment history. Again, those offering work normally regarded as 'low skilled' could be very, very particular about what they wanted. The manager of a small restaurant explained how careful he was in taking people and training them on the job:

> I limit the work they do until they are capable [through on the job training]... It's not like a sweet shop where someone can do the job straight away after one day. Full-timers progress from the floor – I like them to work on the counter and the cooking grill. Part-timers start waiting on tables then go on to dispensing.

Even when formal qualifications were not called for, employers clearly knew what they liked and what they didn't like. For these employers it was not a simple matter of being able to 'make do' with candidates prepared to try new occupations.

When was occupational flexibility reasonable?

There were relatively few jobs open to those who satisfied basic 'suitability' criteria (physical fitness, decent appearance and willingness to work), but they included cleaning, laundering, warehouse and other manual labouring work, and casual and temporary employment. The upgrading of work in some sectors, reductions in the number of unskilled jobs available, and more stringent employer demands, meant that these jobs were falling as a proportion of all work on offer. However, where these jobs were available, employers habitually employed people who had worked in other occupations because their previous occupations were not relevant to the decision to recruit them. They drew from the claimant and non-claimant unemployed.

In the majority of cases, however, taking occupationally flexible candidates was not considered the best option, especially when other labour was available. One's occupational flexibility could not make up for experience or 'hard skill'. One employer explained:

> if you've been glass blowing for 20 years and you're going for a clerical job you will lose out against clerical experience.

Some said that they would only consider 'flexible' claimants if labour market conditions made it absolutely necessary. This was partly due to employers perceiving the unemployed as male manual workers with little or no relevant skill or experience. In some cases it was due to employers' previous experiences. Employers and trade union representatives recalled cases in which those made redundant from industrial occupations had been unsuccessful in making the transition to other work: this had led to dismissals in the hotel and catering sector, or rejections on application. One council had considered 'industrial redundancies' for administrative work but:

> they had problems just filling in the forms, and poor verbal skills. [So] they fell at the first hurdle.

The most successful instances of occupational flexibility occurred in a 'controlled environment', for example in larger firms with training facilities. Hotels regularly trained applicants from 'scratch' once their basic suitability had been established. Similarly, larger firms in sectors such as glass and steel manufacture were contracting and redeploying staff, using a mixture of on and off the job training.

The other 'controlled environment' in which employers had successfully recruited occupationally flexible candidates was when they had made it a deliberate recruitment objective. Some hospitals and retailers, for instance, had targeted older workers, most of whom did not possess relevant work experience. They had been successfully trained and assimilated.

Structured training programmes only existed where employers realised that recruiting ready-trained staff was not possible, or where traditional sources of experienced staff were drying up. Claimants were regularly the beneficiaries. However some employers, in areas like waste management and insurance, tailored their training to those who already had substantial experience in the sector, thus excluding most claimants.

Many firms did not have the time, inclination or resources to train those willing to change occupations. An engineering firm, predisposed to taking unemployed candidates, said:

> we can't use Joe Soap. We have no training facilities and all the people on the shop floor are at least semi-skilled.

The majority of employers were not opposed to occupational flexibility in principle, but they were at pains to stress its limitations. Experience had taught employers what sorts of 'occupational transfers' could be accommodated. Some had learned to 'screen out' certain occupations before interview, while recognising others as indicators of an applicant's probable aptitudes and strengths. For example, security guard companies prized stability and reliability above all else, and so welcomed applicants from the Services and Police Force; by the same token, they rejected 'jobchangers' out of hand.

Marked occupational flexibility was viewed with suspicion by employers. A retailer found it 'curious' that a bricklayer had applied for a baker's job:

> But I see no reason why not, if he explains his circumstances sufficiently.

In a sense, occupational flexibility was regarded as 'all very well', but 'it depends how far you go'. A car manufacturer felt that flexibility beyond certain limitations could not further one's employment prospects. If a production line job came up, and:

> if it's between a trimmer and an estate agent I'm hardly going to give it to the estate agent.

Age, sex, physical and mental limitations: bars to recruitment?

Claimants faced effective 'bars to recruitment' on grounds not associated with their claimant status, which nevertheless meant that they would not be considered by some employers, or for certain types of work.

Fears expressed by claimants interviewed that their age barred access to some vacancies was substantiated by employers. Firms investing heavily in training sought to maximise that investment by employing those they imagined would remain with the firm some time: this regularly excluded those aged over 50. For apprenticeships, employers sought school leavers, with a maximum age of 19 years old (unless the applicant offered particular skills or experience).

There was concern that older workers would be less willing to be supervised in lower grade work than younger workers. When asked whether he would take a 19 year old claimant or 63 year old one to start in office work, one employer said:

> I'd take the 19 year old because otherwise [the older man] would have to accept supervision from someone younger than in his last organisation.

While some valued older workers with stable work histories, particularly for work involving unsocial hours, others felt that those made redundant from 'good firms' would be less willing to stay in work offering lower status and poorer conditions. One employer said:

[they] will be a destructive element asking for a subsidised canteen, safety shoes. I won't take them... It's always the same letter – 'Rockware [Glass], 35 years, now 52, unemployed two years' – that person's chances of staying are low.

While some employers feared the expectations that older workers had, based on their seniority in previous jobs and the quality of those jobs, others were very keen to recruit them in the belief that they would provide stability and maturity. This was the case in retailing, the health service and clerical work. However, recruitment drives geared towards over-50s had not proved successful, employers believing that firms' images as 'go-ahead' or 'hectic' were off-putting.

A variety of jobs were perceived to be gender-specific by employers. Some treated this as 'inevitable'. For example, working in coking ovens was regarded as 'the last bastion of the real, strong man'; other very physical work, such as driver-operators in the waste disposal industry, were all men.

Work in cafes and restaurants was regarded as predominantly the preserve of women and girls because, although school leavers and college students were used casually, employers' experience was that young men did not remain in permanent posts long, leaving for higher wages and for employers offering better career prospects. For this reason employers in small cafes and restaurants had been disappointed with male recruits, including those on Youth Training and Employment Training.

Similarly women were regarded as more naturally suited to work which was dexterous and repetitive. Women were sought after for factory operatives in the clothing, baking, pharmaceutical and cosmetic industries. But only in one instance did this preference mean the exclusion of men. The employer explained:

> Process operating is sad, routine, boring, menial work... Women are better at it than men. Men say 'am I going to be doing this for 50 years' whereas women say 'I am doing this for social reasons' or 'I can buy some shoes for the kids on Saturday'.

He was disinclined to use men as packers because 'they would be a disruptive influence'. He continued:

> If they are sent by the jobcentre we will give them an interview but not a job... [they are] men in dungarees with a *Daily Star* in their back pocket... They say they are between jobs on oil rigs. There's no point taking them on. Anyway we can do the manual dexterity test: the women always get through... Yes, it's discrimination.

Clearly, employers set limits to the work which men and women can take, according to their own views of what the job requires and the commitment that men or women are likely to have in the job. Employers rarely sought to redress the gender images of the jobs they offered, although this was occurring in some occupations which had been traditionally dominated by men, such as engineering apprenticeships.

Perceptions of those with physical and mental limitations differed markedly among employers. Some firms, including manufacturers suffering from high absenteeism rates, favoured those with physical disabilities who, through experience, had shown themselves to be more reliable and productive workers. Their motivation and commitment were deemed superior. Those with mental difficulties, whom employers sometimes referred to as 'not quite normal', were sought after for manual work, such as shelf-filling in retailing, because their work rate and appreciation of the work offered were often higher.

There were indications from some employers that they would have liked to take on more people with disabilities but that, even in cases where their contacts with the Employment Service's Disablement Resettlement Officer were good, they received few applications. Employers surmised that 'self-deselection' was a serious problem.

The majority of employers interviewed said that the opportunities for thos with physical or mental limitations were limited or non-existent. Most limitati ns or disabilities, including health problems, resulted in applicants being 'screened out'. Sometimes employers were prepared to consider those with mental limitations for specific tasks, as was the case in hotels who were happy to use them for work 'round the back', but 'not up front' where customer-contact was necessary.

Very few employers had made specific efforts to make the recruitment of people with physical or mental disabilities more possible. Yet, where they had, as was the case with some who had employed people with literacy difficulties as cleaners by colour-coding the substances used, had found that the effort was well-rewarded.

In many instances employers had firm ideas about the type of workers they regarded as suitable for the jobs they had. Consequently, no matter how flexible claimants were prepared to be in the types of work they would take, and the terms and conditions attaching to them, their age, sex or physical or mental limitations frequently acted as an effective bar on their recruitment – often without their being aware of it, or else their failure to apply for certain types of work was rooted in the belief that employers would exclude them on those grounds.

Occupational flexibility: awareness of and attitudes towards the Act

Employers were not aware that claimants could be expected to be occupationally flexible after an initial period of claiming. Nor were they aware of the changes that had been made to these provisions in the 1989 Act.

There was no indication that employers' recruitment practices had been affected in any way by the expectation placed on claimants that they should show greater flexibility in the types of work they were prepared to take on the expiry of their permitted periods. Those who were able to make most use of the occupationally flexible did draw from the claimant unemployed; but they had always done so, and had experienced few if any difficulties in being able to find willing candidates. (The claimant interviews did not suggest that the changes had made claimants more willing to be occupationally flexible.)

There was widespread concern when it was explained to interviewees that claimants could lose benefit for failing to be sufficiently occupationally flexible. When told that occupational preferences could not constitute legitimate grounds for refusing employment after an initial period claiming, one employer drew the inference that:

> it's as if a brain surgeon is offered a dustman's job, and if you don't do it it's as if you don't want work. It's not even as if the jobs are around.

In practice, interviews with Employment Service staff and claimants clearly showed that claimants were not under pressure to show this type of flexibility. Nor were they expected to fundamentally reappraise the work they were available for after their permitted period. Instead claimants had received the impression that they ought to be considering types of work other than their initial preference as time went by.

Employers sympathised with claimants expected to take the work that they offered. Some believed that the work they offered was not suitable for all claimants:

> If you are trying to help the unemployed get jobs and careers, with a wife and family, they need to look elsewhere,

said one employer.

Others felt that it was 'traumatic enough becoming unemployed without suddenly having to think of other careers'. Although one employer said that:

> if you are an unemployed bank manager, you are not a bank manager, you are unemployed

most objected to the idea that unemployment became 'the great leveller' after only thirteen weeks (that is, the end of the maximum permitted period) because, for many claimants:

> their skill is their identity. It shouldn't be taken away.

At the same time there was some recognition that the injunction to 'be flexible' could have no practical effect where jobs required skill or qualifications, unless the supporting educational and training facilities were in place. Adult guidance counsellors said that there was too much optimism about the room for occupational flexibility among what was a poorly and narrowly trained workforce. In addition existing vocational training and retraining courses did not offer enough assistance in basic social skills, numeracy and literacy – levels of which training providers often over-estimated. This was confirmed by firms who had uncovered poor literacy and numeracy during staff redeployment.

The employment consequences

Occupational flexibility (as opposed to flexibility and broadly based skilling within an occupation) was not considered a good in itself. On the contrary it held few attractions for employers. In the first place, employers were wary of applicants whose work history showed an inability to 'stick' at anything. Above all, they valued skill and experience. As one craft baker put it:

> if he's been a lorry driver, a caretaker, then worked in a shop, that's no good to me.

Those reliant on highly skilled workers feared skill degradation. Many concurred with the view, expressed by one, that

> the last thing we need is a Jack of all trades.

196

Employers did not think that occupational flexibility would assist them in meeting their labour shortfalls in skill shortage areas. This had to be tackled more fundamentally through the educational and training system as a whole, and through greater priority for vocational training starting at school.

Nor was greater occupational flexibility regarded as a solution to labour shortfalls due to high labour turnover. Indeed, if underpinned by benefit sanctions, it was feared that poorly motivated recruits would increase labour turnover as dismissals and leaving voluntarily rose.

How much travelling do employers expect?

Although managerial staff often travelled for over an hour to and from work, employers recruited other staff from more local catchment areas. The exception was when the employer was able to organise transport for groups of workers arriving and leaving work at the same time.

No employers expected staff to travel each way – to and from work - for an hour every day. That claimants could be expected to do so was not considered beneficial by any employers. This was because they were able to recruit sufficient numbers from the locality. They felt

> if you are looking at their motivation you have to think about them getting knackered just coming to work.

The effect that travelling was thought to have on employees' motivation, and their likelihood of turning up for work, meant that expecting workers to travel more than short distances was considered 'risky'. Since employers usually had the choice, this meant that that staff below managerial level regularly lived in the vicinity.

Particularly for those offering shift work and weekend work, it was impractical to take people living outside the immediate vicinity, unless they had their own transport. Employers were frequently critical of public transport systems which, they believed, made travelling some distance impractical. A number shared a view that it was unreasonable to expect applicants to commit themselves to travel far when they were dependent on a precarious transport system.

In sectors such as the security industry, one's own transport was an absolute prerequisite for being offered work. But for most employers, preparedness to travel:

> is not a deciding factor in offering a job, though they should convince us that they can make it.

Only one employer believed that workers who lived further away were more motivated. For most, if faced with identical candidates, employers said they'd choose the one who had a shorter distance to travel.

It was rare for employers to offer work to applicants who refused it on the grounds of travelling. If they were concerned about the travel involved applicants – claimants and non-claimants alike – did not attend the interview. Some had found, however, that new recruits having to travel some distance, had underestimated their difficulties, and had left after only a short period. Where this had occurred it had made employers more wary about taking staff outside the locality.

Hours of work

Employers had some difficulty filling vacancies which involved unsocial hours, weekend work, short hours or – as in the security industry – long normal hours.

The most intractable problem was attracting staff prepared to work part-time. For example, at peak demand hours in restaurants and shops. It was only in part-time work that contractual hours were regularly negotiable – because, by altering staff shift patterns, employers could engineer adequate staff cover. Otherwise applicants were faced with taking or leaving what the employer offered.

Ideally, many employers found that they would have welcomed more part-time staff, in order to meet peak demands. This almost invariably meant staff prepared to work for less than 24 hours per week. Consequently it was work which claimants did not have to be available for and, in the main, did not want. The legislation does not require claimants to take work of less than 24 hours, while financial and family commitments, as well as the net income effects of taking part-time work, meant that claimants usually sought full-time work.

Employers were aware that some of their part-timers were 'double jobbers', working in at least one other job. This was regarded as a sign of the 'right attitude' to work by most, although some prohibited staff working for other employers. Some 'screened out' those already engaged in physically demanding work.

Sometimes employers were favourable towards applicants who had few outside commitments; but decisions not to recruit applicants were only related to hours when employers were concerned that childcare responsibilities would occasionally take precedence over work attendance.

Unless applicants were unaware of the working hours expected before they attended the interview, they were rarely questioned by those seeking full-time employment. Once or twice employers had received the impression from an applicant that s/he did not want to work for the stipulated hours; these candidates were not recruited, but employers did not regard it as their business to inform the benefit authorities.

Applicants' refusals of job offers

There were three ways in which applicants refused work. They did so by contacting employers after interview – these applicants usually explained their reasons, citing concerns about pay and conditions, career prospects, hours or travel, or the fact that they had accepted another offer. Some firms monitored applicants' reasons for refusal, seeking to do what they could to make their employment more attractive.

Secondly, applicants failed to turn up for work having accepted the offer, often at the interview. Depending on when this refusal to attend occurred – before any work had been done, or after a very short time in post – the applicant could be subject to benefit penalties for refusing employment, neglecting to avail himself of an employment opportunity, or for leaving employment voluntarily. Thirdly the applicant could effectively 'refuse employment' by deliberately appearing unsuitable at interview.

Employers regarded the first situation as acceptable, though they sought to rectify matters. Leaving voluntarily after a short period was considered to be an inevitable part of high labour turnover by some, while others had altered their recruitment techniques, successfully reducing early leaving. They were most galled by applicants failing to turn up for work without contacting them: it inconvenienced them, requiring them to seek a replacement and, for example in process plants, could severely disrupt production.

Few made distinctions between claimants' and non-claimants' propensity to turn job offers down. Some associated explicit refusals or failure to attend on the first day with jobchangers who were able to command other offers. Making oneself unsuitable was associated with jobcentre applicants who were not attending voluntarily – invariably these candidates were not actually offered work.

Although some would have welcomed tougher enforcement of benefit penalties as punishment for claimants, none thought that it would prevent claimants refusing work or making themselves unsuitable for work they did not want. Indeed, there were concerns that benefit penalties compounded employers' difficulties in weeding out unsuitable candidates.

Some had sought to make their own changes in recruitment practices to bring down job refusals and early leaving. In sectors such as hotel and catering and retailing, where turnover was high and where employers relied quite heavily on jobcentre applicants, the practice was to offer the applicant the job 'on the spot' – that is, at the interview, because employers had observed that non-attendance on the first day was associated with the time that applicants had to wait before the job commenced. As one hotelier explained:

> if they are claiming benefit, they want work immediately.

12   Regional variations

The intention of the legislation was that labour market conditions would play a crucial role in determining how the 1989 Act is implemented at local level. The legislation and Adjudication Officers' Guidance require Employment Service staff to have a detailed knowledge of the local labour market:

- when a claimant restricts his or her availability yet claims that s/he has reasonable prospects of obtaining employment despite those restrictions;

- when decisions are to be made as to what constitute the steps to seek work which offer the best prospects of obtaining employment;

- when setting the length of the permitted period (because it involves judgements as to the availability of work in the claimant's usual occupation);

- and when offering particular jobs to claimants (because guidance requires offers of jobs reflecting conditions generally available in the locality, and requires counsellors to offer jobs with the highest pay rates for that type of work first).

This chapter considers the issues raised in Chapters 8 to 11 from a regional perspective, focusing on the dissimilarities between the four very different labour markets that were selected for this study.

The search for work

Labour market conditions

Appendix 2 outlines the salient characteristics in the four labour markets that were studied, including the demand and supply of labour and information on the operation of the Employment Service.

The conditions in which claimants were searching for work were deteriorating markedly but unevenly in all four labour markets during the course of the research. Between October 1990 and January 1991 the stock of unemployed claimants rose by as little as 7.5 per cent in Hammersmith to 21.1 per cent in Hove. In Hammersmith and Fulham, and Brighton and Hove employers said that, over the last year, the markets they recruited in had turned from 'seekers' markets' to 'employers' markets'. In St Helens employers had only felt the benefit of increasing unemployment since October 1990, a fact ref'ected by a relatively stable claimant stock over the year to January 1991, but substantial increases when compared to the count at October 1990.

However, the implications of that deterioration for job seekers are not apparent from unemployed stocks alone. The fall in the number of vacancies remaining unfilled at jobcentres throughout the UK, a trend which began in January 1990, was reflected in the four local labour markets. Competition was intense. In Newport, for instance, of the 1,925 vacancies notified to the jobcentre in the quarter to 5th October 1990,

82 per cent were filled within a week;

10 per cent within 1-4 weeks;

1 per cent within 4-8 weeks;

and only 7 per cent were still on display.

During that period, 75 per cent of Newport's notified vacancies were being taken by the unemployed. This suggests very effective claimant job search and expectations which, even if they were out of line with vacancies available, did not affect claimants' preparedness to take them.

There was evidence that the Employment Service was sensitive to labour market conditions in considering how to implement the actively seeking work requirement. An Employment Service Manager referred to 'the employment situation (being) very buoyant in West London', when explaining possible differences in the way that they actively seeking work provisions could be interpreted in London and in Barnsley, Yorkshire (letter to M. Morrell, Hammersmith Unemployed Workers Centre, 29th March 1990). The letter coincided with the pilot study in Hammersmith and Fulham, which revealed a 'seekers' market'. However, that changed rapidly so that, between April 1990 and January 1991 when the claimant interviews were carried out, the stock of unemployed claimants had risen by 1,292 – 17 per cent.

Although all four labour markets had witnessed the 'stripping out' of many full-time permanent manufacturing-based jobs in the 1980s, the process of industrial restructuring had had the most profound impact in Newport and St Helens because their industrial bases were larger, and the process of restructuring was still in progress.

While Newport had experienced rapid shrinkage in its primary manufacturing and heavy industry sectors (steel, dock work and coal) in the first part of the 1980s, large numbers of workers in pharmaceuticals, glass and chemicals manufacture were still being made redundant in St Helens. According to the council's economic development department:

> in the last six weeks [prior to the interviews in September] there have been 800 redundancies of highly skilled, motivated people.

The unemployment benefit office referred to them as the 'long term employed'; that is, those who had worked within the same firm for most of their working lives. This was a feature that distinguished St Helens from the other labour markets. According to employers it reflected the 'conservative' behaviour of local inhabitants and the great divide between a large, but shrinking primary employment sector – dominated by large manufacturers – and a small secondary sector of less secure, poorer paying jobs.

Between August and October 1990 3,006 fresh claims for benefit were made in St Helens, a large number being the 'long term employed'. They presented a problem for the Employment Service because, as the unemployment benefit office said, when it came to seeking new work:

> they have no idea where to start.

The Employment Service had to concentrate resources on such claimants because they had had little recent experience of unemployment or job search. The situation was similar in the southern labour markets where Employment Service counsellors increasingly found themselves advising those who had been made redundant from financial and professional occupations.

However, it was also the case that such workers were highly sought after by employers for their stable work histories and recent experience. Consequently, they were often more successful in obtaining the full-time permanent vacancies which arose. This had the effect, which was particularly acute in St Helens, of reducing other claimants' access to the 'better jobs'. It was regarded by the Employment Service and council development officer as contributing to the 'stickiness' of long-term unemployment which, although it had fallen by around one quarter in the year to January 1991, still affected four in ten of all claimants in St Helens.

In Brighton and Hove, Hammersmith and Fulham and Newport claimants' access to 'better jobs' was also limited through daily net in-flows to the area, with other job seekers attracted to the area for employment. Newport, for example, has an official Travel To Work Area of 95,000 people, extending high into the Valleys. Likewise, Brighton and Hove provide 40 per cent of the employment in East Sussex.

Partly because employees stayed in post so long, and because those with recent work experience were first in line for vacancies as they arose, the younger unemployed regularly had little or no work experience. An economic development officer in St Helens council said:

> half of the long-term unemployed have never had a proper job; they've been recycled through schemes.

This was a feature of all four labour markets. Employment Service staff in Hammersmith and St Helens said that it was often hard to know what to do with young claimants once they had been through the schemes and training that were on offer through the Employment Service. However, the problem was particularly pronounced in St Helens because of the shrinkage in the traditional sources of 'good jobs' and the difficulties in replacing them. The council had pioneered a business-oriented economic growth strategy, rather than an employment-growth strategy, so that the rate of job creation was not high. The work sought was conditioned by the perception that there were few jobs available. A careers and adult guidance counsellor said:

> there are not many jobs in St Helens. People have grown up with that. Some are prepared to do anything.

Employment Service training scheme take up was high in St Helens and Newport. However, the interviews with claimants in St Helens revealed a 'tiredness' with Employment Training, for instance, which stemmed from a belief that there were few jobs to 'step back' into, as much as a concern about the quality of the training on offer. This contrasted somewhat with claimants in Newport, some of whom were currently undergoing Employment Training. They believed that it was of benefit in acquiring basic learning and confidence skills, as well as City and Guilds qualifications. The 'stickiness' of long-term unemployment could reflect, in part, increasing opposition to being 'recycled' through government training programmes. Increasingly claimants were seeking 'real work' rather than 'stepping stones back into work'.

For this reason it seemed that St Helens' council's emphasis on self-employment as the only real alternative to long-term unemployment was unlikely to appeal to many claimants. The claimant interviews revealed concerns about the levels of risk involved, coupled with uncertain rewards. That said, one claimant had successfully begun a taxi cab business through the Enterprise Allowance Scheme and some said they would consider self-employment more seriously if they could be sure of commanding an adequate income during the initial stages.

'Openness to anything' was associated not only with those who had little or no work experience, but also those who were qualified or experienced in work that was no longer available.

An Employment Service Regional Director believed those made redundant from steel works and mining were prepared to search for other work following a decade in which they had accepted that the 'old' jobs were not going to return.

But this preparedness to search for other types of work was not unlimited. One interviewee in Newport, explaining his move down from the Valleys said:

there's nothing to do any more in the Valleys. The steel and mines are gone... all the male jobs. There are just a few units now paying £70-80 a week. That's OK for women as a second wage. But a man [with a family] can't live on that.

There was evidence of some concern – initially at least – among local Employment Service staff that redundant workers were not necessarily prepared to look for the type of work that was available in Newport. An advice worker said that an unemployed centre had been set up to assist those made redundant from Llanwern in the early 1980s, because claimants had been expected to actively seek work at that time. More recently, following the passage of the Act in 1989, actively seeking work provisions had been enforced vigorously in the case of redundant mineworkers. According to a representative of the South Wales NUM, the effect had been to drive men into the mineworkers' redundancy scheme because it exempted them from the requirement to seek work.

Brighton and Hove was a very different labour market. As one of the unemployment benefit office staff remarked:

Brighton has an image. It attracts people down...'Think of a sunny resort: Brighton!'... Brighton is a low pay blackspot, but people always think of it dripping with jobs. The sky is always blue and it must be booming. They think of getting away from the drudgery of signing on in Bolton or Manchester.

Many came to Brighton expecting to find work, but as the claimant interviews showed, the labour market competition was very intense. A planner in Brighton Council emphasised that:

the young people down from Wigan with a dog on a string, they're only one element of those searching.

There is a large daily in-flow, with few job prospects in the rest of East Sussex, and a large resident population who have chosen to live in Brighton. Together these elements created 'labour market congestion'.

It was matched by congestion in the housing market. Although the private rented sector was large, demand for housing was high, with people moving into the area for work finding that there was little or no live-in accommodation offered by employers such as hotels. Rents were expensive, as were house prices. Indeed Brighton had the largest house price/earnings 'affordability gap' in Britain.

The vicious circle of 'joblessness' and homelessness was a significant part of the labour market in Hammersmith and Fulham and Brighton and Hove. In both of these labour markets claimants described the difficulties in obtaining work without a permanent address: employers were loath to 'take a chance' with applicants without permanent accommodation and seekers had to overcome a number of practical difficulties in making themselves presentable for interviews. Employment Service staff normally took account of these problems in deciding what steps it was reasonable for claimants to take in seeking work. However there was evidence in Fulham that the signing procedures for claimants of no fixed abode were being tightened up. A proposal to require Personal Issue claimants to present themselves each day at Elephant and Castle DSS had resulted in strike action among DSS staff.

Another feature of the Brighton and Hove labour market worthy of mention was the large student population. They sought casual part-time and temporary posts during their studies. These were readily available. But when they had completed their studies they were keen to remain in Brighton, only to discover that there were few full-time permanent graduate posts on offer. They broadened their job search accordingly.

Travelling in search of work was less of a problem in Newport and St Helens, both being relatively self-contained. But Brighton and Hove stretched some miles along the south coast, while claimants in Hammersmith and Fulham were prepared to seek work throughout London. Claimants in Hammersmith and Fulham said that their search had been hampered by the lack of Employment Service assistance in meeting travel costs. In the early 1980s Brighton lost many of its manufacturing jobs located on industrial estates throughout the area. A council planner said that many claimants were now 'marooned' on outlying housing estates, expensive and intermittent bus connections making it very difficult for them to reach jobs concentrated in Brighton town centre.

Job search methods used

In all four labour markets informal search methods were regarded as the most effective in obtaining work. But it was rare for claimants to rely on informal methods alone.

Jobcentre use featured most heavily in St Helens. This was not due to a larger proportion of vacancies or good vacancies being registered there than with the other jobcentres studied, but because there were fewer search channel options. For example, there were very few private employment agencies. Those that existed catered for a narrow range of occupations. In Newport claimants regularly used the jobcentre in conjunction with the local newspaper, *The Argus*. As in Brighton (which also had an *Argus*) claimants felt that they would be able to 'cover' all the vacancies in the locality by visiting the jobcentre and buying the newspaper on the 'jobs day'.

But claimants' perception of jobcentres was far more negative in the two south eastern labour markets than in St Helens and Newport. This was due in part to the chronic under-resourcing of the Employment Service in the south east. An interviewee at Fulham jobcentre said:

> the quality of work and the service to claimants is particularly bad in London, reflecting high staff turnover.

Morale was very low:

> up North ours are seen as good jobs. Down here it's like working for McDonald's.

But resources were just as overstretched in Brighton and Hove. An interviewee at Hove unemployment benefit office said that they had lost a number of staff in the course of the year, but that, although they disputed the calculation of staffing levels with the Employment Service Area Office, they had overshot their yearly budget, so that they would only receive extra staff if their placement ratios improved.

In both of the south eastern labour markets overstretched resources had led to the early closing of jobcentres and a more rapid rundown in services to non-claimants than was the case in St Helens or Newport.

The Employment Service Regional Director for the south east said that most of the difficulties related to inner city areas where there were 'one to one' difficulties with clients, and to long-term unemployment. The nature of these clients' problems involved heavy resource commitments, for example through inner city job teams geared to matching claimants to jobs. These difficulties had been compounded by the flow of newly redundant professionals on to the claimant register: because the sectors they had worked in were suffering from the recession they needed intensive counselling assistance in finding work.

The differing attitudes to jobcentres as search channels also related to claimants' experiences of claiming benefit. Whereas new claims were taken at the unemployment benefit offices in St Helens and Newport, they were taken at jobcentres in Hammersmith and Brighton. It meant that in these cases the jobcentres were associated with the 'hassle' of claiming. All new claims, restart and counsellor interviews in St Helens took place in the unemployment benefit offices. Because claimants did not associate the St Helens jobcentre with the pressures of claiming benefit they were more positive about using it. A receptionist at the jobcentre estimated that half of the people he saw were non-claimants – however, this was likely to change with the jobcentre's relocation away from the main shopping arcade.

At the same time there was evidence that the new claims process was more disconcerting for claimants in the south eastern labour markets. It was in these areas that claimants reported feeling 'intimidated', whereas in St Helens and Newport claimants laid emphasis on their embarrassment in claiming. Only in the south eastern areas did claimants report difficulties in registering their claims. Comments such as:

> they would rather give you a job there and then than your benefit

typically expressed concern that benefit was being denied.

Local Employment Service staff confirmed that they collected statistics on those who had visited but not claimed benefit: they were called 'non-pursuals'.

Because feelings of 'intimidation' were more prevalent in the south east, and because in the labour markets studied claiming was associated with jobcentres as well as benefit offices, claimants did not like using jobcentres for job search. However they remained popular with non-claimants in search of part-time and temporary employment.

Those able to use agencies in St Helens, such as those seeking work in the transport sector, had very negative attitudes towards them. They were regarded as 'exploitative' in the wages they offered and the commission they took. By contrast they featured strongly in Brighton and Hove and Hammersmith and Fulham. The manager at the Office Angels recruitment consultancy estimated that only one in forty or fifty of her registered clients stated that they also used the jobcentre. Although many of their clients were currently in work or unemployed non-claimants, she had noticed an increase in their use by claimant groups such as redundant white collar workers. As with other private employment agencies in London, those in

Hammersmith and Fulham dealt with a wide range of occupations sought after by claimants.

Plenty of jobs in London?

On the basis of research conducted in 1988 the Government expressed particular concern about the job seeking activities of Londoners. In a White Paper (*Employment in the 1990s*, HMSO, 1988) which foreshadowed proposals which were to become the 1989 Act, it stated:

> unemployment in London could be considerably reduced and many vacancies filled if unemployed people looked more intensively and more effectively.

This view is refuted strongly by the research in Hammersmith and Fulham. The interviews with claimants revealed strenuous job search efforts akin to those in the other labour markets (this was also confirmed in research conducted by the council's Economic Development Unit in 1989). Jobcentre vacancy turnover rates matched those in the other labour markets studied. Counsellors had informed some of the claimants interviewed that they were unlikely to obtain work that they preferred because labour demand was so low. And, as in the other markets assessed, success in obtaining employment could not be reduced to the 'effectiveness' of job search. Claimants with good job search techniques – particularly longer-term claimants – regularly lost out in competition with seekers offering recent work experience or qualifications.

Awareness of and attitudes towards actively seeking work

Awareness of the requirement to seek work was vague in all four labour markets. However, its practical significance varied between areas.

In St Helens most claimants were explicitly told that they were expected to seek work and that their benefit could be threatened if they did not. In Newport, on the other hand, although claimants knew that they were expected to seek work, there was little awareness of what could happen to benefit if the claimant did not look regularly.

In Brighton and Hove younger claimants and students were more aware of the Employment Service's expectations than older claimants and those who had been unemployed for some time. Targeting of the requirement was also apparent in Hammersmith and Fulham, where students, new claimants and women returners had all experienced pressures to seek work.

In St Helens there was strong resentment at the prospect of losing benefit for failing to seek work, especially those seeking family wages. One claimant said that it was:

> all very well suspending benefit and expecting people to change... but there's no work there... [so you] can't go out and pick a job out of thin air.

It led to the belief that the regulations could in no way be used to assist claimants in their search, and that their only purpose could be punitive. In practice, although they were informed of the requirement to seek work, they were rarely asked for proof. And yet, according to the employer interviews in St Helens, the provisions had had a striking impact on claimants' search, at least early on, with claimants requesting search proof from employers, and seeing people they would not normally have expected to see. St Helens illustrates how the provisions have had some impact on search behaviour, even though the claimants were only told of their obligations, with no further action being taken.

In Newport the strong antipathy to the requirements was largely confined to men. They referred to being 'messed about' by requirements which could not help them find work and were not inclined to keep proof of their job search. However, they were safe in the knowledge that the local Employment Service staff did not request it. They felt that the local Employment Service staff did not like enforcing the provisions; some cited friends who had been claiming for some time without having to prove their search for work. That staff appeared to be 'going through the motions' was not considered surprising in view of the small number of vacancies locally available. Despite this, most of the women claiming had kept job search records.

Jobsearch checking was much more evident in Hammersmith and Fulham, with some claimants being asked for proof regularly by Signing Clerks. There was also evidence of warning letters being issued shortly after the Act's introduction. Since then claimants perceived the threat to benefit to have diminished because of Employment Service staffing and resource problems. This was also the case in Brighton and Hove. In the two south eastern areas the only discernible impact that the regulations had had on claimants' activity was their ability to procure and manufacture job search proof in order to fulfil the eligibility requirements. There had been no discernible impact on claimants' job search patterns.

The regulations were not generally needed to ensure that claimants broadened their job search. Those with debt problems, including students and itinerants in the south eastern areas, needed no other impetus than financial necessity. An advice worker in Brighton said that those in couples could not rely on a sole earner:

> both need to work... There is tactical stuff on who should claim. These things are much more important than actively seeking work when it comes to decisions about work.

The 21-hour rule

Since the late 1970s claimants have been able to receive benefit while studying for less than 21 hours per week, provided they remained available for and capable of full-time work.

In St Helens the introduction of the actively seeking work provisions has had no effect on the '21-hour' claimants. However it was a major concern in Hammersmith and Fulham where the council's Economic Development Unit regarded the provisions as:

> effectively discouraging unemployed people from taking up educational courses to improve their job prospects (paper for consideration by the Planning and Economic Development Committee, 3rd July 1990).

The development unit staff were concerned at the 'increased pressure' to leave studies faced by 1,000 students on concessionary fees at the Hammersmith and West

London College. They included participants in 20 adult course programmes for claimants studying under the 21 hour rule. These included Access courses (return to learning courses, office skills) and English as a second language courses. There was

> clear evidence in local colleges to suggest that the fear of losing benefit and the pressure exerted by the Employment Service is leading to marked reductions in enrolments (ibid).

There was concern that many were transferring to Employment Training merely to satisfy the requirement to seek work. The unit had also recorded cases of claimants being required to leave their courses for work that they regarded as wholly unsuitable (even though claimants can only be expected to leave their studies for 'suitable' vacancies (IS Gen Regs. reg. 9(1)(c))).

In addition, the local Employment Service were interpreting the requirement to seek work in such a way as to prevent claimants taking advantage of Department of Environment funded vocationally oriented training and non-college based construction industry training. This was because the regulations require training to be institution-based, and to involve training rather than retraining. The development unit feared that claimants participating in estate-based training courses, and those such as women returners undergoing retraining, could be subject to benefit loss if they did not leave the course. The council was pushing for the 21-hour rule to be amended to allow claimants to engage in such training as a restart 'positive option'.

Threats to benefit had resulted in local colleges setting up job markets to assist claimants in seeking work, and the appointment of tutors with special responsibility for claimants' job search. Such developments had not taken place in the other labour markets, although adult training providers said that their students had been expected to provide timetables detailing their course activity and the times in which they intended to search for work.

Clearly, regulations requiring claimants to take those steps which offered the best prospects of obtaining job offers, which in practice discourage claimants from pursuing courses which they regard as an essential part in moving back into work, need to be reconsidered.

Looking for workers

Jobcentre use

Jobcentres were quite widely used in all four labour markets but the precise extent to which they were used and what employers expected from them varied between regions.

Employers perceived Newport to be an area of historically high unemployment. They did not regard the unemployed as 'untouchable'. Indeed many welcomed the recent growth in the unemployment pool, believing that it would improve the quality of applicants. At the Hilton National, Newport, there had been 37 applicants for one full-time maintenance worker and one part-time chambermaid. Such large jobcentre responses meant that employers did not need to resort to costly recruitment methods such as newspapers.

A similar attitude to the unemployed was expressed by employers in St Helens. The widespread use of seasonal contracts (in the pharmaceuticals, waste management and bakeries sectors for instance) and probationary contracts for factory process and clerical work meant that employers relied heavily on the unemployed for recruitment. The majority of those already in work were not prepared to jeopardise existing permanent contracts.

However, employers using jobcentres felt that they would not miss them because, in the first place, it was a close-knit town where informal networks allowed employers to reach those seeking work. In the second place, labour demand was low in the town due to labour reductions and redeployment among the primary manufacturers and lower labour turnover, workers being content to 'sit tight'. So employers frequently relied solely on internal and speculative applicants. In fact, Surefil Packaging, Wiseacre Engineering, Smith Kline Beecham and Fred Davies (Storage) had all been inundated with applicants following jobcentre notification of a vacancy. This proved a positive disincentive to using jobcentres.

The jobcentre in Brighton had a particularly poor image with employers. It was associated with itinerants, those 'not prepared to make an effort', and with low paying temporary and seasonal work. The Personnel Manager at the Grand Hotel said:

> if I had to rely on the jobcentre I'd have no staff.

And yet the jobcentre was used extensively by employers. In sectors such as hotels and catering, retailing and private nursing homes, vacancies with high labour turnover (such as cashiers and hotel service staff) were on 'continual placement' with the jobcentre. In addition firms such as British Telecom PLC used it for technical and supervisory grades, often in conjunction with the local *Argus* newspaper, in the belief that these were the two channels most frequently used by job seekers. Part of the reason for this seeming discrepancy between employers' thoughts and actions lies in a comment from a Brighton jobcentre staff member who said:

> employers use us because they don't have to pay. They are prepared to spend the time interviewing unscreened candidates.

This was borne out by Eaton Gardens Nursing Home and the hotel personnel managers interviewed who, because the number of jobcentre applicants was usually high, were able to find suitable people.

Brighton and Hove had experienced a very dramatic shift in labour demand during 1990. During 1989 Brighton council's Leisure and Recreation Department, for example, had had to run a concerted recruitment campaign which had included British Rail posters and newspaper advertisements throughout the country in order to recruit staff. Employers had had low response rates to newspaper advertisements, and had relied upon employment agencies and taking temporary staff as permanents in order to fill vacancies. That had changed dramatically, so that American Express, for example, had only 1 per cent of their job stock vacant in November 1990, yet were receiving 3-400 speculative applications per week. The Hospitality Inn reported 15-20 speculative visits per day mostly from the unemployed. The ability to rely on speculative applications had resulted in a fall in jobcentre notifications and press advertisements.

Brighton and Hove illustrate how dramatically jobcentre usage can alter with labour market conditions.

In Hammersmith and Fulham a variety of recruitment methods were popular with employers (free newspapers, council 'contact points' for council posts, 'bussing in' staff) so that jobcentres had only a marginal role.

Recruitment consultants played a more central role than in the other labour markets. Employers depended heavily on agencies' screening techniques, because they were the most risk-averse of the employers interviewed. In consequence those vacancies notified to the jobcentre were largely part-time, temporary and seasonal. Despite the promotion of progressive employment policies and equal opportunities elsewhere, the council – one of the largest employers in the area – frequently placed part-time and seasonal posts with the jobcentres but not their full-time and permanent equivalents.

The local economy in Hammersmith and Fulham was dominated by smaller businesses. The council's Economic Development Unit said:

> when we talk to small employers they want a simple, cheap means to recruit.

It was not quite so simple, with some small firms such as Claxton Laundries being almost totally reliant on them, while others in search of more highly skilled labour, such as W J Marston's financial department, were wholly ignorant of their whereabouts, depending instead on private agencies.

The belief in the south eastern labour markets that there were 'jobs to be had' made employers very wary of the long-term unemployed. This in turn influenced their propensity to use jobcentres for full-time permanent posts which claimants were normally in search of. However, in each of the labour markets, jobcentres were also considered important in reaching those seeking part-time and casual employment – namely students and women.

This had been the case for some time in the south eastern labour markets. Securicor Cleaning (recruiting in Brighton for Sussex and Surrey), for instance, took most of their part-time cleaners through jobcentres. The personnel officer there considered the recent spate of jobcentre closures and mergers to be 'criminal', forcing them to consider newspapers and agencies. In Newport, however, attracting women returners was considered a more recent development. Some such as Avana Bakeries had used jobcentres for this purpose for some time, but others were considering using jobcentres for this purpose for the first time. TSB Insurance were going to advertise telephonists' posts there; the Great British Burger wanted 'midday fillers' while Compton Sons and Webb believed they could attract more women returners for full-time sewing machinists posts.

Some of this interest in women returners was occasioned by concerns at reductions in the number and quality of young people seeking work. This had resulted in the discontinuation of YTs by some employers. It was a much bigger issue in Newport than in the other labour markets.

It was in Brighton and Hove that employers had experienced the greatest difficulties with jobcentre applicants. There was concern at the quality of applicants supplied. Two employers had complained to jobcentre staff that they had frequently received wholly unsuitable applicants. Nevertheless, they tended to sympathise with the task of jobcentre staff rather than blaming them for failing to screen sufficiently. When complaints had been lodged by employers jobcentre staff had responded positively. Despite the difficulties suitable applicants could normally be found among the large numbers applying – except in skill shortage areas such as nursing and cookery, where some reported having to take candidates who were not totally suitable.

A key problem, reported by nearly all the employers in Brighton and Hove, was the failure of applicants to turn up for interviews. Although the council's Tourism Department and a large high street retailer had tackled the problem through letter or telephone contact prior to interview, most tended to accept poor attendance rates. Hotels associated non-attendance with jobcentre candidates whereas the Hospitals Unit said that the problem was with jobchangers, jobcentre applicants having a good idea about what the vacancy entailed from the jobcentre.

In Hammersmith and Fulham employers' greatest concern was that some jobcentre applicants were being 'forced to attend'. Those like Novotel, who had introduced the requirement to fill an application form, and were introducing pre-interview screening sessions, were confident that they would be able to 'weed out' unwilling candidates.

Rather than facing difficulties in persuading jobcentre candidates to turn up, as was the case in the south eastern regions, employers in St Helens had problems fielding the numbers who applied. Being inundated with applicants was a major factor in dissuading employers from using the jobcentre.

In terms of the actual applications made by jobcentre candidates, employers in Brighton and Hove regarded them as generally poor, often encouraging jobcentre applicants to fill the forms at the interview. A manager at Rentokil Group suggested that jobcentre applicants were less motivated than speculative applicants who, he felt, were 'better quality'. In contrast St Helens employers were largely impressed by the amount of preparation jobcentre applicants had put in. A personnel officer at British Gas PLC, for example, felt that jobclub applications were 'very well presented. They have obviously had a lot of good guidance.'

Attitudes to the Employment Service

By and large employers were familiar with the service offered at their local jobcentres. The exceptions were in Hammersmith and Fulham where some employers did not know where their local jobcentre was, or what services it offered them. They tended to blame the Employment Service for their ignorance, believing that it was up to jobcentre staff to 'sell themselves' to employers.

This poor employer liaison is largely the result of overstretched local resources. A member of staff at Fulham jobcentre said:

local labour market information was the flavour of the month. We had visits to employers... but we have done none since the beginning of the year, since staff losses. Yet they are essential in keeping good relations with employers.

Some employers in Brighton had sought to build up a rapport with the jobcentre but had been frustrated by high levels of staff turnover in the jobcentre and the sporadic nature of the interest shown in them. The closest relationship was with a high street supermarket near to the jobcentre: the Personnel Manager had spent some time visiting the jobcentre to discuss job specifications and the procedures for submitting candidates to interview. Employers found that they needed to make quite an effort to get the most out of their jobcentre.

It is likely that the priority given to employer relations is largely determined by the call on resources from other quarters. In St Helens, where the jobcentre was not engaged in counsellor interviews, the thrust of their work was related to job placement, rather than benefit checking. Perhaps because of this employers in St Helens had found the jobcentre generally efficient and helpful.

Newport and Risca jobcentres had provided premises for local employers to carry out recruitment interviews. This had proved very beneficial to TSB Insurance when they had relocated to Newport and to Avana Bakeries in recruiting seasonal temporary staff.

Actively seeking work

Employers' awareness of the actively seeking work provisions was extremely limited in the south eastern labour markets. There was some aversion to knowing anything by some who felt that social security regulations were not the proper concern of employers, but of the government agencies who had to 'deal' with the unemployed.

In Newport awareness was largely confined to those who were advising staff on redundancy matters. There was evidence that the Employment Service locally were more concerned not to upset employers by sending unsuitable candidates than they were in enforcing the requirement to seek work. The Manager of the Great British Burger Restaurant, which was very close to the jobcentre, said:

> if they were putting the frighteners on at the jobcentre this is the first place they would come. They haven't come.

The situation was different in St Helens, where employers were very aware of the provisions. They had been asked by applicants to provide proof of their job search; they had noticed a substantial increase in the number of jobclub applications, and identified the timing of speculative applications from the unemployed, and their subsequent falling away, as related to the requirement to seek work rather than rising unemployment. Indeed the rates of speculative applications and trends in unemployment had cut in different directions.

There were variations in the extent to which Employment Service staff contacted employers to check on claimants' interview attendance. In Brighton and Hove and St Helens jobcentres did not check on claimants' attendance, although they did check on whether vacancies had been filled and by whom – information necessary to update their vacancy listings and record 'positive outcomes' by successful claimants. In

Hammersmith and Fulham interview attendance was checked, suggesting that the Employment Service was taking some action to enforce the requirement to seek work.

Employers in the south eastern labour markets had perceived no impact on the quality or quantity of applicants. Those in Newport had not noticed a fall in the quality of applicants which would have been consistent with claimants 'going through the motions' to satisfy the provisions. On the contrary, they felt the quality of applicants had improved with rising unemployment.

There were no regional variations in employers' attitudes to the requirement to seek work. In St Helens, the only region in which employers were aware that claimants were expected to seek work, most felt that the expectation was reasonable, but that proving that search was unfair, relying as they thought it did, on employers' willingness to furnish evidence.

Attitudes to taking work

The major factors affecting claimants' attitudes to taking work varied little between regions. The findings in Chapters 8 and 10 concerning claimants' aspirations; their flexibility in taking work; and the awareness and impact of the legislative changes, were applicable in all four labour markets.

There were differences which this section points to, but they should not be over-emphasised. The most obvious differences related to treatment by, and attitudes towards the local Employment Service, and the special features of local labour markets (some of which have already been covered in the section on seeking work in this chapter).

Pay flexibility

In all four labour markets there were no serious problems with claimants' excessive wage expectations. Staff at Hammersmith unemployment benefit office and Fulham jobcentre agreed that 'there's a high take up of low paid jobs in this area'.

The Member of Parliament for Newport West, Paul Flynn, drawing on the contacts he had with constituents through surgeries, pointed to a 'culture in the area', wherein wage expectations had been driven down by rising unemployment in the 1980s. Claimants in our sample showed a strong willingness to take work at the pay rates locally available. One claimant had taken a £60 per week wage cut when moving from night work to day shifts, while another had returned to his last job following completion of Employment Training, despite a substantial wage reduction, out of 'desperation'.

For the jobcentre in St Helens pay expectations were 'a sore point'. But:

> it's more a problem of the pay on offer – £1.85 an hour for a security guard, you can get that, although the majority are £2 - £3 an hour.

An adult guidance counsellor wondered if it was 'a Merseyside thing':

> the complaint isn't that work is below them but that the wage is too low.

Despite this, there had been no benefit penalties for refusals of employment or restricting availability on the grounds of pay in St Helens since the introduction of the Act.

Claimants in Brighton and Hove emphasised the importance of being able to cover their housing costs and meeting debts they had incurred through homelessness, personal difficulties or college. But for the majority this meant taking work as a 'stop gap', rather than refusing it in the hope that something better would come along. Wage flexibility featured strongly among those who had arrived in Brighton and Hove from other parts of the country. A staff member at Brighton jobcentre referred to:

> ruck sack people, so desperate that they are prepared to work for relatively low wages... [Although they are] initially staggered at the low wages, the dreadful thing is that they accept it after a while.

This influx was one factor in keeping local wage rates below those offered for similar work in the environs, such as Horsham and Crawley.

Employment Service advice on taking work offering pay rates that were low relative to previous earnings and benefits was limited in all four labour markets, partly because mechanisms for reviewing claimants' expectations after the expiry of their permitted periods were not in place.

Widespread hostility to in-work benefits by claimants in Hammersmith and Fulham meant that counsellors tended to confine their assistance on pay to altering claimants' excessive wage expectations on initial claim forms. It helped them avoid restricting their availability and thus losing benefit.

In St Helens and Newport there were fewer objections in principle to in-work benefits. Instead criticisms of family credit, for instance, centred on how little it helped. Claimant Advisers in St Helens had access to hand-held computers enabling the calculation of possible entitlement. Those who had taken work with wages topped up by family credit said it had done little to raise their net incomes because gains were offset by losses in housing benefit. One St Helens claimant with a wife and four children had received little family credit because his net earnings were pushed up by overtime hours – he felt penalised for working long hours:

> I was doing 60 hours a week, over, and taking home £90..I used to get family credit but it was a waste of time. £3 odd a week, working 60 hours. Six of us in the family.

Because the expected gains were so small, top-ups did not feature in claimants' decisions to take work. In fact, some had not taken work despite family credit eligibility because it did not compensate for the extra costs of moving into work.

Similarly in Newport family credit was not felt to be 'worth the effort'. But one or two claimants who had been interested in in-work benefit assistance said that they had had to pursue Employment Service staff for it. Between July and September 1990 only 278 claimants were given advice about in-work benefits in Newport, whereas there had been 4,875 interviews attended for new claims, restart and other counsellor interviews.

Government agencies and the council's economic development department in Newport suggested that a 'culture of not working' had arisen due to redundancy pay offs in the early 1980s. In addition, research conducted by the Training Agency Intelligence Unit in Wales (*Valleys Skills*, 1990, part of the Valleys Programme) suggested that occupational expectations were:

> realistic in the light of previous occupations but whether they matched current demand is questionable.

Although the Valleys Initiative did not cover Newport itself, it had implications for the types of people who would be seeking work there.

The interviews with employers and claimants suggest that claimants were more flexible than the Training Agency research and government agencies believed. One interviewee expected to be made redundant from his printing job in two weeks time. He typified interviewees' attitudes when he said:

> I'll do my best not to [leave printing] but if I run out of time and it's 13 weeks – which I didn't know anything about until I come here... I want to keep on printing but if there are no jobs about then I'm gonna have to do something else obviously.

In contrast to the view that workers made redundant from heavy manufacturing and mining industries were less willing to take other work available, the bulk of the evidence from the local labour markets suggests that workers accepted that the jobs they had prized so highly were not going to return. A welder in St Helens said:

> there's no point wishing to go back to welding because there's nothing to go back to.

This applied to older and younger workers alike. A NUPE representative for manual workers, referring to caretaking, said:

> they often come off the dole and are often older workers. Around here they have come from steel and mining... There aren't a massive number of people who have made careers in caretaking or portering.

A recent report (*Training and Education: The Experience and Needs of Redundant Miners at Cynheidre and Betws Collieries in South Wales*, C. Trotman and T. Lewis) found that the average age of miners made redundant between October 1989 and January 1990 was 34. They discovered that:

> a large proportion of redundant mineworkers interviewed are now in low paid, non-unionised employment... men working outside their craft, on low pay and on training found and paid for by themselves.

The problem for young redundant workers in the Valleys was not the 'culture of not working' so much as the problems of transition to other work without adequate retraining structures. As the report concludes:

> in an industry where skills are specific, the policy or reemployment can't be successful without priority to training.

For older redundant workers the difficulties in obtaining new work were compounded by employer attitudes. This was most marked in St Helens where large scale redundancies were most prevalent (the majority of those in Newport having occurred in the early to mid 1980s). A receptionist at an unemployment benefit office there said that those made redundant in their late 50s were:

unlikely to get new work if they have been working in the glass industry all their lives.

The employer interviews confirmed that they were concerned that older workers would not settle to new work where terms and conditions were poorer, or where they were expected to take work of lower status alongside much younger people.

In Hammersmith and Fulham Economic Development Unit the concern was that, with the loss of large numbers of engineering jobs, skill degradation was occurring. Workers from the GEC Valve factory which had closed were 'all going to be waitresses and goodness knows what'.

For claimants in general, occupational flexibility was more deeply ingrained in Newport, than in Hammersmith and Fulham for instance, because – as was the case in St Helens – so many claimants had little or no work experience, had been 'recycled' through government training schemes and were eager to take work whatever it entailed. In addition, claimants in Newport and St Helens in particular were used to responding flexibly because the work on offer was frequently of a temporary nature, and because their working lives had been frequently interrupted by lay offs and redundancies.

Whereas in St Helens and Newport certain groups of workers experienced obstacles to obtaining work in new occupations (with employer objections to older workers, or poor retraining facilities) in Brighton and Hove there was a more general feeling that being occupationally flexible was not a great advantage in obtaining work. Because labour market competition was very strong claimants believed that inexperience and long-term unemployment were frequently insurmountable obstacles.

One claimant in Brighton described the stigma of long-term unemployment:

[employers] look at you and think there is some sort of problem there, rather than..you just haven't been able to find work... Somebody who's unemployed has got a problem, and they might be taking that problem on board.

Graduates in particular felt difficulties competing with more experienced candidates – even for non-graduate posts. One said she had tried to get waitressing work through the jobcentre but that employers had informed her she was not experienced enough. She said:

I can see the employers' point, but how do you get experience if no-one's going to give me the opportunity.

Travel restrictions

Travel restrictions were an important issue in Hammersmith and Fulham. According to the Regional Director for the Employment Service in London and the South East:

people do have a restricted view of moving to work and their preparedness to travel on public transport, even in London... By far the most important restriction relates to travel to work... People are remarkably immobile.

However, although one claimant had been warned that her benefit could be affected if she persisted in objecting to travel of one hour each way per day, most were content to travel for this amount of time, provided the costs incurred were met. One claimant said:

> it must cover the costs of going to work otherwise you are getting less in the end [than if you were on benefit].

The position was similar in Newport, although the council's economic development department pointed out that, because claimants were used to taking work in the city, they were loath to consider the work that was available in the Valleys. Securicor said that they found it slightly more difficult to fill posts based on sites outside Newport, but this was largely the result of poor off-peak public transport facilities, rather than claimant inflexibility.

In all four labour markets there was an acceptance of the need to move to 'wherever the work is'. But it was most marked in St Helens: there appeared to be little attachment to the town, most agreeing with one claimant who said it was:

> a dump... There's nothing here is there? It's a dump, St Helens, let's face it.

So they were prepared to leave permanently if they were offered suitable work.

Short-term work

Whereas many claimants in Brighton and Hove, Newport and St Helens accepted that they had to take fixed-term and other forms of temporary employment, because it was frequently all that was available, those in Hammersmith and Fulham were more wary of trying to move between temporary work and benefits because they feared difficulties in reestablishing their claims to benefit. One interviewee currently in employment said signing on for benefit occasionally was

> too complicated... [it's] fruitless for a week or so. I'd be waiting 4-5 months for money, if I'm allowed the money, so I don't bother... Work is uncertain so I often rely on selling a jumper here and there or what have you.

A staff member at the Hammersmith unemployment benefit office said that:

> living week to week on benefit deters job takeup because they have to wait a month for a wage... They ought to have something to tide them over. They used to get something from DSS but they don't any longer.

Attitudes to Employment Service advice on jobs and schemes

Claimants in Hammersmith and Fulham had felt the most pressure to take work or other 'positive options'. It was exerted at restart, not before. Restart Counsellors were regarded as 'insensitive' to what claimants wanted, 'dictating what you can and can't do'.

218

One claimant who was certain as to what she wanted said:

> they would have pushed me on to any job really [if I hadn't been sure], just to keep their [unemployment] figures down.

Another, who said that 'they are determined to make sure that you end up with a job' described how she had lowered her occupational expectations once the jobcentre had told her that she ought to consider work outside her fashion and design qualification because they were rarely notified of such vacancies. She felt that her agreement to take clerical work, which she had done in the past as a 'stop gap', was due to counsellors' pressure.

The staff member interviewed at the Fulham jobcentre had taken her current post following a restart interview:

> that's how we get casuals, at restart. And that's how I got my job. They said 'we happen to have a job here'.

Although some claimants said that they had taken work they did not really want their decisions were not associated with the penalties related to refusing employment opportunities, of which they were largely ignorant.

Still, job suggestions were rare. One claimant joked that counsellors only ever asked claimants to take specific jobs in 'cuckooland'.

On the whole offers at restart involved Employment Training, jobclub and Enterprise Allowance. A staff member at Hammersmith unemployment benefit office said that:

> if you refuse them all they get you on refusing suitable training... We can do it... There's no way you can't take up anything unless you sign off.

Those who did refuse all 'options' were 'continually hassled'. The claimants who had taken Employment Training had done so in the belief that their benefit would have been threatened otherwise.

Employment Training was also 'sold' actively by the Employment Service in Brighton and Hove. As was the case in Hammersmith and Fulham, there was evidence from advice agencies that their volunteers had left following pressure to join Employment Training schemes. Although none of the claimants interviewed had felt any pressure to join Employment Training or move into work they did not want, Brighton Unemployed Workers Centre and Brighton Advice cited a number of cases they were aware of. The Unemployed Centre had run a campaign against the 'creeping compulsion' it associated with Employment Training, which had begun with its introduction in 1988. Claimants interviewed in Brighton and Hove were not interested in ET because they did not think that it would be a 'stepping stone' back into work. The unemployment benefit office had been 'selling it hard' to 'special groups' in the past according to the staff interviewed there, but reductions in ET resources meant that would no longer be possible.

The picture was more mixed in Newport. One claimant said that he had been explicitly informed that, if he refused all the 'options' available, then his benefit would be stopped and that he had taken up ET because:

I was nominated by the dole office. If I didn't go on it my money would stop. The lady actually told me.

But others who had joined ET as one of the 'special' groups well before six months registered unemployment were far more positive about the scheme and had felt no pressure to join. Two women returners had taken it for confidence building and City and Guilds qualifications while a dyslexic was hoping to return to it for basic learning skills.

The majority of claimants were neither wholly committed to ET nor explicitly informed that refusal would result in benefit penalties. For most the mix of counselling and benefit checking created confusion. This was apparent in the comments of an older claimant in Newport which depicts the fine line counsellors have to tread between counselling and persuasion:

> in the [restart] interview she said 'well, you've got to take something'. I said 'you told me it was voluntary and the other lady told me it was voluntary'. She said 'yes, it is'. I said 'so what are you saying, if I don't like it you're going to stop my dole?'... She said 'no'. I said, 'well, that's what it sounds like'. She said 'no'. It went on like that and in the end I said 'put me down for it'. She said 'oh, that's no good to us', and then she terminated [the interview]...

According to Newport Employment Service statistics, 30 per cent of referrals to ET in the six months between April and September 1990 came from Restart Counsellors; 24 per cent from New Claims Advisers; 9 per cent from Client Advisers; and 23 per cent during the course of other jobcentre work. Overall, only 34 per cent of referrals had led to ET starts. But the highest start rate was achieved through straight jobcentre referrals (40 per cent), compared to only 28 per cent from Restart Counsellors. This appears to confirm that claimants are liable to react against the pressure they feel exerted on them through restart.

Employment Service 'pressure' was least visible in St Helens. Nobody could recall being offered jobs by counsellors. However, when counsellors informed claimants that the jobs they wanted were not available through the jobcentre, this advice was usually supplemented with suggestions about what other search channels to use, in contrast to Hammersmith and Fulham where other, less desirable jobcentre vacancies were suggested.

Although none could recall direct job suggestions by counsellors, 80 per cent of St Helens' vacancies (which were displayed in the jobcentre and unemployment benefit offices) were filled by unemployed claimants. The proportion in Newport was 75 per cent.

With a greater proportion of its claimants long-term unemployed than in the other three labour markets, there was, as the St Helens unemployment benefit office staff interviewee said, 'a lot of activity around ET and EAS'. However, whereas those who had not felt 'pressured' were confined to the very long-term unemployed and those on the fringes of sickness and invalidity in Hammersmith and Fulham, others in St Helens, such as men seeking a 'family wage', said that the 'positive options' had been presented to them as options, not as obligatory or compulsory.

Claimants in St Helens expressed similar views to other claimants interviewed as to the Employment Service's intentions in offering ET. They said that it was 'to change the [unemployment] figures'; to 'make work for themselves and keep 'em in a job'. One commented:

> to me it's just something to get you off their figures when they stick 'em on the telly and they say unemployment's gone down by x amount... It's a big swindle for the unemployment figures because people are on different schemes and all that.

So some had refused ET, but they had felt able to do so because there ·vas no imminent threat to their benefit in doing so. Disillusionment with gove nment training schemes meant that take-up was likely to fall from traditionally high levels. One claimant commented:

> they've pushed me like, you know, and then they've just relaxed, 'cos they know I've done like what they've said, been on ET schemes and things, so now they've relaxed 'em for a few months. And then they'll start again sort of thing but I'll not take it this time.

This attitude is reflected in local Employment Service figures. Although there was a 40 per cent start rate on referrals to ET from all sources between April and December 1990, the 1,921 restart interviews in the three months to December 1990 produced only 99 ET starts (along with 1 EAS start, 6 restart course starts, 80 jobclub starts and 5 job starts).

DSS and Employment Service

Claimants frequently confused the DSS, which they called 'the social', and the Employment Service – 'the dole', in discussion about government agencies' intentions and the experience of claiming. This was particularly noticeable in St Helens.

It meant that attitudes towards using jobcentres and claimants' understanding of Employment Service objectives were sometimes influenced by their experiences with the local DSS. For example, negative feelings about the Employment Service's refusal to assist with travelling costs were sometimes confused with social fund claims. More fundamentally, it is possible that attempts by the Employment Service to provide helpful guidance and counselling has been compromised on occasions by claimants' failure to differentiate between the two agencies.

Employing the unemployed

Employers' recruitment decisions, and their awareness of and attitudes towards the legislation covering refusal of employment and restricted availability were very similar in all four labour markets.

Demands for labour were primarily determined by employers' size, activity, sector (manufacturing, services, financial, construction), and ownership (public or private). Location was not an important determinant so that, for example, large hotels' recruitment practices in each of the labour markets had far more in common than they did differences.

The regional differences that were apparent related almost exclusively to labour market circumstances.

Pay and recruitment

Pay levels and pay policies were used by employers as recruitment and retention tools. The problems faced by employers in each region differed. Downward wage flexibility was least feasible in Brighton and Hove and Hammersmith and Fulham.

In Brighton and Hove, although employers did not find it hard to attract applicants, it was difficult to attract 'the right sort of people'. In order to do this local wage rates varied considerably. For example Securicor Cleaning offered a range of hourly rates to their part-time cleaners, depending upon precisely where in Sussex they worked. Wage reductions in Brighton and Hove were not practicable given the already low level of wages in the city and intense competition among employers to recruit.

Brighton and Hove's employers were also experiencing major problems in retaining staff. According to Brighton jobcentre some were paying just enough to recruit staff but not to retain them:

> if people are willing to accept a wage that's what they employer will offer. Some pay the minimum to recruit and wonder why turnover is so high. They have no concept of the costs of staff turnover.

There were those who, because they were party to nationally agreed rates, were limited in their ability to use pay to alleviate recruitment and retention problems. Employers like the Hospitals Unit would have welcomed the opportunity to raise rates but were unable to do so. Others, who had full control over their pay scales had found that raising pay rates had had little effect on high turnover levels. Eaton Gardens Nursing Home were recruiting 'unsuitable' workers despite raising pay rates to fend off 'poachers'. The owner said:

> it's a good place for a nursing home, but bad for staff.

Recruitment and retention problems were also prevalent in Hammersmith and Fulham. However, with the exception of emerging recruitment difficulties in the hotels sector and between those seeking women for part-time employment, these labour market pressures were largely absent in Newport and St Helens. According to St Helens Economic Development Officer:

> nobody has difficulties recruiting or retaining staff. Turnover is very low according to a survey of 8-900 companies we have undertaken – except in management.

This was confirmed by the employer interviews: Yorkshire Bank and Smith Kline Beecham's, for example, said that staff only left voluntarily for maternity, retirement or if the family was leaving the area. In Newport the Hilton Hotel reported fewer problems getting and holding staff than any other in the south west region, and the Great British Burger Restaurants in Newport experienced amongst the lowest turnover rates in the country. At Llanwern, British Steel reported a 0.5 per cent turnover rate per annum.

In Newport and St Helens claimants' wage expectations were low enough to allow employers to lower wage rates without experiencing recruitment and retention difficulties. Surefil Packaging in St Helens said that they could lower their hourly rates by one fifth to £2.00 because 'desperation leads the way', while Newport Restaurants believed that they would still get waitresses at £1 per hour. As was the case in all four labour markets, the only serious difficulties that employers experienced with applicants' wage expectations was among jobchangers and managers who were in a position to negotiate.

However none of the St Helens or Newport employers said that they would contemplate wage reductions when offering posts to claimants. Although there were a number of reasons for this including likely deteriorations in the quality of staff available at lower rates, St Helens employers were more constrained by union-negotiated pay rates. In Newport there were very strong moral objections to lowering pay rates – an act which was described variously by employers as 'immoral', 'criminal' and 'exploitative'. These views were also expressed vigorously in Brighton and Hove where differential rates for equivalent jobs were considered just cause for staff uproar. It was considered the type of issue on which union organisation was based.

Nevertheless, employers in Newport did point to the extent of 'wage undercutting' that already existed in the local economy. Tulsa (Holdings) and Newport Restaurants said that they already had to compete with firms recruiting staff in the 'informal economy', where Wages Council rates, national insurance contributions and taxation were ignored. They feared that 'encouraging' employers to take claimants at lower rates of pay than other staff would merely reinforce the current practice so that:

> they will pay very low rates... it would encourage people on the dole to work for £1 an hour off the books.

Similarly, Wiseacre Engineering in St Helens regarded it as a 'probability not a possibility that employers will reduce wages to the unemployed' if made aware of the legislative changes. Their Secretary felt this was made possible by the levels of unemployment locally.

Perhaps because large scale redundancies were more frequent in St Helens than in the other regions, employers expressed a particular concern about taking those previously paid more elsewhere. The Personnel Manager at Smith Kline Beecham remarked:

> if I was Surefil [Packaging, a firm which also used packers] I would never recruit someone from Beecham... because they are used to a higher wage.

Interestingly, one of the Surefil directors concurred, believing that this would introduce a disruptive influence because, as with those made redundant, it was felt that they might come 'with a bit of a chip'.

Occupational flexibility was not considered a great merit among applicants in any of the four labour markets. Indeed, those who had exhibited it were frequently distrusted as 'jobchangers' and therefore liable to prove unreliable.

In Hammersmith and Fulham and Brighton and Hove, where competition among applicants was very intense, employers were often capable of attracting well-qualified and experienced applicants so that reliance on less suitable candidates' flexibility was usually unnecessary. But this state of affairs was contingent on a labour market favourable to employers. The Personnel Manager at Brighton Council's Leisure and Recreation Department explained:

> 12-15 months ago we were struggling to get people to work – [we had] 30 enquiries for a job; now the same job would attract 120-130. It means we are taking on high quality [staff] at every level.

Where there were serious difficulties in recruiting staff, as was the case for example with nurses and cooks in Brighton, claimants' preparedness to show occupational flexibility could not bridge the skills gap which employers sought to fill, at least in the short term.

The only employment opportunities that could present themselves to claimants prepared to be occupationally flexible were with firms capable of training those with aptitude. There were a broad range of employers able to do this in Brighton and Hove (including American Express, British Telecom, Hospitality Inn, Rentokil) and in Newport (Compton, Sons and Webb, the Great British Burger).

In St Helens larger employers like Smith Kline Beecham and British Steel had successfully redeployed staff who had shown great occupational flexibility. But employers showed less preparedness to take older workers who had been made redundant from 'better' jobs. Some had had to, despite their misgivings, as was the case in the engineering sector which was suffering the repercussions of reductions in apprenticeships in the 1980s.

What St Helens manufacturing employers did value was intra-occupational flexibility, that is the preparedness to be occupationally flexible within an occupation. But the tendency towards this was seen to be driven by job requirements rather than the requirements of the benefits system.

Particularly noticeable among the interviews in Newport and St Helens was a tendency among employers to stereotype the posts they offered by gender. At Surefil Packaging this precluded men being taken on as packers. At British Gas where women were being encouraged to apply for engineering posts, a personnel officer was disappointed at the poor response which he attributed to 'conservatism' shown by local job seekers.

Attitudes to taking the unemployed

According to the Economic Development Department at Hammersmith and Fulham Council employers:

won't take the unemployed until they are absolutely desperate... They need selection criteria, so unless they come across phenomenally credibly, why should an employer take the risk?

This sentiment was echoed by employers in both of the south eastern labour markets where employers were regularly able to take applicants already in work, or those offering relevant experience and/or qualifications. They were even prepared to take applicants from beyond the locality before considering those currently unemployed. The stigma of unemployment, and particularly long-term unemployment was strongest in the south east because employers felt there were 'jobs to be had', so that many of those claiming were considered 'unemployable'. If an applicant did not have 'a good reason' for being out of work for some time, the employer was likely to 'screen' him or her out before interview.

Because of this wariness of the unemployed among employers in the south east, many would not consider taking the unemployed 'at discount' unless, as was the case with private employment agencies' clients, there was some guarantee as to the applicant's basic suitability.

Employers such as Avana Bakeries and Great British Burgers in Newport and Surefil Packaging in St Helens were much more reliant on taking applicants without experience, partly because of the quality of the labour available. Group 4 Total Securities in Newport said that they would even consider candidates who had been unemployed for 7 years if they could show a good reason, 'which is not unusual around here'. Newport council's Economic and Development Department said that the local jobcentre felt the unemployed were becoming:

> more difficult to employ... [they are hard to place because of] literacy and social problems which mean that they are not suitable for jobs.

Employers in Newport were looking forward to rising unemployment over the coming year because they thought that it would raise the quality of the labour on offer.

Only in St Helens were there signs of positive discrimination in favour of the unemployed – in Smith Kline Beecham and British Gas, both of whom were prepared to interview applicants who were unemployed who they may otherwise not have interviewed. But the prevalence of initial probationary contracts in St Helens meant that employers were much more prepared to 'try out' claimants than in any of the other regions.

Part 4
UNEMPLOYMENT POLICIES
FOR THE 1990S

13 The process of claiming benefits: Conclusions and recommendations

In this chapter we bring together the conclusions relating to the process of claiming benefits following the 1989 Act and make recommendations based on the research findings.

The effects of the 1989 Social Security Act

Contrary to many predictions the 1989 social security changes did not lead to an increase in the number of claimants being disallowed on grounds of doubtful availability, or disqualified for refusal of employment, leaving work voluntarily or through misconduct. On the contrary, the total numbers disallowed or disqualified under all these headings fell from 331,000 in 1989 to 270,000 in 1990.

The numbers disallowed on grounds of actively seeking work were small, probably not much more than 5,000 in the whole of 1990.

There was a noticeable increase in the numbers disallowed because of failure to attend restart interviews, following the introduction in April 1990 of a more stringent procedure. There is considerable confusion about the numbers disallowed because two sets of official figures do not tally. On figures which are directly comparable, there was an increase from just over 700 disallowances in 1989 to over 2,600 in 1990. However, figures from the Chief Executive of the ES suggest that this jump is from over 13,000 in 1989 to over 21,000 in 1990. Either way, it is clear that there has been a considerable increase in such disallowances.

The biggest change numerically has been in the number disallowed unemployment benefit because of the introduction of the new rules concerning part-time work and the lower earnings limit introduced in December 1989. This effectively limits unemployment benefit to part-time workers to those earning less than the lower earnings limit. (£46 in 1990/91.) The Government's estimate was that it would affect about 5,000 claimants; in the event it led to the disallowance of almost 110,000.

There has also been a very large increase in the number of disallowances of contribution credits, which jumped from 46,000 to 73,000 between 1989 and 1990. This will weaken the contributory base of unemployment benefits still further, continuing the trend since 1980.

Largely as a result of these last two factors the number of disqualifications and disallowances in total rose by 80,000 between 1989 and 1990, reversing recent trends. This has probably led to the removal of many of these from the unemployment register.

Despite there being over 72,000 claimants disallowed benefit in 1990 on grounds of doubtful availability and actively seeking work there were fewer than 3,000 hardship payments made. These are supposed to be considered automatically following any disallowance, but it is clear both from these figures and from our reported evidence that they are not. This important safety net is an almost complete failure.

The 1989 Act and the New Framework

Among our main findings were that, in the views of those working both within the ES and the DSS, many of the procedures envisaged in the New Framework were not working and the intentions of the 1989 Act were not being carried out.

The main reason given was the lack of staffing to do the job properly. Staff had been cut in some places, remained static or had lagged behind the increases in the numbers of new claims at the same time as both the numbers of claims had increased considerably and the paperwork demanded by the New Framework and legislative changes had also much increased. The net effect was staff were working under great pressure, often with very low morale.

Despite the partial implementation of the Act, staff in the ES generally agreed that things had got tougher for claimants following the new legislation and the New Framework. Form-filling was seen as hazardous and could easily lead to loss of benefit on spurious grounds, and the overall emphasis on policing benefits, even though only partially carried into effect, had made many claimants feel intimidated. Some staff felt it had prevented some of the unemployed from claiming at all, especially after leaving their job voluntarily. There was general agreement that, from the claimants' point of view, the experience of claiming was now less helpful and more threatening.

Advice agency workers felt both that the new regulations had generally either been largely ignored or had been sympathetically enforced, yet claimants still felt under more pressure when claiming. Many felt under increased pressure to take jobs or training even when this was unsuitable, or to leave the register.

The reasons given by advice agency staff about why the regulations had not been more strictly enforced were a) staff shortages in the ES and DSS and b) that staff in the ES were thought to be often out of sympathy with the coercive nature of the regulations and so chose to ignore them. This was especially true in places of high unemployment.

Because of staff shortages some offices had closed earlier in the day than usual; claimants found it very difficult to get through on the 'phones, which were constantly in use; there were frequently delays of two weeks or so before a claimant had a first interview, which further delayed payment of the claim which in any case was paid two weeks in arrears. All had the effect of worsening the service to claimants.

Both ES staff and advice workers agreed that the new regulations on restricted availability, refusal of employment and actively seeking work mostly affected those claimants who were foolish enough or honest enough not to provide the "right" answers when filling in the forms. The supposed "hard-core" of the unemployed would still not be touched by them, while the vast majority of claimants had been made to feel harassed. Those with literacy or language problems were particularly vulnerable to penalties.

Despite the changes in the regulations on other aspects of benefit control, it was still the disqualifications for leaving work voluntarily that were seen as the biggest issue.

Restart interviews were seen as having become much less user-friendly and more intimidating. These perceptions are supported by the figures for the outcomes of restart interviews; in 1990 only 1.1% of all interviews led directly to a job placement; only 12.4% of interviews led to any kind of positive outcome (e.g. ET, EAS, Jobclub etc.). By contrast, 2.4% led to disallowance for failure to attend, while another 1.8% led to referral to AOs for doubts about availability or actively seeking work. In other words, on being invited to attend a restart interview, claimants had four times as much chance of being disallowed benefit as they had of getting a job as a result. Compulsory restart courses are likely to exacerbate that effect in future.

There was a good deal of agreement among the claimants we spoke to that jobcentres were of little use to them. Hardly any could remember ever having found a job as a result of an interview at a jobcentre, and many of those that had gone on ET had felt pressurised into it under the threat of benefit loss. They had subsequently found the training to be of poor quality. They would have welcomed good quality training.

With few exceptions, interviews at jobcentres were felt to be at best well-intentioned but useless, at worst insensitive and degrading. The control function of jobcentres, i.e. checking on availability and jobsearch behaviour, was seen to be much their most salient feature. Claimants reported feeling that the main function of the interview was to reduce the claimant count, regardless of the needs of the individual claimant.

Back to work plans were described as suggesting the "stunningly obvious" and of little use; few could remember ever having been given any advice on in-work benefits, and no-one had been given any specific information about how they would affect a particular job offer.

Claimants recognised that staff in the ES were themselves under a lot of pressure and therefore had little time for each claimant.

Claimants anticipated trouble rather than help on attending for interview, and prepared accordingly. They had their own ways of avoiding the possible penalties, largely by giving the answers they knew were expected of them and by going through the required motions.

Claimants' awareness of benefit penalties was often incomplete; they knew there were penalties, but were often unsure of the details, making their experience of claiming uncertain and unpredictable.

Most had heard about the need to be actively seeking work and all agreed that the sanctions were more of a threat than a reality; none had been penalised. They did not think it would help them find jobs and saw it much more as a hurdle to be got over on the way to benefit. It was an irritant which contributed to a sense of being pressurised not into useful job searching activities but into either the pointless recording of fruitless efforts at chasing non-existent jobs or into the fabrication of evidence, which they felt to be more than justified by the futility of the regulations. Far from enabling claimants back into work it contributed to their sense of frustration and annoyance and actively encouraged them to be dishonest. That it was all as yet only a mild irritation was because the staff of the Employment Service had generally had the good sense to moderate the requirement in the light of the lack of available jobs.

Liaison between the ES and DSS

Both sets of staff agreed that liaison between the ES and the DSS was poor. Various attempts to set up co-ordinating machinery had been ineffective.

Consequences for claimants were often delays and sometimes the payment of wrong amounts of benefit. Delays occurred especially at the new claims stage, when delays in seeing a claimant for a first interview in the ES led to delays in the payment of IS, and variable policies with regard to the payment of hardship payments.

The dependence of the DSS on the ES in matters concerning decisions about whether to disallow benefit or to disqualify claimants was seen as problematic by staff in both departments. Because it is the ES that makes decisions about claimants' availability for work even where the claim is for income support only it is quite possible that many claimants for IS are being disallowed at the new claim stage by ES staff using regulations applicable to unemployment benefit even though the rules applicable to IS are sometimes different. A secondary consequence of the DSS's dependence on the decisions (or opinions) of the ES is that inevitably the decision making process is slowed down. By the time a claim for IS has been referred from the ES to the Adjudication Officer in the ES, the decision sent back from the Adjudication Officer to the ES and then forwarded to the DSS it was not unusual in one southern region for six weeks to have elapsed, during which time the claimant would have been without benefit and without a decision against which to appeal. In London the delay could be far longer, with many cases taking as long as six months.

Recommendations

These findings reinforce the recommendations relating to the labour market effects of the new legislation. In particular they point to the need to:

232

- Separate the counselling functions of the ES from its benefit policing functions. Without this separation claimants will continue to view the help offered by the ES staff with the suspicion that it is not offered in their best interests. This is the biggest single change which would have effects on all other aspects of the claiming experience and would counter the growing sense that claiming is an intimidating, risky and unhelpful process.

- With or without this separation of functions claimants need much better information about the likely consequences of pursuing different options. This includes better information both about possible penalties, the right to appeal, and about possible in-work benefits.

- Increase the staffing levels in both the ES and DSS.

- Improve liaison between the ES and the DSS at local level. This could be done in one of three ways. At the simplest level, the need to establish effective local liaison machinery must be given a much higher priority. A more effective improvement would be the alignment of the UB and IS regulations. At the moment these differ in significant ways without any clear rationale why they should. The resulting confusion leads to wrong payment of benefits and makes it impossible for claimants to understand the rules under which they are being treated.

- A still more fundamental alignment would be that of the two systems of benefit. At the moment, only about 22% of claimants qualify for UB, (some with and some without IS), while 62% qualify for IS only. (The remainder fail to qualify for any benefit – *UB Statistics, Summary Tables*, 1990, Table 8). There is therefore a strong case either for abandoning the contributory principle or of restoring it once again to the central position it had under Beveridge. Obviously either proposal raises fundamental issues beyond the scope of this research project. What we can say is that the existence of two systems of benefit now causes many delays and inaccuracies in payments of benefit and makes both systems unintelligible to claimants.

The quality of adjudication

About one in three of all new and renewal claims for unemployment benefit and income support are referred for adjudication every year. In 1990 this amounted to 1,173,000 claims being referred. Whilst awaiting the outcome of the Adjudication Officer's decision benefit is usually either not paid at all or reduced. The reasonableness of the judgement to make the referral and the time taken in processing the referrals are therefore both important for the claimants.

There is evidence to show that many referrals from ES staff to AOs are based on poor information or poor judgement. In 1990 half the claims referred were allowed by the AOs, calling into question the decision to refer. In respect of claims referred on grounds of doubtful availability, actively seeking work or refusal of employment the proportion subsequently allowed rose to roughly two thirds. In 1990 270,000 claims were allowed after referral. Most of these would have resulted in delayed payments for claimants.

Internal management documents from the ES show that poor quality referrals from ES staff is a persistent issue, resulting in unnecessary delays before the claim can be considered by the AO.

Once a claim reaches the AO it is meant to be dealt with in 14 days. Whilst official figures show that between 85% and 90% of claims in respect of doubtful availability and refusal of employment were dealt with in under 4 weeks ES staff suggest far longer delays are not unusual, especially in London. The attempt to reach a decision in 14 days appears to have been abandoned as impractical because of staff shortages; delays of up to six months were mentioned.

The quality of AOs' decisions has been described as "in need of much improvement" by the Chief Adjudication Officer. He described the quality of decision-making in the DSS as "disappointing" and in the ES as "unsatisfactory". Giving insufficient evidence for their decisions is the main reason, though one in six of availability decisions were based on the inaccurate application of the law. Decisions about availability were the least satisfactory.

Staff shortages were again seen as a cause of poor decisions, especially when shortages of AOs were met by the use of upgraded clerical officers.

The quality of submissions to appeal tribunals was also heavily criticised by the Chief Adjudication Officer. Absent or deficient argument, ignoring of matters raised by the appellant, and citing relevant legislation and caselaw inaccurately were among the main reasons for the criticisms.

A quarter of all decisions are revised in the appellants' favour before they reach the tribunal, again calling into question the wisdom of the original decision.

Recommendations

- The time taken to reach decisions must be reduced at all stages, i.e in referral to the AO, in the decision of the AO and in reaching an appeal tribunal.

- Performance targets must be set, e.g. the requirement in the Social Security Act 1975, (Sec. 99) that the AO should reach a decision in 14 days must be binding, and similar targets should be set for the other stages in the process.

- Staffing levels must be increased to make these targets possible.

- Whether or not a faster system is in place, given the high proportion of claims referred and subsequently allowed, claimants whose initial claim is referred for adjudication should have the option of receiving benefit at the full rate pending the outcome of the decision. This would make a substantial difference to the financial circumstances of thousands of claimants who now get no benefit pending the decision (apart from a tiny handful who receive hardship payments) yet whose claims are subsequently allowed. Where the claim was eventually disallowed claimants who had opted to receive the benefit would have to repay it.

- Similarly, where claimants lodged an appeal at the time of being given an adverse decision on a claim for benefit they should also have the option of receiving benefit on the same terms as above pending the outcome of the appeal.

- Staff at all levels need much better training in the meaning and application of the regulations.

- This also means that staff must be paid enough to stay in the service once trained.

- AOs should be encouraged to review decisions when invited to do so by claimants or advice agencies rather than leave the outcome to appeals tribunals.

Availability and restricted availability

The procedures for assessing availability have tightened since 1989. The practice has developed of no longer permitting claimants to give general answers to questions about wages or type of job required, but to give specific answers can lay the claimant open to disallowance.

Claimants often do not understand the significance of their answers to the UB671, especially about desired wage levels. Mostly ES staff advise them to change their statements to avoid disallowance, but sometimes they do not, which results in unnecessary disallowances. Claimants also say they want a particular wage but often look for work at lower wages.

There was evidence that the regulations were being harshly applied in a number of areas.

Those out of work are expected to have a higher standard of availability than those in work; for example the need to attend hospital or clinics for the odd day was taken as a sign of unavailability in a claimant, though an employee would probably be allowed the time off.

When claimants are in receipt of UB and a doubt arises about their availability their benefit continues in payment until the AO reaches a decision; there is no equivalent procedure for IS only claimants, whose benefit is suspended pending the AO's decision. There is no justification for this unequal treatment.

Permitted periods are not always given, and even when they are some claimants are still disallowed for restricting their jobsearch within it.

Claimants are often given a forward disallowal of benefit although there is no provision to do so within the regulations. This results in unnecessary and wrongful loss of benefit.

One result of the new regulations has been to create artificial barriers between claimants and their benefits. One way they have learnt to deal with these is by telling ES staff what they want to hear; the regulations encourage dishonesty.

The effects of the regulations have been moderated by claimants adapting to the new rules, by the reluctance of many of the ES staff to enforce them, and by the breakdown of the follow-up procedures due to staff shortages.

Recommendations

- The practice of requiring claimants to name a specific wage for which they are prepared to work should be discontinued. It is no real indication of the wages claimants will in fact work for, and results in unnecessary disallowances.

- Claims for income support should be judged by the standard of what constitutes availability under the regulations applicable to income support and not those applicable to unemployment benefit. That is to say claimants who are available for 24 hours or more in a week [regulation 7(1) of the I.S. (Gen.) Regs.] should be judged available for IS purposes even if they fail to meet the stricter UB test.

- The requirement that claimants have to prove immediate availability should be relaxed. Women may be genuinely available for work but may need a few days in which to organise child care; it is unrealistic to expect everyone to be available for work at 24 hours notice.

- The regulations governing restrictions on availability should be brought more into line with those governing "good cause" for refusal of employment. Under regulation 12E(2)(c) [S.S. (U., S. etc.) Regs.] carers may have their responsibilities taken into account as "good cause" for refusing a particular job offered. Because no similar defence exists for carers under the restrictions on availability regulations, [7B, S.S. (U., S. etc.) Regs.] it is then possible for the same person who successfully refused a particular job to be judged to have restricted their availability and so to be disallowed benefit. This ought not to be possible.

- Similarly, where claimants have to attend hospitals or clinics the same standards of availability should be applied to them as would be applied by a reasonable employer if they were employees. That is, they should not be disallowed benefit because they have to attend a clinic rather than a job interview any more than an employee would be sacked if he or she had to have a day off work for similar reasons.

- When someone on IS has their availability questioned and the issue is referred to the AO they should have the same right to continue to receive benefit at the full rate pending the outcome of the referral as UB claimants now have.

- Staff need better guidance and training on the significance of "permitted periods".

- The common practice of disallowing claimants who have restricted their availability for a named period of future time is illegal and staff must be given clearer instructions not to do it.

- When staff in the ES or DSS have sufficient doubts about a claimant's availability to refer it for adjudication they must inform the claimant at the time of the interview of their doubts and of the grounds for their doubts. It should not be possible for claimants to find their benefit suspended or disallowed without first having been warned of the possibility and the reasons for it.

236

Actively seeking work

There is widespread agreement that the new regulations have not been enforced to any great extent, at least as far as disallowances of benefit are concerned. In 1990 only 5,227 claimants were disallowed benefit on grounds of not actively seeking work. That represents less than 0.14% of all claims for UB in 1990.

The reasons given for this were a) that referring someone to an AO on these grounds involved a lot more administration than using doubtful availability, which staff preferred using; b) the staff were reluctant to use the new regulations partly because they had not been given the extra resources needed to do the extra work involved and partly because many of them disagreed with their intention, especially in a time of increasing unemployment.

Despite the lack of disallowances advice agencies felt that the regulations had nevertheless had an effect, both on claimants' behaviour and particularly in worsening the general atmosphere between claimants and the ES. Yet more barriers have been erected, seen by most people as pointless, between the claimants and their benefits. "Streetwise" claimants had little difficulty in satisfying the requirements.

Staff in the ES sometimes inappropriately invoke the actively seeking work requirements when they should use the availability test.

The regulations apply equally to claimants who want contribution credits only and have been applied to quarterly attenders, who now have to sign on every fortnight, significantly worsening conditions for the over 50s.

Recommendation

- Given that the requirement to be actively seeking work has been so little used and yet has worsened relationships between claimants and the ES and DSS it should be abolished. It serves no useful purpose and there are already sufficient safeguards against abuses of the social security system in the availability and refusal of employment regulations.

Part-time students

The actively seeking work requirement and the new availability regulations have made it harder for students on part-time courses under the 21-hour rule to prove entitlement to benefit. Although the guidelines in the AOG are sensible they are not always followed in practice. Many advice workers commented on the short-sightedness of preventing claimants from taking courses to improve their employability while insisting that they look for menial dead-end jobs instead.

Given that we already have employment training schemes which require the unemployed to live on benefit plus a small amount extra it seems illogical to prevent them from taking courses which will improve their employability just because they have found the course on their own initiative rather than through the ES. Given the dire need for a better trained workforce it seems the height of folly to stop people from pursuing courses which will improve their skills and require them instead to look for jobs which may or may not be available. If the price to pay for this is that we support people taking these courses from the unemployment benefit or income support funds it is a small and almost certainly cost-effective price.

Recommendation

- Claimants on part-time courses which may ultimately improve their employment prospects should not be disallowed benefit on grounds of doubtful availability, failure actively to seek work, or refusal of employment.

On the margins of capability

Both departments have a financial interest in pushing claimants on to the other; the ES may deal with its long-term unemployed who have been through all the other options by finding them to be incapable of work and redirecting them towards the DSS and invalidity benefit, while the DSS reclassifies its disabled claimants as fit for light work and redirects them to the ES.

The consequences of this for claimants is that they may be pushed towards jobs for which they are unsuitable or that they may have to define themselves as disabled when they would prefer not to. This process is further exacerbated by the performance targets set within the ES, which also encourage staff to send claimants after unsuitable jobs or redirect them to the DSS as incapable of work.

One consequence of the push in to work of claimants who may not be fully ready is that they may take a job but soon leave it and so fall foul of the voluntary unemployment deduction. This was referred to as one of the "most prominent" issues by a London advice agency.

Advice workers commented on the unrealistic list of standard jobs which the DSS used when defining light work. It was this list which usually helped the claimant, when represented, to win an appeal, since often they were unsuitable for the particular claimant or they did not exist in the area.

The requirement to actively seek work had forced many partially disabled claimants to redefine themselves, often reluctantly, as incapable of work in order to avoid the necessity to prove their jobsearching. Advice agencies agreed that it was usually better to opt for a disability benefit than for unemployment benefit as this avoided all the requirements to be available for and actively seeking work. For this reason they advised claimants to appeal against decisions finding them fit for light work even though they had misgivings about doing so as many claimants did not like to think of themselves as incapable of work.

The border area between capacity and incapacity for work is one which gives rise to the possibility of widely differing interpretations of the regulations, with different benefit outcomes for claimants. Disputes about incapacity caused claimants many problems. When claimants have been in receipt of sickness or invalidity benefit and are then found fit for work they may continue to receive IS (subject to a 40% deduction) without the need to sign on as available for work pending the outcome of an appeal providing their GP continues to certify that they are incapable of work.

Evidence from the advice agencies is that this is not always known by the DSS, who erroneously continue to require such claimants to sign on.

There is considerable room for different interpretations about when the restrictions imposed by a claimant's disability reach the point of rendering the claimant unavailable for work. The regulations on both UB and IS seem to afford claimants with disabilities very strong protection since both refer to the need to be available only for work which the claimant can "reasonably be expected to do." Despite this claimants were sent after jobs which were manifestly unsuitable for them and then disallowed on the grounds of restricted availability when they refused to take them.

It is possible for claimants to fall between the criteria of both departments and to be found fit for light work by the DSS but not available for work by the ES. It is also possible to be considered available for work even when in receipt of medical certificates, which, while it means that the claimant is subject to the requirement actively to seek work, does have the advantage of removing the 40% deduction from any IS in payment. Claimants who are on the margins of capability and who place restrictions on their availability or job searching activities may sometimes be required to sign on as available for work and sometimes not; sometimes be considered to be unavailable for work and therefore not eligible for UB or IS at all; sometimes be considered to be available within the limitations of their physical or mental limitations and so receive full UB and IS; or be considered to be unavailable for work and therefore ineligible for UB but allowed to be eligible for IS at a reduced rate.

Which of these many possibilities applies in any one case is likely to be a function partly of which interpretation the particular office takes and partly of whether the claimant seeks the help of an advice agency. The consequences for the claimant vary from having benefit in full, benefit subject to the 40% deduction or none at all.

Recommendations

- To avoid the need to be shunted between departments claimants with more than a very minimal level of disability should be free to choose whether to opt for sickness-related or unemployment-related benefits. They could then define themselves as still within or outside the labour market.

- To remove unnecessary pressures to choose sickness-related benefits the requirement actively to seek work, even if not abolished for everyone as we recommend, should not apply to claimants with disabilities.

- For the same reason, claimants should be made aware that under the current regulations they have to be available only for work they can reasonably be expected to do, and for the number of hours they can reasonably be expected to work.

- It should not be possible for claimants to fall between both departments. They must be found either capable or not capable of work and not left in limbo while each department refuses to accept responsibility. Pending a decision, the department to whom the claim was first made or where benefit was already in payment should pay or continue to pay benefit.

- Pending the outcome of an appeal against a decision of the DSS that a claimant is fit for work IS should continue in payment at the full rate. There is no justification for imposing a 40% deduction when there is no suggestion that the claimant has done anything wrong.

Refusal of employment

Disallowances for refusal of employment or training, and for neglect to avail oneself of a suitable job offer are very rare. They amounted to only 4,317 in 1990, or 0.11% of all claims. The vast majority of claimants want to work, and measures to disallow for refusal of work are needed only as a very last resort. In the light of this it was unnecessary to remove from claimants the defence of being able to refuse a job on the grounds that it is unsuitable, as was done in the 1989 Act. We came across examples of claimants being disqualified from benefit having refused jobs which seemed quite unsuitable to them.

It was also unnecessary to prevent the level of wages being taken into consideration as "good cause" for refusal, and to remove the defence that one would be worse off than on benefit if one took the job offered, as were also done.

The regulations governing refusal of employment are clear as far as UB cases are concerned but complicated for IS claimants by the consideration of whether the vacancy refused continues to exist or not. If it does, IS claimants are disallowed benefit; whether they are eligible for a hardship payment appears to be a matter of some dispute. As soon as the vacancy ceases to exist, IS claimants regain entitlement to benefit but at the reduced rate. This complicated interaction of the regulations means that claimants for IS are sometimes disallowed benefit by ES staff when in fact they could qualify for a reduced rate of income support.

Not many claimants' advice agencies had experience of claimants being penalised for refusal of employment because so few claimants were ever offered jobs and those that were usually took them.

Claimants were not always aware that they were being offered a job and that the penalty for refusing it was disqualification.

ES staff may not always use the refusal of employment procedures when a claimant refuses a job offer; they may refer direct to the fraud section on the assumption that a refusal means that the claimant already has a job; or they may apply the more general restricted availability procedures. As these do not have the opportunity for the claimant to plead that he or she had "good cause", since this does not apply in the case of doubtful availability, claimants may lose benefit because of the application of the wrong regulations. Depending on which course of action is followed the outcome for the claimant could be anything from a reduced rate of IS paid automatically, a hardship payment only, or no benefit at all, with or without an accompanying interview with the fraud section.

240

- The defences for refusal of a job offer that existed before the 1989 Act should be restored. Claimants should be allowed to refuse jobs on the grounds that the job is not suitable, or that the wages will not cover their normal outgoings, or are so low that they will be worse off than on benefit.

- Refusal of a specific job should not be used to justify disallowance on the more general ground of doubtful availability.

- There should be definite procedures both within the ES and DSS to ensure that a claimant is always clear that he or she has been offered a specific job, and what the consequences of refusal may be.

- When a claimant is disqualified by staff in the ES they should always make it clear to the claimant that he or she may still qualify for a reduced rate of income support.

- When a claimant is disqualified for refusal of employment he or she should still qualify for a hardship payment where appropriate, and this should be made clear in the regulations and guidance.

Voluntary unemployment

Issues concerning so-called voluntary unemployment, (i.e. where claimants have left a job without just cause or have been sacked for misconduct,) were said by advice workers to give rise to the largest number of problems. Inordinate delays in reaching decisions about disqualification and the universal imposition of the maximum penalty of 26 weeks, despite Commissioners' Decisions and the guidance in the AOG not to do so, were cited.

When AOs did reach decisions on cases concerning leaving voluntarily and misconduct in 1990 they allowed 56% and 41% respectively of the claims referred.

An emerging issue was the increasing numbers of claimants who had been forced off invalidity benefits and made to find work who then left because they were not really up to the work and were disqualified.

The "employment on trial" provisions of the 1989 Act which allowed certain claimants to leave a job without penalty provided they stayed more then six but less than twelve were largely unknown to claimants, but were welcomed by them when they heard about them.

Although advice agencies claimed to win almost every appeal against the 26 week penalty most claimants do not appeal; many do not even sign on when they have left voluntarily even though they could still be entitled to a reduced rate of IS.

The dependence of the DSS on ES decisions and opinions in respect of disqualifications for both leaving work voluntarily and misconduct and the lack of liaison between the ES and the DSS in respect of appeals against these particular disqualifications meant that some claimants wasted time appealing to the wrong department.

241

Recommendations

- Since AOs are reluctant to abide by their own guidance and the ruling of the Tribunal of Commissioners R(U)8/74(T) that the length of the period of disqualification is a matter to be considered on the merits of each case but instead almost always impose the maximum period, and since this period is usually cut on appeal, we recommend that the maximum period of disqualification be considerably reduced.

- Given the high proportion of referrals to AOs which are subsequently allowed, and given the inordinate length of time it often takes to reach a decision, claimants should have the option of receiving their benefit in full pending the outcome of the decision. If the decision goes against them they would have to repay any benefit received.

- If they appeal at the time they are given the adverse decision, they should have the option of continuing to receive benefit on the same terms until the outcome of the appeal.

- It should always be made clear to claimants when they are disqualified that they may still qualify for a reduced rate of income support.

- Our proposals that claimants with disabilities should be allowed to choose whether to opt for sickness-related or unemployment related benefits without being subject to the requirement to be actively seeking work would remove the pressure on them to take unsuitable jobs and so reduce the numbers being disqualified for leaving them again.

- Employers should be required to return their answers about the circumstances of a claimant's leaving their employment within two weeks rather than four, the present time-limit.

- The employment on trial provisions should be given wider publicity and, in order to encourage claimants back into work without the risk of ending up worse off, should be extended to all claimants.

- Appeals against disqualification on grounds of leaving voluntarily or misconduct should always be treated as an appeal against both departments where both are involved, and procedures should be established to ensure that this happens.

Literacy and those whose first language is not English

Although the stated policy of the ES is sympathetic to those with both literacy and language problems the practice does not always follow the policy. Both groups were reported to have particular problems proving their availability for work and active jobsearching.

The stated policy of the ES is to encourage the presence of independent interpreters. The ES policy of keeping lists of interpreters prepared to work free of charge is not always effective in preventing language difficulties with the result that claimants lose entitlement to benefit unnecessarily.

Some offices took a claimant's inability to speak English as ipso facto proof that they must be unavailable for work.

Wives left at home when husbands returned temporarily to their country of origin might not be treated as a lone claimant or parent, which led to difficulties over benefits.

The different statuses that refugees may have as they go through the process of establishing their claim to remain here give rise to inequities in the way they are treated for benefit purposes. In particular only those with full refugee status are allowed exemption from the need to be available for work while attending an English language course.

Given the length of time it has taken to process applications from would-be refugees it is often difficult both to achieve refugee status and to begin an English language course within twelve months of arrival here. In any case, courses providing 15 hours of pure English teaching are very hard to find and are not necessarily as effective at teaching English as courses in which the language is taught as part of more general studies.

There is no provision for refugees aged 19 or over in vocationally based non-advanced education. This means they are denied the opportunities to improve their employability except through Employment Training.

The actively seeking work regulations bear particularly harshly on refugees, who are often forced to leave courses which would have improved their prospects of employment in the longer term and instead take menial jobs.

Recommendations

- The existence of the ES policy on encouraging interpreters should be more widely publicised.

- Both the ES and the DSS should provide funds to pay for interpreters where none are otherwise available.

- The practice of disallowing benefit simply on the grounds that claimants do not speak English should be forbidden. These claimants should have their availability judged on the same terms as all other claimants.

- The provision in paragraph 16 of Schedule 1 to the IS (General) Regulations that refugees may be excused the requirement to be available for work if they are taking an English course should be extended to include any course which is likely to improve prospects of obtaining employment.

- The time period within which a refugee must start such a course should be extended to two years.

- Because they have just as much need to learn English in order to improve their employability, those with "exceptional leave to remain" should also be eligible for income support without the requirement to be available for work while taking such a course.

- Refugees aged 19 and over in non-advanced vocationally based courses should receive income support without the need to be available for work.

Hardship payments

The award of a hardship payment was very rare.

Claims for hardship were not automatically considered by AOs after disallowances.

Those that were given depended on the particular practices of different offices rather than on the application of the regulations. For the claimants it was purely a matter of chance whether the offices considered the claims automatically or only responded to claims initiated by claimants, and to which particular groups of claimants it was local office policy to grant them.

Claimants were not routinely informed of the possibility of making a claim for hardship payments.

Recommendations

- Claims for hardship payments should be automatically considered following a disallowance on grounds of doubtful availability or not actively seeking work. The only way this can happen effectively is if claimants are informed at the time of their disallowance that hardship payments are possible and they are given the opportunity to present their case for one. Procedures should be introduced to ensure this happens.

- All claimants who are eligible should be automatically considered. Local offices should not be allowed to introduce their own criteria for who is considered to be "deserving".

On the deficiency of the published statistics

The published statistics are deficient in several respects. In particular there is no useable information published on the outcome of claims for income support; since about 62% of all claims are for income support this is a major deficiency. Nor is there any disaggregated information on the outcome of appeals against disqualifications and disallowances, either for UB claims or for IS claims.

Such information as is published is virtually unintelligible without further information and explanation from those who compile it.

Recommendations

- Information on income support claims should be collected and published in the same way as information on UB claims.

- Information on the outcome of appeals should be published by type of disallowance or disqualification.

- Information on the number of claimants for income support who are disallowed contribution credits should be published in the same way as it is for unemployment benefit claimants.

- The information which is published on the decisions of Adjudication Officers in the ES should be presented in a more intelligible form. Relevant definitions and notes explaining what each table in the *Quarterly and Annual Analysis of Decisions of AOs* does and does not include, together with some explanatory notes about the reasons for inclusion and exclusion, should be included in these publications.

14 The effects on the labour market: Conclusions and recommendations

This chapter summarises the findings on the labour market impact of the 1989 legislative changes and the policy ideas they give rise to.

Seeking employment

Claimant awareness of actively seeking work

Claimants were aware that they had responsibilities to seek work and furnish proof when requested, even if they were not familiar with the phrases 'actively seeking work' or 'actively seeking employment'.

Even if, as was usually the case, counsellors had not explicitly linked the requirements to benefit entitlement, most assumed that they were linked. However, few knew what the precise benefit implications were if one failed to meet the requirements – for example how much benefit could be lost and for how long. Nor were they aware of what was expected of them in order to reestablish entitlement.

No claimant was aware that s/he could be expected to broaden his or her jobsearch after an initial period of unemployment.

Behavioural impact

Claimants' response to the requirements was determined firstly by the belief that the use of benefit penalties was remote; and secondly that they were merely 'a hoop to jump through' to obtain benefit, rather than of help in finding employment.

Consequently the provisions had had very little effect on the type of search undertaken by claimants, its intensity or the methods used. Instead their behaviour was geared towards ensuring that they could persuade counsellors of their right to benefit by providing appropriate 'proof'.

The small amount of evidence that there had been any impact on jobsearch included:

- employers stating that they had been requested to provide evidence of job search;

- speculative visits from applicants employers said they would not normally have seen (mainly in St Helens);

- some evidence of an increase in speculative approaches from people employers often regarded as 'unsuitable';

- claimants relating the efforts they had made to procure jobsearch proof.

In each case initial activity in the autumn of 1989 had died down once claimants realised that counsellors were not reviewing their search and rarely asked for search proof.

Employment Service counselling and advice rarely, if ever, proved to be the impetus behind claimants widening their jobsearch, either by reference to the permitted period or indirectly through more general jobsearch advice.

Claimant jobsearch

Most claimants were flexible in the type of work they were seeking from the outset. This reflected the fact that few had had a 'usual occupation' and regarded 'openness to anything' as the best policy for obtaining work. Those with 'usual occupations' or specific forms of work in mind were usually prepared to broaden their search after an initial lack of success.

The majority had experienced more than one spell of unemployment and were therefore adept at searching for work. Most thought that they knew the best methods for obtaining the work that they sought. Many had been repeatedly successful in finding work but the short-term nature of the work available had resulted in frequent bouts of unemployment.

Employment Service advice and action

Counsellors usually informed claimants of the requirement to seek work and furnish proof when requested at the signing on interview. They also informed claimants that their search could be reviewed. In practice they rarely reviewed claimants' search.

The shortness and infrequency of counsellor interviews meant that little jobsearch advice was offered to claimants. Jobclubs and inner city 'jobsearch teams' were the only exceptions.

Claimants could not see how satisfying the ASW requirements could improve their prospects of finding work. They did not regard their jobsearch techniques or intensity to be a major obstacle in gaining access to vacancies. Instead they cited problems such as the number of applicants applying for a small and dwindling number of suitable vacancies; intense labour market competition from those with relevant or recent skills and work experience; and the attitudes of employers towards them.

They felt that they had little to learn about jobsearch from Employment Service counsellors. There were exceptions, including those who had been out of the labour market for some time – for example women returners – and those who found themselves unemployed for the first time after a sustained period of employment. These groups prized structured jobsearch assistance most.

The jobsearch advice given by counsellors was usually considered perfunctory and no more than common sense. Claimants felt that the 'advice' was offered by 'bureaucrats' who were more interested in 'looking after themselves' than in making helpful suggestions. Most complained that they were not treated as individuals but as 'numbers' or 'statistics'.

Fulfilling Employment Service expectations was treated as part of the claiming process, rather than the 'real' search for work. That their jobsearch could be reviewed at any time, and that they could be expected to show proof to 'doubting' counsellors, were illustrative of the 'real' intentions behind the legislation – those of 'checking up' on claimants' benefit eligibility. So the prospect of review interviews was felt to be threatening rather than helpful.

Claimants frequently distrusted the advice given by Employment Service staff because they were wary of the dual function the staff performed – benefit checking and jobsearch assistance. It meant many were less inclined to use jobcentres than they otherwise would have been (this was particularly the case where jobcentre staff took new claims or restart interviews). At worst, claimants' feelings of intimidation meant that the prospect of approaching counsellors for positive advice and assistance was foreclosed.

There was great impatience at the suggestion that benefit could be suspended if claimants' job search was deemed insufficient. Firstly, they often believed they were taking all reasonable steps to find work. Secondly, they pointed to the small number of vacancies available. And thirdly, they questioned the motivation behind Employment Service sanctions.

No claimant felt that the provisions had materially assisted them in finding and obtaining employment. On the contrary, some were aware that their preoccupation with obtaining jobsearch proof had involved the pursuit of employers who would provide job search proof but who they knew could not provide work. This had proved demotivating for some, and detrimental to their 'real' search for work.

Searching for workers

Awareness of actively seeking work

Employers were either totally unaware of the provisions or, if they were aware of them, their knowledge of them was very vague. The exception was in firms who were advising on large scale redundancies.

Awareness was confined to those with personnel or legal responsibilities in larger firms; those aware through channels incidental to their work, for example friends claiming benefit; and through contact with claimants requesting jobsearch proof.

Impact on applications received

There had been no discernible impact on the quality or quantity of applications received from claimants. Where a rise in claimant applications had been noticeable it had been short-lived in most cases, following on from the introduction of the Act in the autumn of 1989.

Although many employers were unable to identify claimant applications and therefore changes in their number, most considered the rise in jobcentre applications over the previous eighteen months to be associated with rising unemployment rather than legislative changes.

Attitudes towards actively seeking work

Employers felt that it was reasonable to expect claimants to seek work. They looked favourably on those who had 'got off their backsides' or 'looked off their own back'.

However employers who knew, and those that were told during interview, that the expectations were underpinned by benefit penalties, considered the provisions to be counterproductive.

Firstly, it forced employers to question claimants' genuine desire for work. As one employer put it:

> are they coming for a job or because they've got to present themselves for a job?

Since willingness to undertake the work offered was considered as the most fundamental element in an applicant's suitability, this put claimants at a disadvantage relative to other groups.

Secondly, employers said that the provisions merely confirmed the image of claimants as 'dependent' – people unlikely to seek work unless forced to do so. The reinforcement of this negative image could, they felt, damage the job prospects of the unemployed.

Some did welcome the fact that claimants could be expected to attend employer interviews, because failure to turn up for interview was a cause of great inconvenience. However, they were not sure whether the provisions were being fully enforced because it was not usual for the Employment Service to check on claimants' attendance.

Although there was sympathy for claimants seeking work, even those who endeavoured to respond to each applicant found that, because they frequently received overwhelming responses to their vacancies, they were unable to do so.

Impact on recruitment practices

Some expressed concern at the quality of service they had received through jobcentres – in particular their seeming inability to 'screen out' unsuitable candidates.

Some had experienced 'unwilling' jobcentre applicants in the past. It was rare for employers to stop using jobcentres for this reason because the advantages outweighed the risks. Many believed that they could screen out unsuitable applicants themselves. However, the more risk-averse employers said that they would have to consider their continued use of jobcentres if the provisions were widely enforced and the number of 'unwilling' candidates increased. On the other hand, some felt that they had a duty to register their vacancies with jobcentres.

Where claimants were responding to ASW by intensifying their search, employers' responses were mixed. Some welcomed the extra candidates from which to choose and were keen to 'offer assistance' to the unemployed. Others were impatient with the flow of unsuitable candidates, to the extent that they a) had warned the jobcentre; b) had desisted from using the jobcentre for recruitment; c) thought twice about notifying the jobcentre of a vacancy, knowing that they'd be inundated with applicants.

Impact on employment prospects

Where there was evidence of increased jobsearch activity there appeared to be little material benefit to claimants. Employers said their vacancies were oversubscribed and that claimants regularly lost out in competition against more suitable candidates. Satisfying the condition to seek work did not enhance job prospects where employers considered applicants to be 'unsuitable'. Claimants were not able to change who they were! Employers did not welcome an increase in applicants per se, only an increase in suitable applicants from which to choose.

That competition for vacancies was intense was confirmed by evidence regarding the turnover of jobcentre vacancies. In Newport jobcentre, for example, 82 per cent of the vacancies had been filled within one week of being registered.

Employers had not noticed improvements in the quality of jobcentre applications generally. Indeed there had been some, for example the use of curricula vitae for waitressing posts, which had appeared wholly inappropriate, leading employers to conclude that some claimants were more concerned with gaining evidence of their job search than obtaining work. It did nothing to improve their job prospects.

Summary: actively seeking work

- Whilst employers saw 'seeking work' as a 'good thing' this was not the case if underpinned by benefit penalties or if it meant more unsuitable candidates coming to them;

- there was no evidence that actively seeking work helped obtain work;

- the requirement had had a limited impact on claimants' jobsearch methods and intensity;

- Employment Service counselling and advice was poor and limited, and was often ridiculed by claimants;

- the impact of Employment Service advice was diminished substantially by claimants' questioning of counsellors' real motives;

- there was little or no follow up or review of on claimants' job search. Penalties were rarely used so there was little chance for the provisions to be truly operative. To that extent, it is unclear what its full impact could be;

- claimants believed that actively seeking work was merely a 'hoop to jump through' to obtain benefit, and of no help in finding work.

Actively seeking work policy proposals

The legislation and changes in the Employment Service were intended to improve claimants' job search techniques and assist them in moving back into work.

The research suggests that this could be achieved more satisfactorily with if the Government pursued the changes outlined below.

- The separation of benefit eligibility checking from counselling and advice.

- The creation of fully trained counsellors – trained in careers advice, confidence building, job search methods, local labour market practices and conditions. Their counselling would continue post-job placement to help overcome initial difficulties encountered by the demands of work.

- The repeal of the requirement to seek work and its benefit penalties thus ensuring that employers can be confident that claimants coming to them are doing so because they want the job; and allowing claimants to make approaches to employers only where they believe the vacancy is suitable.

- Properly trained counsellors should operate on a model more closely related to other employment agencies, by 'screening out' unsuitable candidates, developing a full knowledge of each employer's demand for labour, and developing methods by which claimants can be offered to employers on a 'trial' basis.

251

- The development of services to claimants which improve jobsearch techniques and personal presentation, alongside confidence building courses – including networking with other organisations providing such services to avoid overlap and fully utilise local resources.

- The maintenance of the job ready/not ready distinction and, having removed the requirement to actively seek work, enable the 'not job ready' to concentrate fully on moving towards job readiness.

- Recognising that, as a public job placement service, the Employment Service performs valuable functions which commercial agencies cannot perform – so that it is faced with a greater proportion of 'not job ready' and 'unsuitable/poor quality' seekers, as well as vacancies at the lower end of the job market, the Government should actively gear its resources to encouraging the registration of all job vacancies with the Employment Service, and consciously target/develop services for claimants and non claimants alike because only then will seekers regard the Employment Service as a worthwhile place to seek decent work, and only then will employers be satisfied that the supply of candidates from the Employment Service will be as valuable as other labour sources. Essentially, only then will the stigma attached to the use of jobcentres, users of jobcentres, and jobcentre vacancies be removed.

- The concept of 'positive options' should be altered such that the success of a counsellor's assistance is judged by the jobseeker rather than against government criteria which define what constitute positive outcomes. For this to operate successfully the Employment Service's Framework Agreement objectives need to be substantially reformed, such that its success does not involve removal from the unemployment register or targets for particular government schemes/programmes – a factor currently biasing the advice given to seekers. Placement onto EAS or ET should not involve removal from the unemployment register.

- Greater priority should be given to the efficient servicing of employers' and job searchers' needs, which requires broad, continually up-dated information on vacancies at all offices, including Supervacs. Resources need to be devoted to employer follow ups on the filling of vacancies, vacancies coming up and job specifications. This process might be assisted by a requirement for employers to notify vacancies and no further need to 'check up' on attendance at interview. For claimants the fullest job specifications must be available, including pay rates/ranges, so assisting efficient job search.

- Since the effectiveness of job search is related to financial resources it is important to ensure that benefit is only stopped once an Adjudication Officer's decision is made and not before the claimant has had a right to appeal. Currently an actively seeking work benefit suspension can impair job search directly.

- More broadly, since the quality of competing labour, attitudes towards the unemployed etc are key determinants in getting work, it would be best to put government resources into assisting claimants gain real advantages such as qualifications rather than improving job search; as well as into educating employers about the unemployed.

Attitudes to taking work

Awareness of refusal of employment and restricted availability provisions

Nearly all claimants were aware that they had to be careful in citing their pay and occupational expectations on claiming and subsequently at interviews. Some were aware that 'things have tightened up' since previous claims and that they had to be more specific about what they wanted.

Few if any knew that they had a period in which to stipulate particular conditions, although many had gained the impression from the Employment Service officers that they were expected to be more flexible as time went by.

Many knew that leaving a job voluntarily threatened future claims and that sticking to a certain pay level or job could jeopardise a claim – as could, it was felt, continual refusal to take up options offered to them by counsellors.

Only a few claimants were aware that there were any benefit penalties attached to refusing offers of employment or neglecting to avail oneself of an employment opportunity. Those who did know were not aware of the 1989 changes.

None were aware of the precise benefit penalties which could be applied for different courses of action, or the length of time for which they could apply.

Impact on Employment Service counselling and job suggestions

Claimants' general lack of awareness about benefit penalties attaching to refusal of employment and restricted availability partly reflected the 'dual' role of Employment Service counsellors wherein specific comments about benefit reduction/stoppage were counterproductive in counselling interviews. Counsellors only resorted to such explanations if they felt a warning or penalty was appropriate.

However, interviews were often so short and, in the case of review interviews, so infrequent, that counsellors were usually unable to discuss claimants' availability, job offers and job search, and therefore did not refer to benefit sanctions, even if such a warning might have been appropriate.

This created a paradox. The purpose of the permitted period was to allow claimants time in which to specify pay and occupational preferences which, if adhered to on the period's expiry, could lead to benefit penalties. The objective – to alter claimants' behaviour after that point – was precluded where claimants were unaware of the period they were being given.

Indirectly, however, the legislation had served as a signal to Employment Service officers which strongly influenced the structure and purpose of counselling interviews, in such a way that claimants were often led to fulfil expectations of them without those expectations having to be made explicit.

The lack of awareness also reflected the fact that some actions which triggered benefit penalties rarely occurred. For instance, hardly any claimants were aware that

253

refusing employment could lead to unemployment benefit disqualification and a reduction of up to 40 per cent in any income support entitlement, even though this has been a feature of the system for some time. Needless to say there was virtually no awareness of the changes made to the refusal of employment rules by the Social Security Act 1989. One of the major reasons for this was that Employment Service counsellors rarely suggested vacancies to claimants other than at the restart stage, and often not even then. When they were suggested it was rare for a claimant to turn down the suggestion immediately, or simply refuse a job offer at the employer interview. The claimant was more likely to 'give it a go', even if this resulted in an early departure from the job and a benefit deduction for leaving voluntarily, or else s/he did not turn up for the first day of employment.

Nor had the Act affected the type of work suggested to claimants. Counsellors continued to suggest what seemed suitable in the light of the claimant's circumstances, and did not hold to the letter of the Adjudication Officers' Guidance and regulations which could require pursuit of a vacancy irrespective of financial considerations.

Impact on claimants' behaviour

Claimants' belief that availability restrictions and continued refusal of 'positive options' might jeopardise their benefits did affect the restrictions claimants placed on their initial claim forms and their propensity to take one of the options offered to them, although reasons for taking up Employment Training et al were numerous – including the desire for basic skills and qualifications which they felt would assist in moving back into employment.

Because it was so rare for counsellors to suggest specific jobs to claimants, and because counsellors continued to make judgements as to vacancies' suitability for individual claimants, the 1989 Act had virtually no impact on the jobs claimants had to consider. So claimants had not been faced with choices between benefit loss and accepting jobs offering wages below their benefit levels, for instance.

However, there were some claimants who said that they had taken jobs offering terms and conditions lower than they had initially considered, or in occupations they had not initially considered, partly as a result of counsellor 'pressure' to reduce their expectations. This only occurred in a small minority of cases.

The occupational flexibility envisaged in the Act was already part of the 'natural' workings of the labour market. Most were without a 'usual occupation' and regularly changed occupations in response to turbulent labour market conditions, shifting employer demands, and the termination of short-term employment. Often those with a usual occupation or skills to protect considered a broader spectrum of work spontaneously after a period out of work, or else they were not particularly attached to their usual occupation anyway, so that they showed no disinclination towards occupational flexibility.

When claimants searched for work they were looking for something to help them satisfy a number of aspirations: work was considered as a means to an end rather than an end in itself.

So the determinants of 'job choice' could not be confined to pay and occupational preferences which the 1989 legislative changes concentrated on. However, through the exclusion of occupational and pay preferences in legislation after the permitted period, claimants felt that they could be denied the possibility of fulfilling wider aspirations (for example, to meet family or financial responsibilities). This was why, when the changes were explained during interviews, they were so strongly opposed to them.

The majority of claimants interviewed had shown considerable pay flexibility relative to previous earnings, in the jobs they had already taken, and their current reservation wages. Their wage expectations were usually in line with the wages offered locally. However, they were very resistant to the flexibility envisaged in the 1989 Act – particularly in disregarding existing financial commitments and benefit entitlements.

Most said they would not accept jobs offering below their benefit levels, although some said they would accept such a job if the alternative was a substantial cut in their existing benefit levels. Few, however, had been faced with this choice and there was little evidence to suggest that the existence of the provisions on the statute books had altered the attitude or behaviour of claimants when it came to taking work which they considered to be totally unsuitable.

Citing pay and occupational preferences was associated with benefit claiming rather than as the basis for constructive counselling assistance.

More generally counsellors' advice was rarely treated as helpful but as a means of reducing claimants' expectations from the outset. The advice was not individually-oriented. There was a widespread belief that advisers' chief objective was to reduce the numbers of registered unemployed, so that they were not concerned whether the job obtained was in the best interests of the claimant.

Determinants of work choice

Claimants' pay and occupational flexibility, as demonstrated by their work histories and current expectations, reflected a strong desire to work and to command a better income for themselves and their families, rather than reflecting the benefit costs of not accepting work or not being flexible enough.

Indeed for many claimants the prospect of benefit penalties featured only very marginally in the actions they took. These included constant jobchangers and those moving around the country – ie. groups who either spent only transitional periods on benefit or who made new claims frequently.

The claimants interviewed who had experienced benefit penalties were normally unable to say why their benefit was affected and how. This raises the question of just how effective benefit sanctions can be if claimants are unaware of the reasons for their imposition.

The biggest concerns that claimants had about moving into work were

- possible losses in net income, with wages and benefit 'top ups' failing to compensate for 'work costs', which were broadly defined by claimants;

- the risks to disrupting existing, albeit inadequate, income levels – particularly in the light of the short-term employment often available; the difficulties many had experienced in re-establishing benefit claims; and the withdrawal of means tested benefits with rises in net income.

Family credit had not proved an incentive to take work, even among its recipients, because it was not transparent to claimants how much better off they would be in work, and because most felt that they would only be marginally better off even if eligible for assistance.

Most claimants, particularly those with family commitments, had to feel that they would be substantially better off in work, and that, in the transition into work, their stable flow of net income would remain uninterrupted, in order to take the perceived risk of moving into work.

Impact of flexibility on job prospects

As with the actively seeking work provisions, claimants felt that pay and occupational flexibility would not materially affect their chances of obtaining work; and that the major obstacles to working included labour market competition, particularly the skills and experience of others, and employers' attitudes to the unemployed.

In practice claimants had little opportunity to show just how flexible they were prepared to be because they were faced with 'set' options offered by employers: if claimants were offered employment, it was on the terms initially laid down by the employer. There was no opportunity for a claimant to gain a competitive advantage over other applicants because the employer had already determined the wages and conditions s/he was prepared to offer to the suitable candidate.

In the same way, employers' treatment of occupational flexibility as a 'second best', and their disinclination to employ older workers, men or women for particular jobs, meant that the room for occupational flexibility was frequently limited.

In obtaining work, wage flexibility relative to previous earnings was not a crucial factor. What was crucial was applicants' preparedness to take the wage on offer, so that the previously very low waged were able to raise their wage expectations and still obtain employment at rates employers were prepared to pay.

Claimants felt that the most likely employment outcome if the 1989 changes were rigorously enforced was an increase in labour turnover, and in benefit deductions for 'voluntary unemployment' as people left after taking work reluctantly, or were dismissed by dissatisfied employers.

Employing the unemployed

Awareness of refusal of employment and restricted availability provisions

Although some employers knew that 'something might happen' to claimants' benefit for refusing employment or making themselves unsuitable at interview, and that some did not attend interviews of their own volition, there was virtually no employer awareness of the RE and RA provisions, although they had been part of the benefits system for some time.

Awareness of them was much lower than for the relatively new ASW provisions. Knowledge of the 1989 changes to these provisions was confined to those with friends or relatives claiming.

Even if employers had known that claimants could be expected to show more pay and occupational flexibility than other applicants it would have made little difference to their recruitment practices since most were not aware of applicants' benefit status.

Attitudes towards pay and occupational flexibility

Employers searching for workers normally had a very precise objective in mind: recruiting the right person for the job. Whether an employer recruited a candidate depended upon the suitability of that candidate and others competing for the post.

It did not depend upon the candidate's ability to offer him or herself at a lower rate of pay than others, or on his or her preparedness to show greater occupational flexibility.

Vacancies' terms and conditions were not normally negotiable with candidates. Where they were the employer needed to view the candidate as basically suitable. Often claimants – particularly the long-term unemployed – were unable to clear the 'basic suitability' hurdle, either because they were 'screened out' automatically because of their unemployment, or because they lost out against stronger competition.

Negotiation on terms and conditions could not make up for a candidate not being suitable. And so, for example, the prospect of employing a claimant 'at a discount', whilst attractive to some, was not relevant in deciding whether or not a candidate was right for the job.

Employers only showed interest in taking applicants 'at a discount' where their suitability had been guaranteed, for example by a private employment agency.

Employers did not regard occupational flexibility as a good in itself. Those able to make use of it were already doing so. Most considered it as 'second best' compared to experienced labour. It was considered 'risky' by some who preferred to look more widely or for longer in order to get the right candidate.

Attitudes towards the refusal of employment and restricted availability changes

A claimant who, it was felt, was being forced to take a job s/he'd really rather refuse was regarded as positively unsuitable because a willingness to do the job was treated as a basic prerequisite. Such applicants were not offered employment.

Employers believed the legislative changes would do nothing to assist in tackling the labour shortages that they faced. They originated in high labour turnover – a problem which they thought would be compounded if the legislation was enforced and 'unwilling' candidates stayed for short periods – and in skill shortages, which could not be met in the short-term, no matter what claimants were prepared to do.

Employers said that claimants' wage expectations matched the wages they offered, and most seemed prepared to take the types of work on offer, even if they had little or no experience in the area.

Employers said that there was a danger in relying on increased occupational flexibility given that it was already prevalent among lower grade occupations, and the retraining structures were not in place to facilitate flexibility higher up the occupational ladder.

Their concerns centred on the poor skills base from which they had to draw, the standard of school leavers, and fears that the educational and training systems were not sufficient in fulfilling employers' needs for a better trained, more flexibly skilled workforce.

Impact on the jobs offered

There was no evidence that the changes had altered the terms and conditions that employers offered to claimants.

The legislative changes were largely irrelevant to wage setting. Jobs tended to attract a rate of pay, or a pay band, which was not negotiable with applicants. Employers valued the opportunity to raise wage rates when the local labour market was 'tight', so that they could continue to attract the right quality of labour. On the other hand, if the labour market was 'slack', labour was plentiful at the rates employers were prepared to pay. In both cases legislation enabling employers to offer lower wages to claimants than to other applicants or to those already in post, were irrelevant.

It was factors other than claimants' wage expectations and 'flexibility' which prevented most employers from lowering their wage rates. Practical considerations in setting pay rates included union-negotiated pay rates, national pay scales, and recruitment and retention pressures, and the reactions of existing staff. Occupational flexibility was limited by factors such as the skill demands of the vacancies on offer and the training facilities at the employer's disposal.

Nearly all the employers interviewed objected on moral or ethical grounds to the claimant flexibility envisaged in the 1989 legislation. Their views centred on:

- opposition to benefit penalties for failing to take pay rates below benefit levels, and without regard to existing financial and family commitments;

- concerns that they already offered very low rates of pay which for some, such as those seeking 'family wages', were wholly inadequate;

- a belief that existing pay rates reflected the value of the work done and that to pay below the 'rate for the job' would be unfair or exploitative;

- that paying lower rates to claimant applicants than to others doing the same work was unfair.

Other attitudinal factors, such as some employers' gender stereotyping of vacancies they offered, also militated against employers making full use of the flexibility expected of claimants.

Impact on claimants' job prospects

The 1989 changes had had no discernible impact on claimants' job prospects. It is more difficult to assess what their effect might have been if they had been fully implemented by Employment Service counsellors, and if employers had been more aware of the changes.

However, the practical difficulties in fully utilising the flexibility expected of claimants meant that, even if they had wanted to, most employers would have been unable to substantially alter their recruitment practices.

In addition, claimants who were required to take vacancies or face benefit penalties would not have been offered jobs because their motivations were considered suspect. For that very reason they were regarded as 'unsuitable'.

There were a variety of reasons as to why claimants were not even given the opportunity to show how flexible they could be. Many were 'screened out' before interview stage because of their unemployment, while the segregation of the vacancies market denied claimants access to many employment opportunities. Vacancy market segregation was accentuated during downturns in labour demand when employers tended to increase their reliance on internal applicants.

It might be assumed that, if claimants were offering themselves at lower pay levels than other candidates and existing employees, that employers might be able to take more of them than hitherto. However, there was no evidence that the changes had, or could, enable employers to take on more workers than they currently employed.

There was a limited amount of evidence to suggest that some employers would wish to take advantage of lowering their wage rates to claimant applicants. But those employers were already drawing on claimants.

So, in those instances in which claimants' flexibility had affected employers' job offers, claimants were taking work already available to them, but at lower wage rates. Their flexibility had done nothing to raise employment levels. Individual claimants and claimants as a whole had not benefited.

Summary: availability and refusal of employment

- The nature of the job offer process, as well as practical and attitudinal factors, meant that pay and occupational flexibility expectations were having a minimal impact on job offers and movement into work. Where they were, the outcomes were not beneficial to claimants. The knowledge that such action was underpinned by benefit sanctions had a negative impact on the employers' propensity to take claimants on.

- In their work histories and current aspirations claimants showed considerable flexibility in the type of work they had taken or were prepared to take.

- Despite ignorance about specific sanctions, claimants' behaviour – in their stated expectations and acceptance of 'positive options' – reflected sensitivity to counsellors' expectations that the claimant should be realistic and flexible over time.

- Certain groups of claimants were unaffected by benefit penalties so that their behaviour remained unaltered by the prospect.

- Lack of benefit penalties awareness was inherent in the counselling process.

- Few jobs were suggested by Employment Service counsellors. To the extent that they were, the 1989 Act had not affected what counsellors offered and when.

- Sanctions were rare because a) claimants normally took work offered to them; b) counsellors suggested few jobs, and when they did they considered their suitability; c) when a claimant did not want a job s/he could act in such a way that the employer did not offer it to him or her – the claimant did not have to formally refuse the job; d) it was difficult for counsellors to prove that claimants had refused work or not availed themselves of opportunities to take work.

- Claimants showed flexibility relative to previous earnings and vacancies on offer, which was reflected in intense competition for jobcentre vacancies. However, there was strong opposition to taking jobs close to or below benefit levels, and in-work benefits were not considered helpful in moving off benefit. This suggests that the changes could have a greater impact if fully enforced, although this presupposes a larger number of jobs suggested and offered.

Policy suggestions based on the study of the refusal of employment and restricted availability provisions

The Employment Service currently have an impossible remit, seeking to service employers, claimants and other jobseekers, whilst meeting statutory obligations to check benefit eligibility. They also have to satisfy the Agency Framework's targets agreed with government. These include reducing the unemployment register. Whilst benefit penalties may have a legitimate role in protecting the NI Fund and politically in 'legitimising' the benefit system as one not susceptible to fraudulent claimants,

- their use as a labour market control mechanism sends perverse signals to employers;

- the 1989 Act, particularly the deletion of 'suitability' and the permitted period for occupational and pay restrictions, although only enforced in part and resulting in benefit penalties for a minority of claimants has, alongside other changes – organisational, administrative and political – created what claimants perceive to be a system of 'entrapment' rather than assistance;

- the actual number of claimants penalised by Adjudication Officers for refusal of employment, restricted availability, and neglect to avail oneself of employment is very small compared to the total number of claimants.

So,

- The Social Security Act 1989 changes concerning refusal of employment and restricted availability should be repealed.

- Consideration should be given to the total removal of benefit penalties for refusing employment and not taking opportunities of employment on the grounds that the benefit accruing through the protection of the NI Fund and the 'legitimising' of the system is outweighed by the implicit assumption that claimants do not want work, and thus employers' perceptions of them as unsuitable candidates; and the negative impact these penalties have on the attitudes of claimants in claiming and seeking Employment Service advice.

- There is an argument for maintaining the refusal of employment condition, as a last resort to be used when flagrant breaches of benefit eligibility rules have occurred. However, to ensure that it is not used, or is not perceived by claimants as being used, to channel them into jobs and schemes that they regard as unsuitable, the right of the claimant to refuse an unsuitable job offer must be well-established. The concept of suitability should include statutory minimum pay, training provision etc; and the 'good cause' defence should be very broad, to include existing financial commitments and current training commitments under the '21 hour rule'. This could form the basis for an alternative social security strategy to affect labour markets by denying employers access to a large pool of labour if their job offers failed to meet basic criteria of pay, training and health and safety. In this way the social security system could become a tool for affecting the quality of labour demand.

- A new availability requirement, stripped of the changes made in 1989, needs to be developed. Its intention would be to establish genuine availability for full-time employment, which is accepted as a technical necessity at the start of a claim – rather than an opportunity to intimidate claimants and reduce their expectations unduly.

- It is necessary to introduce 'due process' and 'fair procedures' principles to ensure no benefit stoppage or reduction prior to an AO decision.

In practice the letter and spirit of the Social Security Act 1989 is not being followed due to the lack of resources and counsellors' sensibilities. Yet the threat of sanctions and the feeling that many 'options' are compulsory, contaminate the claiming process in a way which precludes constructive counselling – as well as labelling claimants as 'workshy', thus having a counterproductive impact on claimant recruitment.

15 The claimants' charter

The conclusions in Chapter 13 suggested to us some key features of a charter for unemployed claimants. A jobseekers' charter has recently been devised by the Employment Service (*Employment Gazette*, January 1992) but it does not address the key issues outlined below. Our charter deals with operational matters rather than legislative changes, recommendations for which are made in Chapters 13 and 14.

Any charter should contain all the usual clauses about being able to expect respectful treatment, prompt attention and full information, which would go a long way towards improving the service to claimants. But our clauses would give real bite to the charter and would transform the experience of being out of work and claiming benefit.

The essence of our proposals is the assumption that almost all those who are claiming unemployment benefits would much rather work. Some residual controls will always be necessary for those who would really rather not work, but our research shows that the number of such claimants is minuscule and that a benefit system ought not to be based on policing the few who do not wish to work.

We therefore propose that the charter should contain the following:

- Those wishing to register a claim must be advised of their inviolable right to do so at once, without having to wait for a new claims interview.

- New claimants must be given an interview by ES local office staff within five working days of making a claim.

- Claimants should be informed about the consequences of their comments and actions at interviews and in completing forms which may impinge on benefit receipt.

262

- Except where there is a real fear of violence to staff, claimants should always be told at interview when an adverse recommendation or decision is made about their benefit, and given the reasons.

- On referral to an AO the ES officer must advise the claimant of the reasons, and how to seek a review or appeal if the AO makes an adverse decision.

- If a claimant receives an adverse decision the reasons must be given in writing together with further information on how to seek a review or appeal, and the availability of independent advice.

- If a doubt is raised about a claimant's benefit the claimant should have the option of receiving benefit in full subject to having to repay it if the AO decision is adverse and the claimant chooses not to appeal or seek review. If the claimant does wish to seek appeal or review he or she must continue to have the option of receiving benefit in full subject to having to repay it if the decision is adverse. We envisage that, in the majority of circumstances, Claimant Advisers' doubts about claimants' eligibility should not result in benefit withdrawal, reductions or deductions.

- Where claims are referred for adjudication they must reach the AO within five working days and the AO must reach a decision within two weeks.

- Beyond a minimum level of incapacity claimants should have the choice of being considered capable or incapable of work.

- Claimants should not be expected to work at jobs unsuitable to their financial and other circumstances.

- Claimants should, where practicable, have the right to be given information about the claimant process in their own language and to have an interpreter present at interviews where claims are decided.

- Claimants should be able to expect the best advice to assist them in obtaining work or training according to their personal needs and aptitudes and irrespective of agency targets.

For this charter to become a reality there would need to be a great deal of change within the ES and in its liaison with the DSS and Benefits Agency. The staff charters coming into operation would need to guarantee staff the resources, training and organisational arrangements that would be a prerequisite for its effectiveness.

Our charter would ease considerably the financial penalties faced by those currently suffering benefit penalties, at least during the crucial point when first losing a job. More than this, by reversing the usual assumption that the unemployed are normally to blame for their own predicament, it could begin to remove the shame and stigma of unemployment by proclaiming to everyone – unemployed and workers alike – that no blame attaches to being out of work.

263

Appendix 1
The interviews

This appendix sets out the timing of the interviews conducted and names the organisations from which interviews were taken. People were interviewed for their own opinions so that the research material does not reflect 'company' or 'official' policies.

(T) denotes a telephone interview. Some organisations and individuals requested anonymity.

Hammersmith and Fulham

The 'pilot' study was conducted in April 1990. In November and December 1990 the rest of the interviews were conducted, other than those with claimants and those who had recently left the register, which were conducted on 29th January 1991.

The following organisations were interviewed:

The Barons Court Project. Hammersmith and Fulham Resource Centre. Hammersmith and Fulham Economic Development Unit (three different sections). The Lyric Theatre (T). Baron's Court Careers Office (T). Department of Social Security, Appeals. General Municipal and Boilermakers. Novotel. Transport and General Workers Union. Fulham Legal Advice Centre. Hammersmith Jobcentre. Fulham Jobcentre. Hammersmith Unemployment Benefit Office (twice). Hammersmith Unemployed Centre (twice). Earls Court and Olympia Ltd. Office Angels Recruitment Agency. Hammersmith and Fulham Borough Council, Leisure and Recreation Department. Hammersmith Information Centre. Employment Service Regional Director, London and the South East. Social Security Appeals Tribunal Regional Chair, and the Full-time

Chair for London South. Claxton Laundry Ltd. W J Marston's Ltd. Rolls Royce
Motor Cars Ltd. Shepherd's Bush Advice Centre.

Newport

The claimant interviews were carried out on 19th February 1991, with the others
conducted in September 1990.
The following organisations were interviewed:

Avana Bakeries Ltd. F G Griffiths Bakery Ltd (T). Social Security Appeals
Tribunal member. Great British Burger Ltd. Tulsa (Holdings) Ltd. Citizens
Advice Bureau. Newport Careers Office (T). Compton Sons and Webb Ltd.
Newport Borough Council Economic Development and Planning Department.
Department of Social Security (two interviews). Employment Intelligence Unit
of the Employment Service. Employment Service Regional Director for Wales.
Newport Restaurants Ltd. Paul Flynn MP. Workers Education Association
organiser. Group Four Total Securities Ltd. Hilton National Hotel. An
Education Adviser for Adult Returners. Newport Resource Centre, Director
and Rights Adviser. British Steel Strip Products, Llanwern. Action Aid for the
Disabled. MIND. National Union of Public Employees. Newport Action For
The Single Homeless. Regional Chair and Full-time Chair of SSATs for Wales.
TSB General Insurance. National Union of Mineworkers, South Wales.

Brighton

The claimant interviews were conducted on 28th January 1991, with the other
interviews taking place in October and November 1990.
The following organisations were interviewed:

Brighton and Hove Albion AFC. Brighton Unemployed Centre. Brighton
Borough Council Welfare Rights Unit (Claim It). Disabled Information Centre.
SSAT member. British Telecom PLC. Department of Social Security. Rentokil
Group Ltd. Uncle Sam's Hamburger Express (T). Securicor Ltd. Securicor
Cleaning Ltd. Brighton Jobcentre. American Express Ltd. Brighton Advice.
Citizens Advice Bureau. Eaton Gardens Nursing Home. East Sussex County
Council Planning Division. Brighton Borough Council Tourism Department.
Brighton Borough Council Technical and Parks Division (T). Grand Hotel.
Hospitality Inn. A high street supermarket. The Hospitals Unit. Brighton
Borough Council Planning Department. Hove Unemployment Benefit Office.

St Helens

The claimant interviews were conducted on 18th February 1991. The other interviews took place in January 1991.
The following organisations were interviewed:

Smith Kline Beecham PLC. St Helens Unemployment Benefit Office. St Helens Jobcentre. St Helens Adult Guidance. Fred Davies (Storage) Ltd (T). British Gas PLC. Pilkington Insulation Ltd. Regional Chair of SSATs and Full-time Chair for the North West. Surefil Packaging Ltd. Merseyside Unemployed Centre. Department of Social Security. Waste Management Ltd. St Helens Metropolitan Borough Economic Development Department. Wiseacre Engineering Ltd. Yorkshire Bank PLC.

Appendix 2
Labour market synopses

This appendix provides thumb nail sketches of the four labour markets studied.

St Helens

The area

St Helens Borough has a population of 187,000. The Mintel lifestyle survey in 1988 ranked St Helens in the bottom 15 out of 280 towns and cities. The council describes its main problems as "poor housing environment; high unemployment levels (particularly long term jobless and youth unemployment); rundown industrial and commercial areas; low incomes and dependency on state benefits..." (St Helens Urban Programme, 1991/2).

The council estimates that 47 per cent of its population live in socially deprived areas.

Unemployment

In October 1990 the Borough of St Helens had 7,492 claimant unemployed, of which five and a half thousand were men. By January 1991 this had risen to 8,179. Using a residency-based denominator the Unemployment Unit calculates this to be 9.2 per cent of the labour force. St Helens North has a rate of 8.3 per cent; St Helens South 10.1 per cent – amongst the lowest rates on Merseyside.

Despite a yearly reduction of a quarter in the number of claimants unemployed for over a year, they still constitute 40 per cent of the total count. In addition 42 per cent of the claimants under 25 have been unemployed for six months or more.

Redundancies at BICC, Pilkingtons, ITT and others had totalled over 800 in the six weeks to 10th January 1990. The UBO reported a doubling in the rate of new claims from the week before Christmas. In the quarter to December 1990 there were over 2,500 new claims registered.

Labour supply and demand

St Helens was hit badly by the recession of the early 1980s so that over 20,000 jobs were lost between 1980 and 1987, predominantly from its traditional staple industries – glass manufacture, coal mining, engineering and chemicals. However manufacturing and construction still constitute 37 per cent of local employment and over 12,000 jobs continue to depend on the glass industry.

The demanning, due primarily to the effects of recession and introduction of new technologies, resulted and continues to result in a steady flow of skilled or semi-skilled workers with stable employment histories into unemployment. They tend to snap up the available primary sector permanent employment, as well as soaking up vacancies in larger organisations through redeployment. Consequently large numbers of the unemployed are long-term unemployed or have virtually no employment experience, having been recycled through various work related government training programmes.

Given the strong competition for primary sector jobs, permanent jobs are only available to the unemployed in low paying secondary sectors, or amongst large employers capable of training or retraining.

With demand for many occupations shrinking or vanishing there is a major skills mismatch between the labour on offer (highly inexperienced and underskilled or narrowly skilled and over 50 years old) and labour demand.

The urban regeneration programmes had created few jobs and when they did the real travel to work area (as opposed to the official one) was large and so pulled in non-residents.

Employment Service registered vacancies

In the quarter ending 4 January 1991, 901 vacancies were notified to the Employment Service. Of these 43 per cent were part-time and 27 per cent for six months duration or less. The vacancies fell into the following categories:

Selling and distribution	22 per cent	wages council rates
Catering	18 per cent	wages council rates
Clerical	19 per cent	£90-130 per week
Cleaning/personal services	11 per cent	£2-2.50 per hour
Engineering	6 per cent	£170-200 per wk (HGV) and £90-120 (others)
Others (inc. managerial, security, construction, sewing)	20 per cent	

Source: letter from Mike Fogden, Chief Executive, Employment Service, to John Evans MP, 21st February 1991.

The 5.1 New Client Advisers and 7 multi-functioning Client Advisers and Restart Counsellors were based in the unemployment benefit offices.

Although the Back To Work Plan was agreed at initial interviews the procedures for following up after the permitted period were not in place so that the permitted period had meant nothing in practice.

The New Framework and Active Signing were to be introduced shortly, r arking a new departure which would involve the more rigorous application of the SSA '89, including caseload follow up after the expiry of the permitted period and a commitment to making the BTWP working documents. There remained doubts that the hardcore claimants would ever fall foul of the regulations, no matter how well enforced.

There are five jobclubs in St Helens, all of them external to the Employment Service. In the second half of 1990 their placement ratios ranged from 46 to 58 per cent (Mike Fogden's letter to John Evans MP, 21st February 1991).

Newport

Unemployment

There were 2,471 claimant unemployed in Newport East constituency in October 1990 and 2,686 in Newport West. By January 1991 the numbers had risen to 2,921 and 3,170 respectively – an 18 per cent annual growth rate. 27 per cent of claimants in Newport East and 34 per cent in Newport West were unemployed for twelve months or more in January.

The highest concentrations of unemployment are in Alexandra, Ringland, Victoria, St Woolos, Bettws, and Central.

Newport was just beginning to face a very serious economic downturn when the employer interviews were conducted in September 1990. Claimants were facing its full force when interviewed in February. The unemployment benefit office reported new claims at a rate of 100 a day. Just over 3,000 new claims were registered in the quarter to October 1990. A local burger restaurant reported the lowest level of customer demand since Llanwern's redundancies in 1980-1.

Labour demand

In 1987 there were over 55,000 employees working in Newport. The town was hit badly by the loss of over 4,000 steelworks jobs in 1980 and by the Miners' Strike in 1985. Since then the proportion of service jobs in the Borough has risen steadily to around two thirds, whilst manufacturing employment has fallen back to under a third.

During the employer interviews in September 1990 Inmos reported 150 white collar professional redundancies and AB Electronics announced very poor profits and possible job loss.

There were only 257 unfilled vacancies at the Newport jobcentre in August 1990 compared to 318 in July and 332 in June.

The Borough Council has a very active economic development strategy geared towards inward investment. While it emphasises its success with the Trustees Savings Bank who relocated in 1988, and electronics companies such as Panasonic, there has been concern that the council has been prepared to accommodate employers regardless of the quality of the jobs on offer and that many of the jobs created are taken by non-residents of the Borough.

Despite this the council claims that its urban redevelopment strategy has transformed the town over the last two years. It hopes to continue the process through town centre renewal and the Usk Barrage and riverfront regeneration plan which, it is projected, will directly employ 800 (including 500 recruited locally) to 1995.

Labour supply

Newport's travel to work area is very large, containing a workforce of nearly 95,000. The town's employers rely heavily on workers travelling down from the Valleys – many, like the clothing manufacturers Compton Sons and Webb, bus workers into Newport each morning.

The council has identified high long-term unemployment and the skills mismatch between claimants – many of whom were blue or black collar workers in the early 1980s – as significant problems. There is a recognised lack of information regarding employers' requirements and the skills base of the resident population. However skills shortages are already apparent in construction, electronics and parts of the service sector.

Many inward investors have been attracted by the combination of cheap and relatively well-skilled labour and grants. However there is a belief that much of the blue collar skilled labour has dried up, and in any case a growing proportion of firms recruiting are in the services sectors.

The area has a considerable informal economy, with many people working whilst claiming benefit or doing two jobs. Employers complained that they had to compete for labour with employers who were prepared to offer cash in hand.

Most employers mentioned the difficulties arising form the decline in the number of school leavers.

'Valleys Skills', conducted by Welsh Training Agency Intelligence Unit, showed that the unemployed were flexible in terms of the pay and locations they were prepared to accept. However it found that they were only occupationally flexible relative to their previous occupation, and not flexible enough to meet existing labour demand.

Vacancies notified to the local Employment Service

In the quarter ending 5 October 1990, 1,925 vacancies were notified to the Employment Service. One third were part-time and one third for six months duration or less. The vacancies fell into the following categories:

Cleaning/personal services	17 per cent	£2-2.50 per hour
Catering	16 per cent	wages council rates
Clerical and secretarial	15 per cent	£5-7,000 per annum
Retail distribution	11 per cent	wages council rates
Transport operation	7 per cent	£4.50 per hour (HGV1) and £2.50-3.50 per hour (others)
Skilled engineering	4 per cent	£4.59 per hour average
Construction	3 per cent	£4 per hour skilled, £3 per hour unskilled
Security	3 per cent	£2-2.50 per hour
Others	24 per cent	inc. hairdressing and sewing machinists (wc rates); production operatives (£3.00 per hour); sales reps (commission); nursing (£4-5 per hour private sector).

Source: Mike Fogden, letter to Paul Flynn MP, 18th December 1990

A note on the local Employment Service

The 5.4 New Client Advisers are based in the unemployment benefit offices, as are two of the Claimant Advisers. The jobcentre has one Claimant Adviser and there are two Specialist Advisers located in the Newport Area Office. Restart interviews are conducted in the jobcentre, with 2.5 counsellors allocated for the task.

There are three jobclubs in Newport. The jobcentre jobclub had a placement ratio of 49 per cent, compared to 35 per cent and 80 per cent for the two external jobclubs (Mike Fogden, letter to Paul Flynn MP, 18th December 1990).

Hammersmith and Fulham

During the 'pilot' scheme in April there were 3,649 claimants in Hammersmith and 2,728 in Fulham . By October there were 4,040 and 2,920 respectively. By January 1991 the numbers had climbed to 4,425 and 3,244. With an unemployment rate of 9.6 per cent according to the Department of Employment, it had the eighth highest unemployment rate out of the 32 Greater London Boroughs.

Nearly a third of claimants in Hammersmith and Fulham had been unemployed for over 12 months.

An unemployment benefit office worker said the steep rise in new claims had begun in October 1990. Local agencies reported dealing with redundant workers now, whereas they had only dealt with job changers hitherto.

Labour demand

It is an area which was hit heavily by the industrial shake-out in the early 1980s, although with 84 per cent of its employment in the service sector, it is fairly typical of Greater London. However, it has a disproportionately high percentage of workers in Education, Health, Recreational, Other Cultural and Personal Services (SICs 93-8). This reflects a high percentage of public sector employment in the Borough.

Only 8 per cent of its employment is in manufacturing. It lost nearly 6,000 jobs in manufacturing and construction between 1981 and 1987. The biggest growth has been in banking, insurance and business services, with over 3,000 jobs created in that period.

Between the April 'pilot' study and the December interviews there was a marked deterioration in the local labour market, with private sector employers across the board placing a freeze on new recruits and/or cutting temporary contracts. In the public sector community charge capping has resulted in a total freeze on recruitment of new and replacement staff.

Labour supply

With substantial job loss in labouring occupations and engineering, there are a number of unskilled and semi-skilled manual workers chasing jobs which are increasingly in administrative and technical fields. Growth in employment has favoured women, with projections showing male employment roughly stable to 1995, but rapid growth in female employment.

Employer interviewees reported skill shortages in accountancy and catering. However the labour market, which had been a job seekers' market in April, was now an employers' market.

Brighton and Hove

Unemployment

Of the 15,483 claimant unemployed living in East Sussex in October 1990, 10,104 lived in Brighton's Travel To Work Area. There were 5,609 claimant unemployed in Brighton Borough and 2,380 in Hove Borough. At 8 per cent and 7 per cent respectively, the percentage of the resident labour force unemployed was much higher than East Sussex as a whole (at around 5.5 per cent).

Indeed, a quarter of the whole county's unemployment is contained in 10 wards in Brighton and Hove.

Residency unemployment rates vary dramatically between wards – from around 20 per cent in Regency to 2 per cent in Patcham. The unemployed are concentrated in 'Costa del Dole' (Regency, Pier and into Brunswick and Adelaide in Hove) and on outlying housing estates such as Whitehawk.

In the year to Janary 1991 unemployment in Brighton and Hove rose by over a quarter — to stand at 2,883 in Hove and 6,373 in Brighton. In the same period the number of claimants unemployed for a year or more fell by over 30 per cent in Brighton and almost a quarter in Hove. Nevertheless those unemployed for a year or more still constituted nearly a quarter of all claimants.

Labour demand

Brighton and Hove provide about 40 per cent of East Sussex's employment.

Between 1981 and 1987 there was a massive shakeout in male full-time jobs, with female full-time jobs at a stable level and a large increase in part-time female employment. By 1987, of the 64,000 employees in Brighton Borough 52 per cent were women, and around one quarter were women in part-time employment.

This shakeout of male employment continued in the year to October 1990, with rising unemployment almost exclusively among the male workforce.

Whilst the county as a whole only has 15 per cent manufacturing employment, Brighton has a mere 9 per cent. 40 per cent are in 'Other Services', and 20 per cent in Distribution, Hotels and Catering.

It is this industrial and occupational composition – no industrial base, a low paying service sector dominated by small firms, and a public sector dominated by low paying sectors such as hospitals – which means Brighton and Hove is one of the lowest paying areas in the south east – even lower than other areas in East Sussex which benefit from a higher percentage of manufacturing.

Although the Borough Council wishes to attract manufacturing jobs the opportunities are limited by limited space, and the cost of redeveloping old industrial sites.

Brighton and Hove had witnessed a very significant economic and employment downturn in the six months before the interviews were conducted. Twelve months ago press advertisements received low responses, employers relied heavily on agencies and often took temporary workers on permanently. But the downturn had resulted in marked reductions in staff turnover (at British Telecom for instance) and a limited number of vacancies on offer (one at Securicor Cleaning, and only 1 per cent of the job stock at American Express). In hotel and catering and retailing the slowdown in economic activity has not affected high staff turnover rates.

Labour supply

The move towards part-time female employment and away from full-time permanent posts is continuing in some sectors. Employers such as the council's tourism department and the Grand Hotel are making great efforts through the introduction of flexitime and jobsharing to attract women returners. In the hospital's personnel unit such techniques are well-established. The competition for women returners is high amongst retailers, the financial sector, hotels and process operators.

There is a realisation that more and more women want work: this often means seeking a part-time job to supplement a first job – hotel employers and Securicor Cleaners are aware that the majority of their part-timers are engaged in other work.

The other major source of part-timers is students. Employers actively recruit them through open days (e.g. American Express) and the Polytechnic noticeboard. They

273

are required to work in order to support themselves through college following removal of rights to short-term benefits and the fall in the real value of grants.

Despite high levels of unemployment skill shortages are reported in a number of areas: nurses for Eaton Gardens Nursing Home, chefs for good restaurants in hotels, and skilled labour for the technical and parks division of the Borough Council. In some sectors like financial services this is aggravated by competition from London. However, as far as the service sector is concerned, its development in recent years provides the opportunity for people to pursue their whole career in Brighton without having to leave.

The early 1980s shakeout has left a large number of unemployed men requiring training in order to undertake the service sector jobs now on offer in Brighton and Hove. In the absence of this training to facilitate occupational flexibility, employers are taking workers from outlying areas. Daily commuting involves a substantial in-flow to Brighton which is increasing.

Housing and earnings

A key problem in Brighton is the house price/earnings affordability gap, which is the greatest in Britain. In 1988 East Sussex displayed the lowest average earnings in the south east but its house prices were amongst the highest. The 'affordability gap' grew dramatically in the 1980s. The combination of low wages and high accommodation costs has prevented the hospitals personnel unit from attracting staff from other health authorities to fill skill shortages, although such a policy has been successfully undertaken by the Borough Council's tourism department.

There is a large rented accommodation sector in Brighton. The rents are high and flats difficult to come by, particularly for those arriving in Brighton expecting to find decently paid work. This combination results in desperation and the preparedness to accept very low wages in order to break the vicious circle of no job - no accommodation. The situation is aggravated by the paucity of live-in accommodation for hotel jobs in Brighton and Hove. Some believe that this situation is a factor in driving down wages in Brighton and Hove compared to outlying areas.

Table 1
Unemployment in the labour markets

Area	Count		Yearly change %	LTU	Yearly change %	LTU as % All CLTs
Brighton						
Kemptown	3299	(9.4)	+29.7	734	-34.8	?2.2
Pavillion	3174	(9.3)	+30.1	696	-30.4	?.1.9
Hove	2883	(7.9)	+26.6	658	-23.2	22.8
Fulham	3244	(7.9)	+22.2	941	-35.7	29.0
Hammersmith	4425	(11.3)	+25.2	1349	-34.4	30.1
St Helens						
North	3746	(8.3)	+4.1	1484	-28.3	39.6
South	4433	(10.1)	+2.3	1886	-24.9	42.5
Newport						
East	2921	(9.3)	+22.3	786	-34.0	26.9
West	3170	(10.1)	+19.0	924	-31.7	29.1

Note: These figures relate to unemployment between January 1991 and January 1990. The claimant count used is the official Department of Employment count. Unemployment rates have been calculated by the Unemployment Unit using residency-based denominators. Long-term unemployment (LTU) is defined as registration for twelve months or more.

Table 2
Percentage increase in claimant count, October 1990 - January 1991

Brighton	-	Kemptown	16.2
	-	Pavillion	14.2
Hove			21.1
Fulham			11.1
Hammersmith			9.5
St Helens	-	North	11.2
	-	South	7.5
Newport	-	East	18.2
	-	West	18.0

Note: This table uses the Department of Employment's offical count and gives some indication as to the change in unemployment stocks during the interview stages of the research (largely conducted between September 1990 and February 1991).

Appendix 3
Screening questionnaire

Head Office: 35 NORTHAMPTON SQUARE,
LONDON EC1V 0AX Telephone 071-250 1866

SCPR
SOCIAL & COMMUNITY PLANNING RESEARCH

Field and DP Office: BRENTWOOD, ESSEX
Northern Field Office: DARLINGTON, CO. DURHAM

P5156   January 1991

UNEMPLOYMENT RESEARCH

Household screening questionnaire

We are carrying out a piece of research into people's experiences of being unemployed. We are interested in finding out about the help people receive in finding work, their experience of signing-on, and their views and feelings about being out of work.

To obtain a cross section of people to take part in a group discussion we are looking for a range of people, such as people of different ages, men and women, and people who are either currently out of work or who have recently been out of work.

May I therefore ask you a few basic questions to check whether or not you would be included?

This is completely confidential.

Area ....   Serial No. ....

---

1. Can I just check. Have you been out of work and
    claiming benefit at all since October 1989?   Yes   1 —— Q2
                                                            No   2 —— END

2. At present, are you.....
    PROMPT UNTIL CATEGORY ASSIGNED

working full-time	1
working part-time	2
on a government scheme	3
(eg. Employment Training, Enterprise Allowance)	
in full-time education	4
registered as unemployed	5
unemployed but <u>not</u> registered	6
not working because of permanent sickness/disability	7
looking after home/family	8
pregnant - due to have a baby	9
retired	10
other - SPECIFY _____	11

    1–5 —— Q3

    6–11 —— END

3. IF CURRENTLY UNEMPLOYED ASK
    a)   How long have you been unemployed?   (CODE BELOW)

    IF NOT CURRENTLY UNEMPLOYED ASK
    b)   How long was your most recent spell of unemployment?   (CODE BELOW)

Less than 6 months	1
Between 6 months and 12 months	2
Between 12 months and 18 months	3
More than 18 months	4

    —— Q4

279

| 4. | Sex: | Female | 1 ─┐ | |
| | | Male | 2 ─┴── Q5 | |

5. What was your age last birthday?

    WRITE IN _____ years

	Under 25	1 ─┐
	25 - 45	2 ├── Q6
	46 - retirement age	3 ─┘
	over retirement age	4 ──── END

6. Marital status:
    Are you

	single?	1 ─┐	CHECK
	married/living as married?	2 ├── QUOTAS
	separated/divorced/widowed?	3 ─┘	

END

IF eligible and recruited
    Complete venue details on appointment letter and leave with respondent.

IF not eligible OR quotas filled
    Thank and explain that they will not be troubled any further.

OUTCOME

Recruited:	☐
Not recruited - quotas filled:	
Not recruited - out of quota:	
Eligible but refused:	
Eligible -can't attend:	

NAME: MR/MRS/MS/MISS _____

ADDRESS: _____

_____

TELEPHONE NO. _____

Appendix 4
Questionnaire for group interviewees

Head Office: 35 NORTHAMPTON SQUARE,
LONDON EC1V 0AX Telephone 071-250 1866

Field and DP Office: BRENTWOOD, ESSEX
Northern Field Office: DARLINGTON, CO. DURHAM

P5156 Q1/3

JANUARY 1991

QUESTIONNAIRE

Area _____

Serial No. _____

We would be grateful if you could complete the details below about you and your family. The information is completely confidential and will only be used for the purposes of the research.

1. How many people live in your household? _____

2a. Who lives with you as a member of your household?
    (Exclude any children who have left home)
    TICK ALL THAT APPLY   Husband/wife/partner
                             Children (under 16)   How many? _____
                             Children (over 16)   How many? _____

2b. If you have children aged 16 and over living at home with you how many are....

        Still at school   _____   Working part-time   __
        In further education   _____   On a government scheme   __
        Working full-time   _____   (eg. ET, YT, Enterprise Allowance)

3a. How many jobs (excluding Government schemes) have you had in the past FIVE years?

        Number of jobs   _____

3b. How many Government schemes (eg. ET, YT, Enterprise Allowance) have you attended in the past FIVE years?

        Number of schemes   _____

    IF YOU HAVE NEVER HAD A JOB, OR WORKED ON A GOVERNMENT SCHEME PLEASE GO TO
    QUESTION 7a.

4a. Are you currently ......
    PLEASE TICK ONE BOX   working (full- or part- time)   GO TO Q.4b
                                     on a government scheme
                                     in further education   GO TO Q.5
                                     unemployed   GO TO Q.6·

4b. How long have you been working in this job or government scheme (eg ET, YT, Enterprise Allowance)?
                    WRITE IN   _____

283

4c.   What sort of work do you do?
              Job title   _____
              Type of work   _____

       PLEASE GO TO Q.6

---

5.   What qualification are you studying for?   _____
       When do you expect to finish?   _____

       PLEASE GO TO Q.7

---

6.   Please list your last <u>three</u> jobs (including Government schemes – ET, YT, Enterprise
       Allowance) indicating the type of work you did, how long you were employed, and your
       reasons for leaving. If the job was part of a government scheme please include this
       with a tick.

       START WITH YOUR MOST <u>RECENT</u> JOB

Type of work	How long employed	Reasons for leaving	Government scheme (√)
1. _____	_____	_____	☐
2. _____	_____	_____	☐
3. _____	_____	_____	☐

7a.   What is your <u>net</u> income (ie after tax, National Insurance and other deductions have
       been made)?
       PLEASE GIVE EITHER A WEEKLY, FORTNIGHTLY, OR MONTHLY AMOUNT
              £ _____   PER WEEK
              £ _____   PER FORTNIGHT
              £   PER MONTH

7b.   If you are married or living with a partner, into which group does your JOINT net
       weekly income fall? Please include income from all sources (earnings, child
       benefit, other benefits) after tax and other deductions have been made.
       PLEASE TICK ONE BOX

WEEKLY		MONTHLY	
Less than £50	☐	Less than £220	☐
£50 – £99		£220 – £429	
£100 – £149		£430 – £649	
£150 – £199		£650 – £869	
£200 – £299		£870 – £1,299	
£300 – £499		£1,300 – £2,169	
£500 and over		£2,700 and over	

8a. Do **you** receive any of the following benefits?
     PLEASE TICK ALL THAT APPLY

     Unemployment benefit ☐
     Income support ☐
     Housing benefit ☐
     Family credit ☐
     Child benefit ☐
     Other (PLEASE SPECIFY)

     _____ ☐

8b   If you are married or living with a partner, does your **partner** receive any of the
     following benefits?
     PLEASE TICK ALL THAT APPLY

     Unemployment benefit ☐
     Income support ☐
     Housing benefit ☐
     Family credit ☐
     Child benefit ☐
     Other (PLEASE SPECIFY)

     _____ ☐

9a. Do you have any qualifications?

                              Yes ☐ ➞ GO TO Q.9b
                              No ☐

9b. What is your **HIGHEST** qualification?

     Highest qualification _____

THANK YOU FOR YOUR HELP

285

Appendix 5
Group interview topic guide

Head Office: 35 NORTHAMPTON SQUARE,
LONDON EC1V 0AX Telephone 071-250 1866

SCPR
SOCIAL & COMMUNITY PLANNING RESEARCH

Field and DP Office: BRENTWOOD, ESSEX
Northern Field Office: DARLINGTON, CO. DURHAM

P5156 TG1/4   FEBRUARY 1991

ACTIVELY SEEKING WORK

Local Labour Market Conditions

GROUP DISCUSSION TOPIC GUIDE

Technical terms and procedures not familiar to the group participants are to be explained when necessary

1. BACKGROUND INFORMATION
    (Collected individually)
    *   Employment details
        - employment status
        - current/most recent job
        - length of unemployment

    *   'Signing-on'
        - at which office; FRESH CLAIM; now

    *   Which Job Centre (if any) do they use

    *   Receipt of benefit; postal or personal issue

2. JOB REQUIREMENTS AND EASE OF FINDING WORK
    *   Job requirements
        - what do they look for in a job;
                rates of pay
                location/travelling time
                conditions
                'usual' or range of different occupations
        - views about the importance of these factors; how flexible are they

    *   Have any of them changed their job requirements; how; why

    *   Whether any individual aware of <u>in-work benefits</u>
        - views about taking low paid jobs and claiming in-work benefits

    *   Would they take a job that they were 'unsure' about
        PROBE   Awareness, experience and usefulness of 'employment on
                    trial'

3. **FINDING WORK**

    Looking for work

    - The range of methods they use to look for work
      - which are the most successful methods; contrast agencies and Job Centres

    - Have any of them changed how they look for work
      - how did this come about
      - when

4. **ENTRY INTO UNEMPLOYMENT**

    Process of signing-on

    - How did they go about signing-on
      - what was said to them
      - delays
      - emergency claims
      - any queries about what they had written on claim forms

    - Feelings about signing-on process
      - any changes required

5. **EXPERIENCE OF UNEMPLOYMENT**

    Interviews

    - Whether any individuals called for interview; when; where; length; what was it called

    - Types of issues discussed (Back to work plans, job search advice, employment counselling, job offers, other menu options; benefit advice, in-work benefits; employment on trial)

    - Feelings about the interviews (perceived purpose, sensitivity of interviewer, usefulness)

    - Whether interviews helped them look for/find work

    - Awareness/Experience of consequences of not attending an interview (prior to interview); source of information

    - Whether any individuals had not attended an interview and examples of the consequences
      - were they aware of the consequences BEFORE deciding whether to

attend

- Awareness of consequences of not looking for work

Evidence of job search
- Whether any individuals have been asked to provide evidence of job search and examples of the type of evidence given
  - reaction of employers of being asked for proof

- Experiences of being unable to provide evidence of job search and examples of the consequences

Experience of being referred to interview
i) *Jobs*
- Whether any individuals had received/accepted job offers; examples of what sort

- The range of factors that lead people to <u>considering/refusing</u> ES job offers (**Note: relate to local labour market and job requirements**)

- Ever been followed up by ES after referral to a job

- Experience of not turning up to job interview

- Experiences of turning down a job offer; awareness of consequences

ii) *Other Menu Options*
- Whether any individuals considered/asked to consider/submitted to other menu options (eg ET, Job Club, etc.); feelings about

- The range of factors that lead people to <u>accepting/refusing</u> menu options

- Experiences of turning down a menu option; awareness of consequences

Permitted periods
- Whether any individuals had changed their job search activities and examples of how
  - the range of factors that lead to changes in job search

- Awareness and experience of permitted periods

- views about permitted period in relation to providing opportunities to find work

- Acceptability of looking for work outside usual occupation and rates of pay

Referral of claim
- Whether any individuals had experienced their claim being referred to an Adjudication Officer and examples of circumstances in which this had occurred
  - did the A.O. decide for or against the claimant

- Feelings about referral of claim and consequences (benefit suspension)

Appeals
- WHERE THE A.O. DECIDED AGAINST THE CLAIMANT, any experiences of appealing to a Social Security Appeal Tribunal
  - circumstances of appeal; assistance given; the tribunals decision

- Views about the appeal process (in cases of claim referral)

6. VIEWS ABOUT BENEFIT SYSTEM AND PENALTIES

- Views about ASW regulations in general
- Has ASW increased chances of finding work
  - how
  - how could it be more effective
  - effect of threat of benefit sanctions

- What do they think should be done to help people back to work